IMAGINING
CANADIAN
LITERATURE

LETTER TO J. McCLELLAND

Leonard Cohen

Some of the best times I ever had,
I had with you, Jack. Some of the best
drinks I ever drank, I drank with you,
Jack. The wars we fought and lost are
long forgotten, but your gallantry in
the face of overwhelming odds is not
forgotten. The drums roll as we salute
your incomparable style of Effortless
Heart and Toronto Soul, and the One
named Beauty, whom I worshiped and you
merely loved (or was it the other way
around?), bends down from her great
height to smile at both our misconcep-
tions. I was a punk from Montreal and
you were the Prime Minister of Canada.
You handed me a thousand drinks and
never once talked about writing, except
to suggest, after the five hundredth,
that I might be King David. You were the
real Prime Minister of Canada. You still
are. And even though it's all gone down
the tubes, the country that *you* govern
will never fall apart.
Thanks, Jack.
Love,
Leonard

IMAGINING CANADIAN LITERATURE

THE SELECTED LETTERS OF JACK McCLELLAND

Jack McClelland

EDITED BY SAM SOLECKI

KEY PORTER BOOKS

Canadian Cataloguing in Publication Data

McClelland, Jack, 1922-
       Imagining Canadian literature: the selected letters of Jack McClelland

Includes index.
ISBN 1-55013-953-3

1. McClelland, Jack, 1922- —Correspondence. 2. Publishers and publishing—Ontario—Toronto—Correspondence. 3. McClelland and Stewart Limited—Biography.
I. Solecki, Sam, 1946- . II. Title.

Z483.M32A4 1998   070.5'092   C97-932724-5

The publisher gratefully acknowledges the support of the Canada Council for the Arts and the Ontario Arts Council for its publishing program.

Key Porter Books Limited
70 The Esplanade
Toronto, Ontario
Canada M5E 1R2

www.keyporter.com

THE CANADA COUNCIL | LE CONSEIL DES ARTS
FOR THE ARTS | DU CANADA
SINCE 1957 | DEPUIS 1957

Design and electronic formatting: Peter Maher
Photograph on page vi: Canapress/Boris Spremo

Printed and bound in Canada

98 99 00 01 6 5 4 3 2 1

CONTENTS

PREFACE

In writing a preface to this selection of my correspondence, I am ignoring the advice I always gave to authors: Don't bother with a preface or a foreword because nobody ever reads them. I seldom read them myself, and I have always assumed that I am a typical book reader. In fact, that assumption often guided me in my many years as a book publisher.

As that typical book reader, I would never have believed there was sufficient interest in a collection of my letters to justify the publisher's investment of time and money. In one of the letters in this collection, tongue firmly planted in cheek, I advise Margaret Laurence to save all my correspondence so she can sell it at a later date. "Our mutual correspondence is saleable at both ends," I wrote. "I sell your letters. You should be selling mine." Of course I was joking. When you spend the greater part of your life around talented writers, it becomes hard to believe that anyone would want to read anything you yourself wrote. That's why I was both flattered and surprised when Anna Porter and Sam Solecki proposed this book to me.

Still, when I first read the manuscript, I was a little embarrassed to discover that about sixty-five per cent of the letters are mine. Since I usually wrote at length and most authors didn't—the popular belief was that they should not waste creative time writing letters when they could be working on a new book—I hate to think how many of these actual pages come from me.

One of the few writers who—thankfully—did write longer letters was Laurence, perhaps the finest Canadian novelist yet discovered. There are more of her letters included in this collection than any other author's. I am not surprised; she wrote beautiful letters. The only novelist whose work rivalled hers was Gabrielle Roy, who had the advantage of being completely bilingual. She wrote very few letters and most were in French. As a result, she has only two letters in this selection.

I used to say that one could often tell from the tone and style of a letter whether the writer was likely to be successfully published. This was something I was taught both by my father and my publishing mentor, Alfred A. Knopf. In the early days of my career with McClelland and Stewart, I would travel across the country soliciting "unsolicited" manuscripts from ordinary Canadians. But I always asked these would-be authors to write to us before sending us the manuscript. I soon learned, from reading the letters, which manuscripts I wanted to read and which I did not. As Knopf would always say, "If they can't write a good letter, how can they write a good book?"

In rereading some of the letters in this collection, I have now concluded that this is not necessarily so. Some authors are perfectionists in everything they do, and their letters bear this out. And others really don't waste their valuable writing time on letters. To this latter category belongs one of my favourite writers, Earle Birney.

Although the language he used in his books was superb, the language in most of his letters was atrocious. One time he sent me a letter liberally sprinkled with his customary swear words. Posing as my secretary, Marge Hodgeman, I acknowledged receipt of the letter in Mr. McClelland's absence. As a secretary in a publishing house, I wrote, I should not be subjected to such foul language. Birney's response was swift and typical: "If I can't write to my publisher using any G.D.F. language I choose, then I'll find another G.D.F. book publisher."

If nothing else, reading through this collection reminds me that book publishing is not only a fascinating business, but it also requires extraordinarily hard work, a dedicated and efficient staff, a certain amount of luck—and a thick skin.

I want to thank Sam Solecki for selecting these letters and Anna Porter for publishing them.

Jack McClelland
December 1997

ACKNOWLEDGEMENTS

Jack McClelland's letters are published with his permission and with the permission of the William Ready Division of Archives and Research Collections, Mills Memorial Library, McMaster University. The letters to Jack McClelland are published with the permission of the following individuals: Margaret Atwood; Mona A. Simpson and R. G. Rice (Ernest Buckler); Wailan Low (Earle Birney); Leonard Cohen; Mrs. Robertson Davies (Robertson Davies); Sylvia Fraser; Aritha van Herk; Hugh Hood; Jocelyn Laurence and the estate of Margaret Laurence (Margaret Laurence); Irving Layton; Norman Levine; Shirley E. Woods (Hugh MacLennan); Brian Moore; Farley Mowat; Peter Newman; Michael Ondaatje; Al Purdy; Mordecai Richler; Fonds Gabrielle Roy (Gabrielle Roy); Phyllis Webb.

JACK McCLELLAND:
The Canadian Publisher

Publishers are the midwives of culture, and, like midwives, once
they have delivered the goods they tend to be forgotten. If they
are remembered at all, it is by association with a particularly
famous book or author. Jack McClelland knew more than his
fair share of prominent writers, and he certainly published
some of the most important Canadian books to appear since the
Second World War, but there's no doubt that his stature in
Canadian publishing and literature is more than a simple sum of
his relationships with his authors. In fact, few would dissent
from a rival publisher's comment that "publishing stands at the
centre of Canadian identity. And at the centre of Canadian
publishing stood Jack McClelland."

McClelland's position was so dominant that he was probably
the only publisher whose activities were regularly reported in
the media and who became nearly a household name in those
households concerned with Canadian culture. For nearly four
decades, he published many of the most popular and most
important Canadian writers, corresponded with the most
influential of our policy makers and politicians, and was
influential in determining aspects of cultural policies as
different as censorship, copyright, grants policies, arts' prizes
and subsidies. His speeches alone—to schools, cultural groups
and government commissions—are a record of the vicissitudes
of Canadian nationalism in the modern era.

Since he wrote no books and has so far not completed his
memoirs, his letters are the most revealing testament to his
career and influence. And they record a career as important to
the creation of modern Canadian literature as that of any writer.
For nearly forty years, forests fell all over Canada every time Jack
McClelland picked up his Dictaphone. Like all editors and
publishers in the pre-e-mail era, he produced a stream of
correspondence—up to twenty letters a day—which, in his case,
comes to nearly two hundred boxes in the M&S archives at

McMaster University. His hundreds of correspondents included many of the writers who helped invent modern Canadian literature and our vision of Canada; the most powerful figures in American, British and Canadian publishing and culture; governors general, prime ministers and provincial premiers; as well as ordinary Canadians such as the ones offended by Leonard Cohen's *Beautiful Losers*. It is arguable that no other publisher has ever played as central a role in his country's culture and society as McClelland has in Canada. With the possible exceptions of Northrop Frye and Margaret Atwood, no other cultural figure has been as influential.

It's only a slight stretch to suggest that the postwar evolution of Canadian political and cultural nationalism could not have happened without the development of McClelland and Stewart into a major publisher with a nationalist agenda, an agenda fostered by its head. Claims about the influence of books are always difficult to substantiate, but there's no doubt that the books McClelland published and often flamboyantly promoted created a new awareness of Canadian writing and a new attitude towards Canadian literature, both French and English. The New Canadian Library series of paperback reprints of Canadian "classics," for example, which McClelland began in 1957 under the editorship of Malcolm Ross, has been more important in helping determine the canon of Canadian literature than the work of any literary critic except Northrop Frye. Had the NCL not been launched, Canadians would not have had many of the raw materials essential for the debate about a national literature.

The company that the twenty-four-year-old McClelland joined in November 1946, after distinguished war service as the captain of a motor torpedo boat, had been founded in 1906 by his father, John A. McClelland, and Frederick D. Goodchild. The other major Canadian publishers at the time were Macmillan, Clarke Irwin, Ryerson, Musson and Thomas Allen. Though McClelland and Goodchild, later McClelland and Stewart, published some prominent Canadian writers, much of the firm's business came from agency publishing, the distribution of books by English and American publishers. At different times it had a mildly nationalist orientation that could be seen, for example, in its commitment to the republication of Canadian works of the nineteenth century. McClelland spent his first two years learning the business from the ground up, including periods on the road. By 1952 he had become general manager and executive vice-president and was running the house. He never looked back.

In retrospect, the fifties and sixties were probably McClelland's happiest, most productive and most successful years. Sales were greater and more books were published annually in the seventies, but the first two decades have the freshness and excitement of the early weeks of a love affair. One senses in the letters McClelland's interest and enjoyment in almost every aspect of the company as he seems gradually to sense what he might be able to do with his father's publishing house, a house that, although successful by Canadian standards, hadn't left its mark on Canadian literature in the way that even Ryerson Press under Lorne Pierce had. Sometimes flying by the seat of his pants—a trick he would master in the financially troubled seventies and eighties—he remade the company in his image, taking it in directions no one could have imagined in the forties.

Letters to Malcolm Ross and W. L. Morton allow us to listen in to the planning of the NCL and the Canadian Centenary Series, which would develop into an eighteen-volume history of the country; letters to Irving Layton, Leonard Cohen, Earle Birney and Al Purdy show McClelland's close involvement in the making of modern Canadian poetry, even though he later claimed he never read it; and in his exchanges with perennial best-sellers Pierre Berton, Farley Mowat and Peter Newman, we can see a publisher who knows that he picked three winners who would not only make money for M&S but also create an audience for Canadian books and writing. McClelland often claimed that he "never published a book expecting to lose money," and the comment is certainly true if one thinks of

Berton, Mowat and Newman. But some of his most ambitious projects of the period—Frank Newfeld's beautifully designed poetry books, NCL, the Centenary Series and the Carleton Library—could only have been taken on by a man whose vision regularly ignored his company's balance sheet. There is no doubt about the value of the New Canadian Library and the Carleton Library reprints of important Canadian works in various disciplines, but one suspects that a more financially astute publisher would have realized that they were both more trouble than they were worth.

More surprisingly, at least for a Toronto-based publisher, McClelland also had a career-long commitment to publishing fiction by Quebec authors, such as Gabrielle Roy, Roger Lemelin, Marie-Claire Blais, André Langevin, Jacques Ferron and Hubert Aquin. From Roy's *Tin Flute* (1947) to Aquin's *Prochain Episode* (1967) and Langevin's *Orphan Street* (1976), M&S published translations of many of the important Quebec novels of the period as well as reprinting classics by writers like Ringuet. Roy was his favourite writer—he classed her work with Margaret Laurence's—and his correspondence with her extends over nearly thirty years and includes remarkably frank exchanges about literature and French-English relations. And though he followed his father in not doing any line-editing of books, several long letters to Langevin show the close attention he paid to the in-house editing of novels he admired. His enthusiasm for Québécois literature waned with the Quiet Revolution because, one suspects, of its political orientation and its often experimental nature.

His loyalty to his writers was legendary, and was implicit in his often repeated comment that M&S published "authors, not books." He helped Mordecai Richler with house prices in Toronto and Montreal; he eased Margaret Laurence's return to Canada; he passed on information about orthopaedic surgeons to one of his novelists; and he almost helped start a fund for Earle Birney when Birney, in fact, didn't need the money. Sylvia Fraser has recalled that he often provided "advances on books that he knew could never turn a profit," and published "a shaky second novel in hopes of inspiring a fully realized third one."

With a handful of irascible exceptions, the letters reveal a patient, tactful man willing to do almost anything to make an author happy: he reassures writers suffering through a crisis of confidence; he sends messages and presents to those who feel ignored; he massages egos bruised by a negative review; and he does damage control when books come out with typos and when royalty statements don't make sense or cheques don't arrive on time. But when provoked, as in several exchanges with the feisty Birney, he gives as good as he gets, though often apologizing afterwards.

But if McClelland published authors (not books), he also promoted them as no one had ever done before in Canada and perhaps anywhere else. On the ides of March in 1980, for instance, he and Sylvia Fraser dressed in togas and rode up Yonge Street in a chariot to promote her novel *The Emperor's Virgin*. An unexpected snowstorm stalled the chariot, froze the toga'd attendants and prevented customers from coming to the signing, though it did ensure that the failed event would pass into publishing lore. The chariot driving up Yonge Street through the snow is, in a manner of speaking, only the tip of the iceberg. The quicksilver and golden-tongued McClelland would charm, cajole, hustle, manipulate and twist arms if he had to. Robert Fulford once called him the ringmaster of Canadian literature. If it would sell books and create an audience for Canadian writing, Jack McClelland would consider doing it. The fifties ended with the Meet the Authors Dinner; the sixties saw national tours by M&S poets and a proposed tour by Pierre Berton dressed like a train engineer, which the author vetoed; the seventies had a water-divining contest to promote Laurence's *Diviners*; and the eighties began with the chariot in the snow as well as the Night of One Hundred Authors. My favourite is the promotion "of an otherwise forgettable book on reptiles by sending columnists empty boxes with letters claiming the boxes contained live snakes."

In a perfect world, the seventies would have been the period

of consolidation and business strategies that would have put
M&S on a sound financial basis for the first time in its history.
Instead, two years of financial losses, in 1967 ($69,097) and 1968
($123,533), brought the company to near bankruptcy and exposed
McClelland's Achilles' heel: the balance sheet. He was a great
publisher but a shaky businessman. The various successes of the
1967-85 period were accomplished under the recurrent threat of
bankruptcy and announcements of loans and impending sale,
despite $14 million in sales in 1979. Still, when history demands
to examine a publisher's books, it's not asking to see the bottom
line. What it wants is on the shelves. And by that standard, M&S
published some of the most memorable books of the era: René
Lévesque's *Option for Québec* (1968), Berton's *Great Railway 1871-1881*
(1970), Richler's *St. Urbain's Horseman* (1971), Atwood's *Surfacing*
(1972), Peter Newman's *Canadian Establishment* (1975), Ken Adachi's
Enemy That Never Was (1976), Rudy Wiebe's *Scorched-Wood People*
(1977), Harold Town and David Silcox's *Tom Thomson: The Silence
and the Storm* (1978), Michael Ondaatje's *There's a Trick with a Knife
I'm Learning to Do* (1979) and *Running in the Family* (1982). This was
also the period that saw the expansion of the NCL, the *History of
Canada* (eighteen volumes) and the *Illustrated Natural History of
Canada* (twelve volumes), as well as the launching in 1977 of the
$50,000 Seal First Novel Award. This is a small selection from la
crème de la crème, from those books that McClelland wanted
the company to be remembered for, though as a publisher he
was as supportive of Charles Templeton, Charlotte Vale Allen
and Merle Shain as he was of Gabrielle Roy, Mordecai Richler
and Margaret Laurence.

The letters of the eighties suggest that McClelland realized
that both as a businessman and as a scout or handicapper of
literary talent he had done all he could. Painful as the realization
must have been, "The Canadian Publishers" would be better off
in other hands; the company needed infusions of energy and
money. As the public and private tributes indicated, McClelland
had become part of the history that he had himself helped
create. Matt Cohen catches something of this in his comment

that "Jack McClelland was not only a great publisher, a giant among his peers, but a man instrumental in changing his country's idea of itself, the man who decided Canada should have a literature made to its measure, invented it, published it." And in a playful verse letter, Leonard Cohen told McClelland, "You were the/real Prime Minister of Canada. You still/are. And even though it's all gone down/the tubes, the country that *you* govern/will never fall apart."

The idea of the publisher as "the real Prime Minister" seems startling only if we don't realize that books are more influential in creating or "changing a country's idea of itself" than politicians, who more often than not are concerned with the mundane realpolitik of the state rather than a vision of the nation. Jack McClelland understood this and spent forty years making his vision into a Canadian reality.

Sam Solecki
UNIVERSITY COLLEGE
UNIVERSITY OF TORONTO

The statistics and quotations both here and in the section introductions are from Carl Spadoni and Judy Donnelly's indispensable "Historical Introduction" to *A Bibliography of McClelland & Stewart Imprints, 1909-85: A Publisher's Legacy* (ECW: 1994), Elspeth Cameron's "Adventures in the Book Trade" (*Saturday Night*, November 1983), *Jack McClelland: The Publisher of Canadian Literature* (University of Guadalajara: 1996), and Paul Audley's "Book Publishing in Canada" (in *Getting It Back*, Abraham Rotstein and Gary Lax, eds. [Clarke, Irwin and Co., 1974]).

THE FORTIES AND FIFTIES:
The Education of a Publisher

When Jack McClelland joined his father's publishing house in November 1946, there were no obvious reasons to think that he would revolutionize Canadian publishing and also influence the development of Canadian culture. His parents, Ethel and Jack McClelland, Sr., had opposed their son's career move on the grounds that no one gets rich in publishing. They could also have pointed to his lack of experience. Beyond what he refers to as "a cheap [postwar] B.A." from the University of Toronto and memories of having seen Charles G. D. Roberts, Lucy Maud Montgomery, Ralph Connor and Stephen Leacock visiting his parents, his qualifications seemed to be non-existent. On the other hand, he was ambitious, energetic and willing to work from the ground up. And his timing couldn't have been better. The influence of British publishers was waning, and the flood of American houses to fill the gap wouldn't begin until the sixties. And in 1951 the cultural nationalism of the Massey-Lévesque Report would have long-term repercussions for Canadian publishing.

The company he joined, like most Canadian houses of the period, survived as much by agency publishing—issuing foreign books under a house's own imprint—as by publishing Canadian books. In 1947, for instance, almost half of the M&S catalogue consisted of books acquired by agency arrangements, a situation that would continue until 1963, when McClelland notified twenty-three foreign publishers that M&S would no longer distribute their books in Canada. In the meantime, M&S was the Canadian "publisher" of Winston Churchill and best-selling novelists like Nevil Shute (*No Highway*), A. J. Cronin (*The Spanish Gardener*) and John P. Marquand (*Point of No Return*). Still, scanning the catalogues of the late forties and early fifties, one can see hints that McClelland, who became general manager and executive vice-president in 1952, was moving the company in a new direction, reshaping it to the point that calling it "The Canadian Publishers" would carry conviction.

During the decade in which Canada adjusted to postwar immigration, the cold war, rock and roll, and the Diefenbaker steamroller of 1958, McClelland laid the foundations for the company's glory years in the sixties and seventies. In 1948 he initiated the Indian File Books poetry series, which won three Governor General's Literary Awards and prepared the ground for later books by Earle Birney, Irving Layton, Leonard Cohen and Al Purdy that changed the face of modern Canadian poetry. Coextensive with this is the beginning of a career-long commitment to French-Canadian fiction, with the publication of Gabrielle Roy's *Tin Flute* (1947), Roger Lemelin's *Plouffe Family* (1950) and André Langevin's *Dust Over the City* (1955). The mid-fifties also saw the appearance of the first M&S books by Pierre Berton (*The Royal Family*, 1954) and Farley Mowat (*The Regiment*, 1955), two authors whose reputations grew in tandem with that of the house itself.

But although this program is impressive—especially if one factors in McClelland's championing of Earle Birney's occasionally scatological wartime satire *Turvey* (1949) and his surprising commitment to Sheila Watson's experimental novel *The Double Hook* (1959)—it isn't noticeably different from what other publishers were doing or might have done. His growing confidence as well as the beginnings of his nationalistic vision are more obvious in the two great publishing projects he set in motion in 1954 and 1956 respectively, neither of which would have been launched by a more cautious publisher. The first of the ambitious projects, the New Canadian Library of paperback reprints of Canadian "classics," was the idea of Malcolm Ross, whose lectures McClelland had attended at the University of Toronto, but the publisher took to it like Gordie Howe to a puck. Between them, McClelland and Ross selected the texts that would not only make the teaching of Canadian literature possible but that would form the basis for the often heated debates in the eighties and nineties over the Canadian canon. It may be the only series in the history of Canadian publishing to have had a book written around it and to be discussed at length in graduate theses. Most of these developments would have shocked Ross and his publisher in 1957, when they issued their first four titles: Morley Callaghan's *Such Is My Beloved*, Frederick Philip Grove's *Over Prairie Trails*, Stephen Leacock's *Literary Lapses* and Sinclair Ross's *As for Me and My House*. The last, a major Canadian novel, had been out of print since the war and had originally been published by an American house.

The Canadian Centenary Series, a multi-volume history of Canada, was proposed in 1955 to W. L. Morton, a professor of history at the University of Manitoba and, at that time, best known for his book *The Progressive Party in Canada* (1950). Two years of discussion refined it into a proposed "sixteen-volume history of Canada covering events from 1000 to 1967" that would be issued between 1959 and 1967. The lengthy correspondence between Morton and McClelland, though often concerned primarily with practical details, nevertheless also contains the publisher's first explicit statements of the constitutive connection he saw between publishing and nationalism. The following paragraph from September 13, 1956, is typical and could serve as an epigraph for this volume.

I think this history is needed for the same reason that we needed railways in this country; that we needed a Canadian Broadcasting Corporation and a National Film Board. None of the foregoing are any more commercially feasible than the history, but they are not any the less important because of it. A proper historical record is part of our cultural heritage, and while the consumer market for the books may be virtually non-existent, they are badly needed in our libraries and in libraries throughout the world. They are required by the teachers who will educate Canadian children of the future; they are needed by college students, historians and researchers.

TO EARLE BIRNEY

Earle Birney (1904–1995): Chaucer scholar, editor, novelist (*Turvey*, 1949), and poet. He published several books, including his *Collected Poems* (1975), with M&S despite an often stormy relationship with J.M. One of his obituaries referred to him as "the West's Trotskyite troubadour," an allusion to his politics and to his meeting with Leon Trotsky in Norway in the late thirties. He is one of the fathers of modern Canadian literature. The following letters deal with some of the problems raised by Birney's use in *Turvey* of words that had not appeared previously in Canadian fiction. The novel is still in print as a New Canadian Classic.

May 4, 1949
Dr. A. Earle Birney
Dept. of English
University of British Columbia.
Vancouver, B.C.

Dear Earle:
Enthusiasm for *Turvey* runs high! I think you have written not only an incisive satire on army life and a fascinating character study but also a *sure-fire best-seller*. Who would expect such a thing from a university professor—or better still, from one of Canada's most distinguished poets? It ain't right.

We had a meeting of our book committee on Friday and the vote was unanimous in favour of sending a contract immediately. This decision was subject only to general agreement on the touchy subject of censorship. I know you anticipated this and hope you won't think us too much in the tradition of Canadian publishers in our suggestions. Frankly, there would be little point in the contract or in our publishing the book were we not in accord with you on these matters. We would not wish to go ahead if we anticipated the possibility of our being loath to promote the book to the fullest extent.

Generally speaking, I would say this: we don't want to urge or force you into any deletions which you think might detract from the value of the book or which you might later regret. Our first interest must be *sales*, yours the literary and artistic effect (plus sales). We find many department stores (an increasingly important book outlet) and bookstores loath to sell books which they object to on moral grounds. We would like to have them on our side.

Now for some general suggestions which are probably unnecessary. I realize, of course, that it is your first draft.

(1) We think the manuscript should be shortened as much as possible. There are two reasons for this. First, production costs and second, because we think it will improve the pace and readability of the book. I personally can see no chapters or sections which could be deleted as such, but am thinking more of a general cutting down in the reworking. I believe you intend to do this. One American publisher who read a few chapters thought some of the material dated and old hat. I think there is some merit in the criticism but these parts you will see when you rework it. At any rate, we would like to produce the book at $2.75—not more than $3—and the manuscript is too long at the moment to hope for such a price.

(2) Censorship! I think you have caught the flavour of the army and army talk to a remarkable degree without the use of too many obscenities. Generally speaking, we would prefer to see all vulgar words deleted except where you think they are absolutely necessary. I particularly object to some of the anatomical references, but I think you will too. I am attaching a more detailed list which I made during a hasty rereading of the manuscript. We don't want to quibble; we want to agree with you. Remember that Aunt Emma's 3 bucks is just as good as anybody else's.

"Bucking," I think, is delightful if not overworked. I think you could cut down in some places. "Cr--nt" is quite objectionable. We don't like the word "Jesus" when it would be possible to substitute "Jeezus" or "Geezes," etc. I don't think anyone means "Jesus" when they use the expression, so there is no need to risk offending. An expression such as "bug--y dance" is O.K., I suppose, but does not seem to add much and might as well be out. I hope we can agree on these matters.

Sincerely,

J. G. McClelland

FROM EARLE BIRNEY

c/o Einar Neilson
Bowen Island, B.C.
May 17, 1949

Dear Jack:
I've delayed replying to yours of the 4th until I had time to think over your many suggestions for revision.

First of all, I want to thank you warmly for your encouraging comments in general and for the pains you have taken to go through the MS and make specific comments and suggestions. I'm glad you like *Turvey* and, naturally, I have no objections to the notion it may sell well. I didn't, however, set out to write a best-seller—if I had, I wouldn't have chosen the war as a topic or a novel with so little love interest—and I'm frankly more interested in doing as good a job with the type of novel it is than in tinkering with it to make a best-seller out of it. This will explain my reluctance to make some of the alterations you suggest. I am also somewhat disappointed in some of the clauses in the contract sent me and will be writing separately about that shortly. I do want to say at the start, however, that I hope very much we can come to a satisfactory agreement on *Turvey* because it is certainly with your firm that I prefer to publish it.

Now for the censorship problem. You can't have it both ways; if, as you say, I've caught the flavour of the army talk, it's been partly by a selective use of army obscenities. If I "delete all vulgar words," that flavour goes and a lot of the sparkle and veracity with it. Also, I suspect Aunt Emma reads a lot more of this sort of thing than the parsons and the Babbitty booksellers imagine, and doesn't object. In fact, I know it. I made a point, since I got your letter, of rereading several *Canadian* novelists (and the argument is reinforced if one cites American novelists, but I'll play it the hard way) and here are some of the words, printed in full, in novels which nobody, to my knowledge, ever even talked of banning in Canada. At any rate, they didn't ban them, and a lot of them were sold:

> Bruce Hutchison: *The Hollow Men* (Longmans, Green):
> Suffering Jesus, Holy Jesus, Great Jesus, Christ! Bastard, floozy, bitched himself, backside, pain in the ass, god-damn sonofabitch. (The last two words are used, in one place, to describe a preacher, p. 180, and on p. 145, in a single para, sonofabitch occurs four times and goddamn five times.)

> J. V. Nablo: *The Long November*, Dutton, N. Y. (but widely distributed in Canada; book is a novel of the Canadian Army, World War II): Jesus Christ Almighty, By Jesus, for Christ's sake, goddamit. Bugger all, sonofabitch, suck-holing, stumblebum, crap, shacked up, quickie, a lay, shove it up your keister, tired of being screwed-without-being-kissed.

> Edward Meade: *Remember Me* (Faber & Faber—but by a Canadian and about Canadian army):
> Buggered, dirty bastards, horse's arse, sonofabitch, etc.[1]

One of the interesting things about such lists is that they look much worse distilled like that; met in their context in the dialogue they slip by without much notice, and make the dialogue natural. Remember that when you look over the list you extracted from my book.

Now for your detailed list. My chief concern is to keep the rhythm and general sound patterns of soldiers' talk, of Canadian talk in general, so the exact spelling doesn't trouble me so much. So, you can spell Jesus any way you like, and bejeezis. I'm glad you accept "bucking" which seems to me the only possible substitute, since "mucking" is an actual word used as well, and "fugging" is definitely associated with *The Naked and the Dead* and would look like mere imitation.

I don't know what to do about the standard expression "you lucky cunt" which I heard every day of my army life. What *I* would like to do is keep it in, as James Joyce did, and Malraux, and D. H. Lawrence, and Henry Miller and a host of other great artists. But I offered a compromise in "crunt," and you don't like that either. Well, we could simply have a "c---." Or would you take "twat"? I want to be able to suggest the phrase in a way the soldier will recognize, How about "gunt"?

On the same tack, I'm willing to compromise with "b-lls" for "balls," but not "b----" which could be confused with something else. The rhythm and sound of these things are important for the sense of reality of a spoken sentence.

Well, Jack, this seems as effective a compromise as I can make offhand. After all, I have to sign a contract which makes me wholly responsible financially so what risks are you taking? If there are expressions that all your readers squirm at, then I'll have to reconsider, but so far yours is the first unfavourable reaction I've had to the language; there have been no proposals from your editorial department to change a word on the score of censorship. I see your position and I've tried to meet it halfway. Also I realize that other expressions may come under scrutiny before the book is printed and I'm always willing to hear an argument; but I won't have the language generally devitalized just to make another innocuous false war-novel for Aunt Emma. I'd rather not publish at all, if that's the way I have to publish in Canada. I'm not complaining, of course. You've kindly passed over a lot of weaknesses in the book that pain me still; I realize there's much revision to do. But I'll have to keep my eye on the literary ball,* not on the nineteenth hole, the land of best-sellers and free drinks in the clubhouse. I've been grateful for your suggestions and will be glad to have more.

Sincerely,

Earle Birney

* not to say "b-alls"!

1. Bruce Hutchison (1901–92): distinguished political journalist and editor and author of several books including *The Unknown Country: Canada and Her People* (1943) and *The Far Side of the Street* (1976), his autobiography. He won three National Newspaper Awards and three Governor General's Awards. J.V. Nablo (b. 1910) and Edward Meade have not been traced.

TO EARLE BIRNEY

June 16, 1959
Dr. Earle Birney
c/o Einar Neilson
Bowen Island, B.C.

Dear Earle:
The first point which bothers me is your comment that mine is the first objection or unfavourable reaction to *Turvey* on the score of language. The fact that there has been no word from our editorial department on this score comes as a surprise to me.

Although mine were largely personal views, the whole was based on my interpretation of the feeling of our board of directors. It is my task to express their opinion in matters of editorial policy. Actually, Earle, I don't think we're going to have too much trouble getting together on the book, but there are a few more things I would like to say.

First, please believe that we have no desire to impose

arbitrary standards of censorship. We reserve the right to make
as many suggestions as we think may be in our mutual interest,
but after you have given our suggestions a fair hearing, we must
ultimately be prepared to accept your decision, as the creator of
the work. Now as to our yardstick—

Our suggestions are based primarily on what we consider
good taste rather than fear of court action. Where profanity,
vulgarity or obscenity are required, then we must accept them.
But how is the justification to be determined? Is it not possible
that writers such as Joyce, Lawrence, Malraux, etc. succeeded in
spite of obscenity rather than because of it?

As a publisher, we have a duty to think of sales. Pornographic,
erotic and sexy passages increase sales. It is our belief that
profanity and vulgarity sometimes have the opposite effect.
Turvey could be read and enjoyed in many thousands of homes
throughout Canada if some of the potentially objectionable
parts were removed. If it is published as it now stands, I am
certain that a sizeable market would be lost. Forgetting the
mercenary angle, I wonder if it is fair to these readers. I would
think of you as one might have thought of Gainsborough had he
painted *Blue Boy* with his fly open.

I now come to the point where you list the words used in
three Canadian novels. I doubt if any of these books were
improved by use of the words listed, but it is possible that they
were. That, to me, has nothing to do with *Turvey*, however. I
would be surprised if any of these three books had a very great
sale in Canada. I know for a fact that many bookstores refused
to stock *The Long November* and many others would not
recommend it. This was particularly so in the author's home
town. That in itself is probably more of a condemnation of the
Canadian public than anything else, but the fact remains that
sales were limited because of the nature of the book. I don't
want to labour this point, so will leave it at that.

In your last paragraph, you say that you have signed a
contract making you wholly responsible financially and that we
are taking no risk. I don't understand this remark. We are not

anticipating any court action. Our suggestions are certainly not based on fears of this kind. If they were, we might be a hell of a lot more cautious because you must realize that such a clause appearing in a standard contract means nothing in court. A publisher is always jointly responsible with the bookseller and the author in cases of this kind, and as your publisher, we would certainly stand beside you completely.

You say before closing, "I would rather not publish at all, if that's the way I have to publish in Canada." To me, Earle, this is not quite fair. I don't feel that anything I have said for the firm is particularly Canadian. Our suggestions might have been made by any American, English or other publisher. If we are wrong, it is not because we are Canadian or because of any peculiar pussyfooting attitude of Canadian publishers. When Edmund Wilson[1] submitted the *Memoirs of Hecate County* to his publishers, they recommended that he delete one story which they thought might be considered offensive. He refused to do so. They accepted his judgement and published the book. It was banned in the United States. The author, publisher and booksellers were prosecuted and the book removed from sale. It is doubtful if the book was improved one damn bit by the chapter included.

Well, there it is, Earle. You must, of course, decide for yourself, but please keep in mind the motivation or interest at stake of those people who do or do not make suggestions concerning *Turvey*. I am being perfectly candid and hope you will not think the less of me for doing so.

Kind regards to Esther and yourself.

Yours sincerely,

J. G. McClelland

1. For Edmund Wilson see the memo of August 19, 1975.

FROM EARLE BIRNEY

Department of English
University of British Columbia
Vancouver, B.C.
July 1, 1949

Dear Jack:
Yesterday the final corrected typescript of *Turvey* was sent to
your editorial office by airmail, and the five extra carbon copies
you asked for were shipped by rail express. They should all
reach you well within the July 15 deadline you originally
suggested if the book were to be given fall publication. It was
not physically possible, however, to prepare *corrected* copies of
these five carbons. You will see that there are corrections in the
airmail original on almost every page of the 369; these are
duplicated in my own copy, for safety's sake, but if you want
your own copies to be accurate you will have to get a clerk to
write in the corrections. You may well want to do this—and I'm
sorry there wasn't time to have it done for you at this end—
because the corrections are sometimes important (and always, I
hope, improvements).

For example, numerous changes had to be made in some chapters
at the last minute, on the advice of my lawyer, to ensure that we
would not be liable to libel suits. Of course, any actual people drawn
on in *Turvey* were already thoroughly disguised in name, appearance,
Canadian origin; but I had not realized how easy it is for the
commanding officer of a *specialized* unit to make out a case that a
similarly specialized unit in a novel is a libel on his unit and his
command of it. My lawyer doubts that much damage could be
established, but he advised me to play it safe by disguising the *units* as
well as the people even more than I had. Hence a lot of changes. And
here I'd better have it quite clear that the copies are submitted to you
uncorrected only to speed up your own plans; if you circulate these
copies without having them corrected I won't be responsible for any
suits that might develop. Of course I'm being super-cautious in saying

this; there's just the faint possibility one of your travellers might show a copy to a bookseller who shows it to a relative who fancies he sees himself or his unit in some passage—and the mere circulation might constitute a libel, even without printing. At least that's what my lawyer says, and he is about as cautious a character as one is likely to meet. I'm pretty sure that since following out the revisions he suggests, the book is now foolproof.

I haven't answered yours of June 16 earlier because I've been working hellbent for leather on *Turvey* and didn't write anybody. I think, though, you'll find the final draft takes care of most of your objections. And the length is down by about thirty pages. "Cunt" is out, in all forms; "Jesus" and "Christ" are always misspelled. I'm glad of your interest in these details, though, Jack, and have profited from them, as you can see. *Turvey* will never be a *Blue Boy*, however; he's the sort of guy whose fly was often open, because that's the world he lived in.

Sincerely,

Earle Birney

TO EARLE BIRNEY

September 22, 1949
Professor Earle Birney
5601 President's Row
University Hill
Vancouver, B.C.

Dear Earle:
Our solicitor is concerned about the house painter whose name is Thomas Turvey. He suggests that you contact this man and obtain his written consent to the publication of the book. He thinks a little flattery might make this attainable and says it would protect us from any possible lawsuit. There is a likelihood that if the book is the distinct success we think it will

be, some shyster lawyer may get hold of the painter and sue for the odd dollar.

We are writing to Ottawa to see if there were any other Thomas Turveys in the army. If there were, we will attempt to get similar statements from them, just to be on the safe side. It may be wise to avoid reference to the house painter in future press releases.

Best regards.

Yours sincerely,

J. G. McClelland

TO MALCOLM ROSS

Malcolm Ross (b. 1911): professor of English at the University of Toronto, Queen's University and Dalhousie University. He edited M&S's New Canadian Library for nearly three decades, and his choices, made in consultation with J.M. and others, helped shape the canon of Canadian literature.

January 27, 1955
Mr. Malcolm Ross
Queen's University
Kingston, Ontario

Dear Mr. Ross:
After a good deal of further discussion here, and after a long struggle with costs, we are finally able to turn on the green light and say that we are prepared to go ahead with the [New Canadian Library] project as planned, sink or swim. The one great difficulty that we see now is that there doesn't seem to be a hell of a lot of money in it for anybody. I am most concerned as to your own reaction to the proposal that we are able to make. It will mean damn little remuneration for you in relation to the effort involved. In view of this, you may want to chuck the whole thing. On this score, we hope that you will be able to

take the view that even though there isn't much in it, it is worth making the test, at least on two books, in order to find out whether or not the idea is a practical one. We think, too, to offset the lack of remuneration, that you should take into account the fact that the series will have a certain prestige value as far as you are concerned.

On to the grim facts! We will have to price the books at $1— possibly 95¢ but probably $1. Out of this sum we are able to allocate only 7¢ for royalty. In the case of certain books the split between editor and author will not be important, but in other cases it will assume considerable importance. We suggest 4¢ a copy to you as the editor and 3¢ a copy to the author as being an equitable split and about par for the course. We would like to limit our advance to $100 in each case—i.e., $100 to you, $100 to the author.

We would propose to do the first two books together as soon as we can rush them through. On the back of the cover we would announce the next six titles but would not plan to publish the next two titles until the spring of 1956. Following your suggestion, the first book would be Grove's *Over Prairie Trails*, and the second would be either one of Callaghan's two books, *Such Is My Beloved* or *More Joy in Heaven*. I think he leans to the former. I did, incidentally, discuss the proposal with him. He is interested and there will probably not be any difficulty re the royalty. He would like to have the opportunity of discussing the relative merits of the two books with you before the final decision is made. Thus, it would be well if you could start on the Grove first and hope either to meet with Callaghan or correspond with him before the final choice is made.

If you let me know by return that you are still with us, I shall send copies of the books off to you without delay. I think we would plan to start setting the Grove immediately, adding your introduction when it is ready. Some time could be saved in this way. The books will be printed in England.

Best regards.

Yours sincerely,

J. G. McClelland

TO NORMAN LEVINE

Norman Levine (b. 1923): best known as a short-story writer (*Selected Stories*, 1975) and for the memoir *Canada Made Me* (1958). Levine spent much of his early career in England, where *Canada Made Me* was first published. It was distributed in Canada by M&S, despite J.M.'s strong reservations. The book would be a continuing source of tension in the relationship between writer and publisher. It is still in print.

August 16, 1955
Mr. Norman Levine
12 Quay Street
St. Ives
Cornwall, England

Dear Norman:
Thanks for the copy of your article ["Canadian Writers Come into Their Own"] in the *Times Literary Supplement.* I think it is an interesting piece of work and well put together, although, as could be expected, I would take issue with you on many points. I think, for instance, that you are inclined to overestimate the importance of Richler and Brian Moore in the overall picture, possibly because you are in England and because you know them both. They may become important but I don't think they are yet. Then, too, I wonder how you can say that Ethel Wilson is the only female novelist in Canada who not only shows us the nerves that go under the working of her characters but their guts as well. I have great admiration for Mrs. Wilson's work, but surely Gabrielle Roy, who is something of a stylist too, by the way, does this even better than Mrs. Wilson. Robertson Davies deserves some mention. Klein, as a novelist, is a stylist surely, and there are others. In passing, I have the impression that neither Ernest Buckler nor John Cornish are "young" novelists, although I may be wrong on this. And Len Peterson, as a novelist in the Canadian scene, is hardly worthy of mention'. He hasn't produced a book-length script for about seven years, and even at that he probably showed more promise than anything else. Still,

why the hell should I sit here and pick holes in your article. The *TLS* publishes Levine and they don't publish McClelland.
Cheers!

J. G. McClelland

1. For Ethel Wilson see Hugh Hood's letter of July 24, 1961; A.M. Klein (1909–72): a major Canadian poet whose one novel, *The Second Scroll* (1951), was heavily influenced by James Joyce's *Ulysses*; John Cornish (b. 1914): his novels include *Olga* (1959), *Sherbourne Street* (1968), and *A World Turned Turtle* (1969); Len Petersen (b. 1917): a man of letters, scriptwriter, dramatist, and novelist, best known for his work in the theatre, *The Great Hunger* (1967), *Burlap Bags* (1972), and radio drama, *Evariste Galois* (1984).

FROM EARLE BIRNEY

Because Birney read his royalty statements as closely as he did medieval manuscripts, as well as paying close attention to the promotion and sales of his books, many of his letters to J.M. focus on the particulars of the writer-publisher relationship. The following two letters are representative of many over the next three decades in which the two men spar over everything from royalties to readings. It is worth noting that Birney has the distinction of being the only correspondent who could regularly make J.M. lose his temper in a letter. Several, including Layton, could exasperate him, but only Birney could drive him over the edge.

University of British Columbia
Vancouver, B.C.
October 27, 1956

Dear Jack:
I have just looked over the copy of my last letter to you and to which your outburst of October 18 was a reply. I can find nothing in my letter which justifies the bad temper and

rudeness of yours. The royalty report, by your own admission, was not clear, did not mean what it said. I did not impute or intend to impute any dishonesty on the part of your firm or yourself when I asked for clarification, nor have I "suggested or implied" on previous occasions that you were. I did not know that you sent out novels to stores on a returnable basis. Perhaps you told me once and I had forgotten; in such a case I must ask you to excuse my ignorance and forgetfulness. Please be assured that it is not a policy I am criticizing; I was merely asking for information, and I was certainly not asking for royalties on unsold books. Nothing in my letter justifies your suggesting that I was, or that I was objecting to being charged for author's gift copies.

Now that you have told me [*Down the Long Table*] is going so badly and it is in reverse gear, I can excuse some of your impatience in discussing its royalties, and I am truly sorry that you are losing so much money on the book. I appreciate also your motives in keeping the true facts from me, though I do not at all think it was necessary. I do not, however, like the arrogance and rudeness of your letter. If I cannot write you for further information about an inadequate royalty statement without getting an insulting reply, you must find someone else in your firm to carry on what necessary correspondence there may be with me.

As ever, with best personal wishes.

Earle Birney

TO EARLE BIRNEY

November 6, 1956
Dr. Earle Birney
The University of British Columbia
Vancouver, B.C.

Dear Earle:

Much as I hate to admit it, after rereading your letter and my own—and this took no little courage—I must admit that I am the one who should make the apology. I must have been in a foul mood. Your letter hit me at a bad time and I got mad. It really had nothing to do with the lack of success of the book at the sales counter—this was our mutual misfortune and was not all that bad anyway. It's probably just the fact that you are a university professor, and as you know, I have a chip on my shoulder about Canadian university professors in general because of the many times they have made unwarranted (in my opinion) attacks on the Canadian publishing industry for various reasons but for motives that are beyond my understanding. To prevent a recurrence of this type of incident, however, I have heeded your suggestion and appointed a pretty gal to look after all further correspondence with Earle Birney concerning monetary matters and royalties. Inasmuch as I have accepted your suggestion, perhaps you will accept one from me. That is, that you should remove the framed royalty report from the wall of your office and have it reframed to include a copy of my reply to your letter. This would serve as ample warning to any would-be authors who might venture into your office that when it comes to author–publisher correspondence on the subject of royalties, they had better steer clear of me. Even though the letter may have been rude and unjustified, I still feel that it was an excellent piece of work, and I am proud of it. It is one of the few letters of its type that I have written for posterity. My secretary will vouch for the fact that she types at least one of these a week on a variety of subjects, but that they seldom escape the waste-paper basket in the office.

Cheers!

J. G. McClelland

TO FARLEY MOWAT

Farley Mowat (b. 1921): one of M&S's best-selling authors, principally known for his books about the Arctic (*People of the Deer*, 1952; *Never Cry Wolf*, 1963). Often appearing in public in a kilt, the prickly and playful Mowat was probably the most colourful writer published by J.M.

November 20, 1956
Mr. Farley Mowat
Palgrave, Ontario

Dear Farley:
I have decided that the only way I can ever get this information to you is to let my secretary in on the deal because otherwise I would never get a letter written. So the picture is this. The staff dinner is to be held at Fantasy Farm on Thursday, December 6. It's a Fiftieth-Anniversary dinner but purely a staff affair with the only outsiders being auditors, lawyers, ad agency types, etc. No authors, booksellers, librarians invited, thank God, although we are having an anniversary party for them on December 27, to which party you may receive an invitation if you are still on our list.

Although in many ways what I am asking you to do is a hell of an imposition, I have hopes that it may appeal to your sense of humour. I would like you to appear before the close of the dinner as an uninvited guest. I would suggest that you come up and speak to me first and then I would reluctantly get up and introduce you and announce that you wanted to say a few words on behalf of the authors. You could then start off as if you were going to make a laudatory address about fifty years of Canadian publishing. You could say how important the occasion is, that you had discussed the matter with some other M&S authors— such as they are—and that they had nominated you as a delegation of one to attend this auspicious occasion and speak on behalf of the authors. With a large build-up you could then say that as a matter of fact it is typical of the cheap, mean, one-horse policy of the firm that we haven't even invited any authors to the dinner. At this point, I would try to begin to appear suitably outraged. You could then begin to tick off the gags one by one. As a start you could pull a few out of your own repertoire about *The People of the Deer*. What I want you to do mainly from that point is to tie in as many of our departments as possible so that they will all get a laugh out of the gags. I leave all this to you but a few of the gimmicks are as follows:

I think you could say that all your early dealings were with me, but that you had always suspected that there must be someone more intelligent behind the scenes—that eventually this led to meeting Mr. Stewart, who was very friendly and reassuring and patted you on the back, but called you Sonny Boy because he obviously couldn't remember your name; and Mr. McClelland, who was dignified and reserved but who revolted you by pulling some dirty-looking seaweed, which he called dulse, out of his coat pocket and insisting that you eat it (I don't know whether he has ever done this to you, but if he hasn't you haven't lived).

You should have the lost manuscript paper and our explanation that it went to Dent's in error.

You should have the beautifully designed jacket with your name spelled wrong.

You should have publication day, your visit to the bookstores, no copies of the book in the bookstores, the booksellers have never heard of McClelland and Stewart, and in the one store where they did know the name they said that our man hadn't been around for three months and he certainly didn't mention your book—he was trying to sell something called *Burgess Bedtime Storybook*. Your author's copies were very late in arriving, and when they did there was postage due and there were two copies of *Sex, Marriage and Birth Control*, along with four copies of your book. When you returned these, you received two cartons of *Using Our Language*, Grade 6. When you wrote in complaining about this, you were told that we had no record of your order but would investigate. As you never heard anything further, you sold the books to the local school and ordered six copies of your own book from Longmans, Green, who supplied immediately.

You could have the autographing party at which nobody from M&S arrived and the books didn't arrive.

You can go on with this sort of thing ad infinitum, Farley. You can have the royalty report that says "Nil—net of returns." You write in complaining about this because you know there could be no returns as we didn't sell any copies during the last royalty period and you ask for an explanation. You are told to refer to your contract. You write saying that although a contract was promised more than a year ago, you haven't yet received it. You are then told that if you haven't a contract you have no complaint. You then try the stores again and find there is no stock on hand. They tell you that they can't get the book from us. One bookseller shows you a report from us that states that the book is not yet published. Our publicist then writes you to say that she is sorry that not many reviews have appeared, but somehow, through never-to-be-repeated negligence, the review copies weren't sent out. Finally you manage to find copies of your book in a bookstore, but the jackets are torn and the corners are all bashed in. You inquire about this and the bookseller tells you that all the books he gets from Hollinger House [M&S headquarters] come in that condition—that we apparently pack them in old Canada Bread cartons and what the hell do we expect? At some point in the proceedings, you get fed up and decide to phone me. After you get plugged in to a dead line several times and after innumerable busy signals, the switchboard operator finally tells you that I am not in yet. You call back at 10:30 and she says, "Mr. McClelland is not up yet—I mean, in yet." At 11:30 you call again. You overhear the girl whisper, "Is Mr. McClelland still drinking coffee in the cafeteria?" and then you are told that I am in conference.

Well, that's the general idea. If you thought it out a bit you could have a hell of a lot of fun with it, and it would certainly help to enliven what would otherwise be a none-too-exciting evening, I fear. The thing would be best if it did not go on too long, I think, so it wouldn't become obvious. It might be that I could become increasingly annoyed, eventually call over the head waiter, whisper to him, and have him send over the other waiters who would carry you out bodily.

Let me know what you think. I am hoping you will be in Toronto sometime before that date because it would be well if we could have a talk about this.

My best to Fran.

Cheers!

J. G. McClelland

FROM FARLEY MOWAT

P'grave
November [25?], 1956

Dear Jack:
All right, you bastard, but who the hell *feeds* me, and *wines* me. If you think I am going to come in with the finger bowls, and lean and Cassius-like and have to sniff the Bacchanalian air of a Mc. and S. orgy—balls to you, sir.

I shall be in the drinking lobby of Fantasy Farm not later than 18:45 hours on December 6. I will expect to be met by a smiling waiter who, on inquiring my identity, will explain that the bar is mine, courtesy of King John hisself. I will expect to be allowed to remain in said bar, uninterrupted, until at least 21:30 hours, at which time I will gird my loins, sally into the inner sanctum, and give the whole lot of you what-for.

I shall be guided by that invidious document you sent me, and will embellish upon it as the mood strikes me.

No, I won't be in Toronto again until D day. God forfend. Anyway, I've *been* there twice this year. If you have anything further to add to your instruction, carrier pigeon. Don't trust the telephone for a last-minute briefing. It has been out most of this month. You had better detail the approach plan, though; and let me know exact times, places, etc.

Any bastard who tries to *throw* me out will get an Eskimo dagger between his ribs.

Would you ship a dozen copies of *Lost in the Barrens* tout de suite? Somebody has to buy them.

Cheers,

F.

TO FARLEY MOWAT

November 30, 1956
Mr. Farley Mowat
Palgrave, Ontario

Dear Farley:
Thank you for your very vulgar communication which has shocked and alarmed all the young ladies in the office. It's disillusioning to find that a distinguished author and man of letters can talk so terribly.

I am delighted that you are prepared to don the mantle of a proper SOB in our little drama. Although the visit will put you to considerable inconvenience, I suspect that you have really accepted with alacrity, for it will once again give you the opportunity to trot out the real Mowat who has lurked under a pleasing and gentle facade for lo these many months. I am probably doing you a real favour, for this schizophrenic caper can be damaging to the mind. It was amazing how quickly your name came to mind when I sought someone to play the role of the hard, cynical, suspicious, complaining, nasty author.

On to more serious matters. Actually, this will be rather an exotic affair in that, out of deference to Dad, and because we have a number of fairly young employees, there will be no liquor at the dinner. This situation is offset in two ways: (a) by the fact that I am having a cocktail party at the house before the dinner for the outside guests; and (b) McClelland and Stewart bowling league is taking over at around nine o'clock for a Christmas dance, and once the party has passed from our control they will of course serve liquor. I can't ask you to my place before, because that would give the show away. I shall, however, have the doorman armed with a bottle of rum so that you can have a smash in the anteroom while waiting for your cue. I would suggest that you arrive some time between 7:15 and 7:45. The cue that I would suggest is the completion of the introduction of the head table. According to the program, I will move the thing from them to the more or less formal speeches (of which there will be very few) and all of which will be very brief. I think this would be the ideal time for you to come forward before we get down to the serious part. The introduction of the head table I would judge will take place some time between 7:45 and 8:15, depending on the speed of the waiters and on the clatter that they set up in passing dishes around.

I will have them hold a dinner for you so that you can eat after you have spoken, or perhaps you would prefer to eat elsewhere before—whichever you wish. I'll have them save a dinner, in any case. The dinner itself is supposed to be over about nine o'clock, at which time the dance will start. I don't plan to stay for more than a very short while at the dance because [my wife] Elizabeth will not be there, so I hope that we can move off somewhere and have a few drinks.

That's all I can think of for the moment. Thanks again and cheers!

Sincerely,

J. G. McClelland

TO BRIAN MOORE

Brian Moore (b. 1921): Irish-born novelist who lived in Montreal for eleven years before immigrating to the United States. His novels include *Judith Hearne* (1955), *The Luck of Ginger Coffey* (1960), *Catholics* (1972), *Black Robe* (1985) and *Lies of Silence* (1990). He has twice won the Governor General's Award.

January 7, 1957
Mr. Brian Moore
498 Lansdowne Avenue
Westmount,
Montreal, Quebec

Dear Mr. Moore:
Just a note to tell you how delighted we are that we are to have the opportunity of handling your work in Canada. I have just completed reading *The Feast of Lupercal*, and it was a rare and pleasant experience indeed. We shall do our very best to give it the promotion and display—and more important, the sale— that it so richly deserves.

While in Boston recently, I found myself in dispute with Arthur Thornhill Sr. [of Little, Brown] as to whether you consider yourself an Irish writer or a Canadian writer. We both understand that you are a naturalized Canadian, but he is under the impression that you prefer to be considered an Irish writer while I, justifiably I think, took the view that we didn't give a damn about that and would consider you a Canadian writer as far as our own promotion is concerned in Canada. As a matter of fact, Little, Brown have used a quote in their catalogue referring to you as one of the great contemporary Irish writers. It's a hell of a good quote, but I still think you should be a Canadian writer.

It's entirely possible that you couldn't care less about it one way or the other, which is a fair point of view except I do think it could begin to matter over the long term, and I think a clear decision should be made now, if you have not already done so.

Nothing would delight me more than a letter from you saying that you wear a Maple Leaf in your lapel and a beaver hat, for I should take great pleasure in sending this on to Arthur Thornhill. On the other hand, if you are to be an Irish writer I should so instruct our promotion department.

If you come up this way at all, do give me a call.

Yours sincerely,

J. G. McClelland

FROM EARLE BIRNEY

Galiano Island P.O., B.C.
August 6, 1957

Dear Jack:
Your letter of July 24, appealing for news of the Watson MS, went to the U. of Iowa, thence to the hamlet of Anamosa, Iowa, recently celebrated in *Life* as The American Small Town (but this is all irrelevant), thence to UBC and so here. But long ago I wrote you I was returning the MS, and indeed I sent it from UBC last week. It was *schrecklich* of me to bear the script away, and so far away, and I am so penitent I have decided to ask for no fee at all, though I did read the MS, or tried to, and made notes, benefit of which I will now confer on you, gratis. (You must understand the psychology of a $25 whore—it's that, or love; this $10 stuff is only for the poxed old bags.)

The Double Hook is certainly a remarkable piece of writing—there is a sustained poetic-cryptic style with a false simplicity about it which reminds me of T. F. Powys,¹ but without his humour. Unfortunately I think it is a stylistic *tour de force*, monotonous, self-conscious, artificial and lacking in real fictional interest. There is a complex family and community life going on in the novel, but it is all abstracted from ordinary concerns and motivations, and the exposition is so sparse and cryptic that it does not explain and we are left floundering, made to go back again and again to find narrative clues and ways of keeping the characters apart, and never really succeeding. At least, that was my experience. I just don't know what the damn novel is about, or I didn't till it was almost ended. I would read on for the beauty and surprise of the style, then get fed up with its unvaried affectedness, put it down, take it up again (mainly because you wanted an opinion, not because in ordinary circumstances I would have carried on). One trouble, narrative-wise, is the disconnectedness of events, the attempt to keep half a dozen stories going like a juggler, without ever getting properly *in* to any of the stories. As for Coyote, he, or He, seems to me a desperate shift to achieve unity by way of a most unreal totemic deity, meant to be terrifying and turning out to be just funny. No, I would not publish this novel. Sheila Watson has remarkable gifts as a writer, but necessary fictional clarity isn't one of them, yet.

Am I off the double hook?

Cheers,

Earle

1. T. F. Powys (1875–1953): brother of John Cowper and Llewelyn Powys, and author of *Mr. Weston's Good Wine* (1927), a lively allegorical novel in which God returns to the world to hand out Love and Death.

TO ANGUS MOWAT

Angus Mowat (1892–1977): librarian and writer of *Then I'll Look Up* (1938), *Conversations with Young Librarians* (1945) and *Carrying Place* (1944). Al Purdy has written an affectionate essay about him, "Angus," in *Starting from Ameliasburgh: The Collected Prose of Al Purdy* (1995).

November 26, 1957
Mr. Angus Mowat
Director of Public Libraries
Department of Education
206 Huron Street
Toronto, Ontario

Dear Angus:
I enjoyed our lunch the other day. I am sure they didn't know how to do Poached Eggs à la Mocambo, but you must give them points for trying. In view of the fact that Farley and I started downing a few noggins again only a few hours later, I am quite surprised that I remembered the two things that I promised to do.

First, I am sending you, under separate cover, a copy of a book called *Princess New York*. This was published either this spring or last fall—I can't remember. In any case, as I mentioned to you, we haven't been able to sell it. I think the subject matter may interest you, and if you have a moment someday I wish you would let me know why you think it hasn't sold.

The second item is that I was to remind you that I take strong exception to the fact that the Canadian Library Association has apparently decided to join forces with the American Library Association to celebrate in March what is to be called a National Library Week. Now I think that a National Library Week is an extremely good idea. As a Canadian, however, I am offended by the very thought that we should share a National Week of a cultural nature with our neighbours to the south. I recognize that there may be certain practical advantages in doing so. C. D. Howe¹ tried to sell us to the United

States and was eventually booted out of office. Now it's the CLA, and even though that body represents some very dear friends— and some of our best customers—I hope the same fate greets them.

I think the CLA should recognize that we are Canadians, that we want to continue being Canadian, and that if we want to continue to be Canadian for very long we can't follow a course of passive acceptance of everything American and everything that seems easy. Because of the proximity of the United States, Canada, I think, stands less chance of surviving as an independent entity, politically or culturally, than almost any nation in the world.

I am not sure that you will agree with my sentiments entirely. I hope that you will, and if you do, I hope you can fire a shot in the right direction. I think the whole thing is appalling. I hope those in the CLA that are responsible come to their senses, and I am prepared to be quoted in the strongest possible terms on the subject.

It was good to see you again. Best regards.

Sincerely,

J. G. McClelland

1. Clarence Decatur Howe (1886–1960): one of the most powerful Liberal politicians of his time. He entered federal politics in 1935, was Minister of Munitions and Supply during the Second World War, and introduced the Trans-Canada Pipelines bill, which led to the Pipeline Debate and the defeat of the St. Laurent government in 1957. In 1979, M&S published Robert Bothwell and William Kilbourn's *C. D. Howe: A Biography.*

FROM NORMAN LEVINE

2 Park View
Bucks Green
near Horsham, Sussex
May 7, 1958

Dear Jack:

I am not surprised by what you say in your letter, although the bit you quote from the reader's report I do not consider criticism. The only thing I would like to comment on is the statement: "We don't think it [*Canada Made Me*] is an honest book."

I don't know the best way to answer that, except that I would be a fool, as a writer, to write dishonest books. I grant you there are other aspects of Canada which I don't know about, or which don't interest me, and I feel quite certain that had I done this trip in a Rolls with several thousand dollars' worth of traveller's cheques, it would have been a different book—but to say that what I have done is "dishonest" I think is unfair.

I don't think that a writer is of much use to his society if he takes the values of his society for granted. I think his job is to rub the labels off things. I think he should also be able to say, "Well, that's all very well for you, but this is the picture as I see it."

Norman

TO NORMAN LEVINE

May 16, 1958
Mr. Norman Levine
2 Park View
Bucks Green
near Horsham
Sussex, England

Dear Norman:
Thanks for yours of May 7. Certainly I don't think you have
written a dishonest book. I don't think the book is honest from
the standpoint of Canada; that is to say, I don't think it presents a
fair or valid picture of this country. Certainly, though, I wouldn't
suggest that you have been deliberately dishonest about it. I
think you have not been particularly objective and I think you
have not been a very good reporter. I wouldn't question the fact
that you saw what you reported. The pity of it, to me, is that you
didn't see a hell of a lot more. But to hell with it! This isn't the
sort of discussion that one can carry on by mail. We can talk
about it when next we meet.

We will do our best to sell the book. Of that you can be sure.
Anything you can do from your end will be helpful. I think you
should get as much publicity through CBC as you can. Once the
book is published, I think we will find ourselves in the midst of
a fairly stormy controversy, and you should be able to make a
real contribution at that time.

Best personal regards.
                              Yours sincerely,

                              J. G. McClelland

TO NORMAN LEVINE

January 9, 1959
Mr. Norman Levine
2 Park View
Bucks Green
near Horsham
Sussex, England

Dear Norman:
By the time this letter reaches you, the *Time* piece will have appeared, if it is to appear at all, and the story will be told. They are unpredictable as hell. Because [*Canada Made Me*] was not published in the United States, I think you can count on the fact that it will appear only in the Canadian section, which in turn appears only in the Canadian edition, although parts of it are occasionally used in the American and Overseas editions. This isn't the normal procedure.

It is a very strange outfit. I don't know whether you're familiar with their method of operation—although I judge you are becoming so now. I judge that about five thousand words of copy are filed for every ten words they use. Most of their stories are filed by telegram, and you can imagine how much this costs. The chap who writes the story has absolutely nothing to do with what finally appears. New York editors cope with that end of it. They want to know every detail, down to the brand of toothpaste that you use. They are thorough, if nothing else.

They did a piece on me a while back and it was an appalling experience. I had about three lengthy meetings with the chap who did the piece. He became a good friend and eventually showed me the story that he filed. I rather liked it. When it finally appeared, the only stray bits remaining were those that had an element of controversy. I had nothing to complain about, really, but I was intrigued by their method. They set up a photographer who shot pictures from every angle, none of which were used. They phoned friends, enemies, etc., and really did a fantastic job just to pick up a few lines of copy. Someday somebody will write a helluva of a good book about *Time* magazine.

One thing I can say in their favour is that this is by long odds the most influential periodical as far as books are concerned in Canada. A notice in *Time*, favourable or otherwise, usually affects sales. I don't think the same can be said about any other publication in this country. My only real criticism of *Time* is the fact that they do slant the news. Normally, editorial comment and news are segregated. They mix the two together, and as a result *Time* magazine becomes a dangerous weapon. One cannot come to any intelligent conclusion from reading *Time*—the facts have been carefully selected and the conclusions are underlined in advance. If they were always right, one would have nothing to fear, but they're not.

In looking over some of your comments about reviewers' reactions, I think it fair to conclude that you expect far too much from them. To begin with, there are not many good critics in this country—perhaps Robertson Davies is the only one, and even he has serious limitations, but quite apart from that I think you're expecting too much of any critic. I don't think the book gives the impression of having been as carefully written as it apparently was. Often your intention must remain obscure because the reader has been lulled into an unperceptive state; what I am trying to say is that I think you have defeated your own purpose by putting the reader into a mood where he is not anticipating subtlety or expecting any symbolic pattern. My difficulty here is that I know what I mean but I don't seem to be able to explain it very well. To hell with it!

All the best.

Sincerely,

J. G. McClelland

TO MORDECAI RICHLER

Mordecai Richler (b. 1931): Montreal-born novelist whose books include *The Apprenticeship of Duddy Kravitz* (1959), *St. Urbain's Horseman* (1971) and *Barney's Version* (1997). He and J.M. corresponded frequently for nearly three decades. Among their more interesting letters are those in which they disagree about Canadian nationalism.

March 2, 1959
Mr. Mordecai Richler
5 Winchester Road
London, England

Dear Mordecai:
Although I almost forgot about it, I am sending to you today under separate cover a copy of *Lolita*. Since it was a gift to me from the Canadian publisher, I am able to pass it on to you in the same way. I hope you're not arrested because of it. I read somewhere recently that Mr. Weidenfeld might test the obscenity problem by showing it to his partner, Mr. Nicolson,[1] who would in turn sue him for having exposed him to the obscene book. Presumably, you take the same risk by having it in your possession. I can imagine that there is nothing that you would enjoy more than to be arrested for possessing a copy of *Lolita*.

Cheers,

J. G. McClelland

---

1. Co-founders of the British publishing firm Weidenfeld and Nicolson.

TO JOHN HUNTINGTON

John Huntington was the managing director of Putnam and Co., the British publishers of Norman Levine's *Canada Made Me*. M&S was the Canadian distributor of the book.

April 7, 1959
Mr. John Huntington
Putnam and Company Limited
42 Great Russell Street
London, England

Dear John:
Thanks for your letter of April 2. I don't know what I can add to the reports that I have already made regarding [Norman Levine's] *Canada Made Me*, but I shall do the best I can.

The sole reason that we haven't reordered is that we still have ample stock on hand. We have approximately 125 copies in our warehouse, quite apart from a reasonably substantial number of copies that are still in various bookstores, on a fully returnable basis. Certainly, we would prefer to have the 125 copies in the bookstores rather than in our warehouse, but there isn't really very much we can do about that. You ask if we are pushing the book. The answer is, yes, we are, although we are not doing any consumer advertising, as such. You are quite right when you say that the book has had a great amount of publicity here. If the story in *Time* and if the radio and newspaper reviews won't move the book, I think you will agree that there is nothing that we can do by way of advertising to make it sell.

I realize that our handling of the book may be suspect, particularly from the author's point of view, and possibly from yours as well, because of the fact that my view of the book is no secret. I can only say what I have said before. I don't admire the book and I wouldn't, as a Canadian publisher, issue it over our imprint. Acting as your agent, however, we have handled the book precisely as we would have handled any other book with

an extra measure of promotion because it was written by a
Canadian author. We have advertised it. We have distributed it
widely for review purposes, and we have tried to place it in
every library and every bookstore in Canada. In the major
centres we have checked and rechecked stock from time to
time. The only thing that hasn't been done is that I haven't
recommended the book personally to anybody and I won't. It is
possible that personal enthusiasm on my part might have
helped, but I refuse to mislead anybody on that score. Some
booksellers like the book; others don't. Most booksellers in
Montreal—since Levine specified Montreal stores as being out
of stock—have the book in stock and have had since
publication. Others bought it initially and have refused to
reorder because they don't want to recommend the book to
their customers. There's not much that can be done about that.
Any bookseller in Montreal or anywhere else in Canada, as far as
that's concerned, is prepared to order the book specially for a
customer if they don't have it in stock, but we can't guarantee
much beyond that.

There are three reasons why I think the book hasn't sold
here. The first is that the press on the whole has been
unfavourable in a damaging way. The reviews have not been of a
nature to encourage buying. A reviewer can criticize a book
severely, as you know, and enhance sales potential at the same
time. This hasn't happened in Canada. There have been one or
two good reviews, but for the most part the press has been bad.

The second factor is that the book has lacked word-of-
mouth recommendation. It is probably as true in England as it is
here that in order to really move across the counters the book
must be talked about and recommended by people who have
read it. It's my guess that this hasn't happened. Nobody has
become very excited about the book. It hasn't become a subject
of cocktail party conversation. Despite the impression that you
may have to the contrary, Levine is not all that well known here,
nor is he, I may say, regarded with too much sympathy.

The third reason that might be advanced for the book's lack

of success here is that it is by no means everyone's cup of tea. I didn't admire or enjoy the book in manuscript, and I told you so at the time. I have yet to meet anyone here who has liked it. I didn't think the book would sell in Canada, although with the publicity that it received I hoped for a while that I might have been wrong. I thought that if the book were going to be a success anywhere it would be a success in England. I can't really imagine why you or your chairman think there should be a big market for this book in Canada.

I have, as you know, great respect for Norman Levine as a writer. Because of that, I am prepared to concede that there could be a level on which this work is a success—a level that is beyond my personal comprehension and literary judgement. If this is true, more power to him, for he has accomplished something worthwhile and at least one or two reviewers have recognized it. The market for a book at that level, however, is an extremely small one, and he can't have it both ways. Please don't misunderstand me here—I don't think for a minute that the book has this quality. It is still, in my opinion, a bad book and I'm glad that Levine has it out of his system. All I am conceding is that there could be merit in the work that I am personally incapable of recognizing.

Well, that's about the full story, John. We have done everything we could do within reason, and within the limits that I have reported, to help the book. If Levine is disappointed, he has only himself to blame, as far as I am concerned. By all means send a copy of this letter to Norman and let him tell me who his friends in Montreal are and where they tried to get the book.

With all good wishes.

Sincerely,

J. G. McClelland

TO MORDECAI RICHLER

November 24, 1959
Mr. Mordecai Richler
5 Winchester Road
London, England

Dear Mordecai:
It was good to hear from you. It sounds terrific—this business of being in the chips, I mean. I did go to see *Room at the Top*, by the way, in company with Irving Layton. He thought it was terrific, a great piece of work. I thought it was lousy and was ready to leave the theatre at any time, all of which goes to show you there is no accounting for tastes. Under great pressure I would probably concede that Layton's reaction was at least as valuable as mine. I might even forgive you if you gave his opinion more weight than mine. I thought, by the way, that the gal—the one who ended up in a pool of blood (I can't remember her name)—put on a tremendous performance. A great actress in my judgement.[1]

I just looked at your letter and see that you find Layton a bore. Oh, well, the hell with it! I don't. I think he's a truly gifted individual, both as a writer and as a person.

Canadian reviews have been good here as far as *Duddy* is concerned. I think it will sell. Several of the Jewish shops tell me that they are a bit afraid of it but they love the book.

I envy you your trip to Rome. Have fun. Drop a line when you have time.

Cheers!

J. G. McClelland

1. J.M. is referring to Simone Signoret.

TO MALCOLM ROSS

December 7, 1959
Dr. Malcolm Ross
Department of English
Queen's University
Kingston, Ontario

Dear Malcolm:
I have just finished rereading *Earth and High Heaven*, by
Gwethalyn Graham,¹ and my opinion, for what it's worth, is that
it should be included in our series of classics. I'm not suggesting
it, by the way, for our next group, but I think it could well be
included in 1961. I think inclusion is justified on grounds of
subject and fact content rather than form or style. I am inclined
to think the book will live. It's a strong and important Canadian
theme. She understands it and has handled it well. From the
standpoint of writing, it's probably adequate, although it's no
masterpiece. I think you should look at it again yourself.
    All the best!

Yours sincerely,

J. G. McClelland

1. Gwethalyn Graham (1913–1965): Canadian journalist and novelist who won a
Governor General's Award for each of her novels, *Swiss Sonata* (1938) and *Earth and
High Heaven* (1944). The second was translated into ten languages. In 1963 she co-
authored *Dear Enemy*, with Solange Chaput-Rolland, an epistolary exploration of
the Anglo-French conflict in Quebec.

THE SIXTIES:
"The Canadian Publishers"

The fifties ended with a bang and a foretaste of McClelland's public relations gambits when M&S joined the Canadian Library Week council and the *Toronto Telegram* in organizing a Meet the Authors Dinner in Toronto. Sixty-nine writers and nearly seven hundred others attended a dinner and a show at the Royal York Hotel "ostensibly to raise money to repair the porch of the Stephen Leacock Museum" in Orillia. McClelland's central role in the event, to be repeated countless times during the next two decades, was another indication of how far he had come since taking over the management of the house in 1952.

But despite the obvious accomplishments of the fifties and the growing celebrity of Berton and Mowat, M&S still lacked the kind of serious creative writer who could establish the reputation of a house the way that Hugh MacLennan had done for Macmillan. The NCL reprints of Leacock, Grove, Ross, MacLennan and others had, at best, lent the house a reflected glory. What was needed was a stable of M&S novelists, and that is precisely what McClelland gathered during the sixties, as Margaret Laurence, Leonard Cohen, Rudy Wiebe, Mordecai Richler, Brian Moore and Margaret Atwood enlivened the catalogues and the press releases. They also made possible the high-profile book launches and tours that became M&S trademarks during the remainder of the McClelland years, and that caused Robert Fulford to compare the publisher to the ringmaster in a three-ring circus.

Laurence, Cohen, Wiebe, Richler, Moore and Atwood all won Governor General's Awards, though Cohen, in a gesture perhaps prompted by Sartre's rejection of the Nobel, refused his. Cohen, of course, would make his mark as the most popular Canadian poet of his generation, as an international singer and as the most controversial novelist ever to appear in Canada. *Beautiful Losers*, his 1966 novel about sainthood and sexuality, was one of the most talked-about novels of the sixties and probably caused his publisher more sleepless nights than any book he published in the period. Like Birney's *Turvey* and Laurence's *Diviners* (1974), it extended the boundaries of what the Canadian novel could say. It shocked Canadian literature into shedding its provincialism and pushed it into the modern era.

Different kinds of controversies—and the free publicity they brought with them—surrounded Peter Newman's *Renegade in Power* (1963), his polemical study of the Diefenbaker years, George Grant's *Lament for a Nation* (1965), Walter Gordon's *Choice for Canada* (1966) and René Lévesque's *Option for Quebec* (1968), a book as pessimistic about Canada's future as Grant's, though for very different reasons. As a group, these volumes indicated a turn towards books with a more contemporary political orientation. At its best, this would result in an extended commitment to Gordon, Newman and Richard Gwyn; at its worst, it would produce self-serving collections like John Turner's *Politics of Purpose* (1968) and Brian Mulroney's almost instantly forgettable *Where I Stand* (1983).

Still, from the point of view of business, *Politics of Purpose* was more important than *Lament for a Nation*, especially for a company that had been expanding during the decade. In 1959 M&S had published nineteen books, but in 1969 it published more than seventy, and as McClelland admitted to various friends, quality control suffered even as sales figures climbed from $1.5 million in 1961 to above $5 million and 2,000,000 copies in 1967. As the decade ended, M&S was the flagship of Canadian publishing and had earned its title of "The Canadian Publishers." It had a stable of authors second to none, and Jack McClelland was a household name. On the other hand, the publishing house was deeply in debt and had just survived an extended financial crisis. As McClelland moved ahead with plans for further expansion, he couldn't know that 1970 would bring the controversial sale of Ryerson to the American-owned McGraw-Hill and that he would be forced to put M&S up for sale within a year.

TO MARGARET LAURENCE

Margaret Laurence (1926–1987): best known for her Manawaka novels, *The Stone Angel* (1964), *A Jest of God* (1966), *The Fire-Dwellers* (1969) and *The Diviners* (1974). The Laurence files are probably the most consistently interesting in J.M.'s correspondence. He liked her and admired her work, while she was comfortable enough in the friendship to tell him things she suspected he might need but not want to hear.

May 17, 1960
Mrs. Margaret Laurence
3556 West 21st Street
Vancouver, B.C.

Dear Mrs. Laurence:
The St. Martin's Press suggestions seem reasonable, but we are not able to evaluate them sensibly without a copy of the manuscript [of *This Side Jordan*]. However, since you, the author, feel that a number of these changes are worth making, we can only favour them. If I had any thought that you were being intimidated by them I should be very much concerned, but I gather that this is far from the case and that you really feel that these suggestions have been useful.

I don't know how they will react in London. I don't know how far typesetting has proceeded—although I'm sure they have started—and how much the proposed changes will affect them. I don't think that these changes can be forced on the Macmillan Company, but I expect that if it is at all possible they will accept them. I don't think we at McClelland and Stewart can interfere, and we shall go along with their decision.

If it should happen that the book appears in two versions, I don't think you should be upset about this. There are all sorts of precedents on record. It happens all the time. It has been our experience that American houses insist on very comprehensive editing; that English houses as a rule require little or none and are inclined to go along with the author's script almost without query. The Canadian practice is just what you would expect—a middle-of-the-road course. We think the Americans edit too heavily and interfere with the author's rights. We think that the English publishers don't take enough editorial responsibility. Naturally, then, we consider our editing to be just about perfect. There's no doubt about it, we Canadians are a superior breed!

Because of the involvement I am afraid that we have not taken much editorial responsibility in this case. As a result we are faced with the disadvantages of a triumvirate. On future books we shall be in a position to follow a better procedure. This would involve submitting the script simultaneously to the three houses, working with only one editor directly (probably here), correlating the three reports at the same time, and doing a final revision for all three in the light of accumulated suggestions. You would then be in a position to say that this is the revised script, I have done all I am going to do and this is the way it is to be published.

I think you are perfectly right in thinking that you would end up with a short story if the revision went on too long. As a matter of fact, that's not a bad idea for a short story for the *New Yorker*. A story of the writer who had a novel accepted by three houses and tried to accommodate their editorial suggestions (which would have had to conflict like mad) and ended up with a short story which was then sold to a magazine. Another publisher seeing the short story wrote to ask you if you could write a novel. You submitted the original draft. It was accepted without change and became an international best-seller. That's not a bad thought. If you don't use it, I think I will.

Sincerely,

J. G. McClelland

TO BRIAN MOORE

Moore's *The Luck of Ginger Coffey* was awarded the Governor General's Award in 1961, and J.M's letter refers to the awards' ceremony.

April 26, 1961
Mr. Brian Moore
150 West 15th Street
New York, N.Y.

Dear Brian:
Thanks for your note. It was wonderful to see you both. The only thing I find completely unpardonable is the fact that you made me appear a real bum by taking the long walk up to Rideau Hall. (I think that's what they call the place.) Had there been any photographers in the bushes, I'd certainly sue you without the slightest hesitation. Next time I shall have a caleche waiting at the gate in case you get any more such extraordinary whims.

I reassured Mordecai re the Guggenheim Foundation, but found I was too late. He had already phoned to ask them point-blank whether or not he had won the grant. I gather that he phoned collect. Apparently they alarmed him somewhat by not being able to find his name on the list. Then when it became clear that he was a Canadian, he was told unofficially, but officially, that he was in business. He has probably told you all this anyway.

I sent a copy of the Stanley Knowles' *New Party* to [your wife] Jackie. I am told it's rather uninspired reading. It just goes to show that we'll do anything to make a buck. Re Berton, I overestimate him. But that's my function in life. My doctoral thesis "Publishing Is for Pimps" will surprise no one but it should make damn good reading. But to hell with all that! Get back to your typewriter. Incidentally, did I remember to tell you, or did the Canadian Authors' Association tell you, that we refused to pay your travelling expenses to the convention in Toronto? We also refused to pay Irving Layton's and Wilder Penfield's,[2] so there's nothing personal in it. They got back at us by inserting in their program that "Author X will speak (compliments of his publisher); Author Y will speak (compliments of his publisher) and Brian Moore will speak—." It's just that we don't think too highly of the Canadian Authors' Association (not for quotation) and while we cooperate with them from time to time, we don't like being used by them in this way. We feel that if they want you—and they do—that they should pay for it. We'd sooner use our money to have a party or develop some other line of promotion for you while you are here. I probably told you about all this in Ottawa, but I can't recall doing so, the tail end of the trip being something of an alcoholic fog, as far as I am concerned. In any case, it was wonderful to see you both.

Cheers!

J. G. McClelland

1. Stanley Knowles (1908–1997): long-time CCF and NDP member of the House of Commons, and author of *The New Party* (1961).
2. Wilder Penfield (1891–1976): surgeon and author. He was professor of neurology and neurosurgery at McGill University, and established the Montreal Neurological Institute. His historical novels, such as *No Other Gods* (1954), had a wide readership.

FROM HUGH HOOD

Hugh Hood (b. 1928): essayist, short-story writer and novelist, best known for a handful of classic short stories and the twelve-novel sequence *The New Age* (1975–). The manuscript discussed in the next two letters was published in 1962 by Ryerson Press under the title *Flying a Red Kite*.

Apt. 1, 2541 Maplewood Avenue
Montreal, Quebec
July 24, 1961

Dear Mr. McClelland:
Last Saturday morning I received in the mail the manuscripts of a dozen stories which I submitted to your house in June, as the basis of a possible book-length publication.

Prior to the arrival of the rejected manuscripts, I received no announcement that they were to be returned to me, not a letter, not even a printed rejection notice. It is customary, throughout the publishing business, so far as I know, if a book-length manuscript has been given at all serious consideration, to send the announcement of the adverse decision a day or two before the manuscript is returned. I have dealt with every sort of house, from the largest and most commercially successful (Doubleday, Harper, Scribner) to the newest (McDowell, Grove) and the most august and conservative (Knopf), and I have never yet had material returned to me so gracelessly and summarily as this. That the letter of rejection should precede the manuscripts is a matter of common courtesy, as I should have supposed obvious. That you fail to observe the rule I consider an insulting slap in the face.

As far as the reasons for your decision to reject my submission are concerned, they can be boiled down to two: either the possibility of financial risk deters you, or the stories seem to you insufficiently meritorious artistically.

I have never before this questioned an editorial decision, feeling as I do that the editor must follow his own judgement.

But this one seems to me so far out of line that my self-respect compels me to protest.

If simple financial necessity compels the leading publishing house in Canada to turn down this book because of its lack of sales potential, then no new fiction which is at all artistically responsible can be published in Canada. Of course my book is perfectly well enough written to bear publication. If you can't afford it, then who can? And what we have is another example of the grotesque ugly provincialism that strangles the life of the arts in Canada.

On the other hand, you may judge the book adversely on artistic grounds. Very well, show me two other writers of my generation—a year or two this or that side of thirty—in English-speaking Canada who can produce a collection of twelve stories as good? There aren't two. Is there one? Who? Mordecai Richler, on the evidence of *A Choice of Enemies* or the pieces in *Maclean's*? David Lewis Stein or Dave Godfrey[1] on the evidence of the stories recently printed in *Tamarack*? Who? There isn't a more competent short-story writer with a wider range in the country, and you must be aware of it—I'm excepting the very few established writers like Ethel Wilson or Morley Callaghan.[2]

If this were the U.S. where there are two hundred young writers as good as I am or better, I would understand and even go along with and perhaps applaud such a decision, but here— who is there as good in Canada, at thirty? Nobody!

It is perfectly true that I haven't published widely, but I *have* published and what is more I have had my work taken quite seriously and encouraged in correspondence by Whit Burnett, William Peden, Evan Connell, Arthur Mizener, Rust Hills, Bob Weaver, Morley Callaghan, Jim Silberman (Dial Press), Madeleine Tracy Brigden (*Mademoiselle*), Don Hutter (Scribner), John Crowe Ransom,[3] and a dozen other equally competent editors, writers and critics. And given the state of fiction in Canada, I deserve publication and if your readers can't see this, then they are incompetent.

This is the first rejection I have ever felt impelled to question and dismiss in such emphatic terms. I'm not an avant-gardiste, but by God I can see why they strike out for themselves in those pathetic little publications.

And, at last, I can forgive the rejection as a matter of your (erroneous) personal judgement; but I cannot forgive the egregious rudeness which simply dumps the rejected MS in my lap, without a line of explanation or justification. Even if the stories were bad, unprofessional, ludicrous, this would be inexcusable. In the case of a writer whose work you must have had the sense to look at with some care, it simply passes understanding.

I won't forget this. And naturally I have no intention of risking another such slap in the face. I won't submit to McClelland and Stewart again, and the loss is yours.

Yours faithfully,

Hugh Hood

1. David Lewis Stein (b. 1937): journalist (New York *Herald Tribune* [Paris]; *Toronto Star*), short-story writer and novelist (*Scratch One Dreamer* [1967]). Dave Godfrey (b. 1938): publisher, short-story writer and novelist. *The New Ancestors* (1970) received the Governor General's Award over *Fifth Business*. He also edited M&S's *Canadian Writers* series of critical monographs from 1968 to 1972.

2. Ethel Wilson (1888–1980): late-blooming short-story writer and novelist whose books include *The Equations of Love* (1952), *Swamp Angel* (1954) and *Mrs. Golightly and Other Stories* (1961). Morley Callaghan (1903–1990): novelist and short-story writer, best known for *Such Is My Beloved* (1934), *More Joy in Heaven* (1937), *The Loved and the Lost* (1951) and the memoir *That Summer in Paris* (1963), which contains vivid portraits of Ernest Hemingway and F. Scott Fitzgerald.

3. These are mainly American editors and writers. Whit Burnett is the author of *Story: The Fiction of the Forties* (1949); William Peden wrote *The American Short Story: Continuity and Change 1940–75* (1975); Evan Connell wrote *Mrs Bridge* (1959) and *Mr Bridge* (1969); Arthur Mizener is best known for his biography of F. Scott Fitzgerald (1951); Rust Hills is the author of *Writing in General and the Short Story* (1977); and John Crowe Ransom (1888–1974), poet and essayist, was one of the fathers of American New Criticism and the influential editor of *The Kenyon Review*. Robert Weaver

(b. 1921) was a very influential CBC producer, anthologist and editor (*The Tamarack Review*, [1956–82]). His several radio programs, especially "Anthology," provided writers, often at the beginning of their careers, with a forum for their work. Beginning with *Canadian Short Stories: First Series* (1960), he published a succession of short-story anthologies with Oxford University Press.

TO HUGH HOOD

August 2, 1961
Mr. Hugh Hood
Apt. 1
2541 Maplewood Avenue
Montreal, Quebec

Dear Mr. Hood:
I was rather surprised to receive your letter of July 24. I should have replied before this, but I was in Montreal last week and tried to contact you without success because I was unable to locate a telephone number. In any case, as you will now have learned (I trust), our rejection letter went out to you on the same date as the manuscript. I presume it was delayed in the mail and reached you the following day. Why and how this would happen I can't imagine, but it is something that could only be explained by the post office.

I do not think that I can add much to what has already been said in our editor's letter. Our decision was based partly on commercial consideration, partly on considerations of artistic merit. As a commercial publishing house, we are seldom able to segregate the two entirely. Commercial risk does not deter us when we find a manuscript that our editors feel must be published. When they feel less strongly than that, we strike some balance between commercial consideration and our wish to publish.

Our readers felt that your collection was uneven—that some of the stories are very good indeed; that others are far less so.

This, of course, is to be expected, but our conclusion was that your material is not yet ready for publication in book form. As I am sure you know yourself, the short-story collection has traditionally been a very difficult commercial proposition. There has been some improvement in the situation of late, but even at that, very few authors are in publication in this way until they have a considerable body of published work behind them.

We are interested in your writing, as I have told you before, and we would like to keep in touch. If you are up this way, I should like to have a chance to talk with you and explain why we don't feel it would be in your long-term interest or in our own to publish the present collection. I would not expect you to agree with our conclusion—and there is no reason why you should—but I would be happier if I thought you understood the real reasons behind the decision. In closing, I can't help suggesting to you that unless you plan to open your own publishing house, you refrain from writing too many letters to publishers of the sort that you have sent to me.

Yours sincerely,

J. G. McClelland

FROM MORDECAI RICHLER

The autobiographical manuscript mentioned below was not published.

August 31, 1961

Dear Jack:
Just a short note to say:

1. Davies's [*A Voice from the Attic*] and *Maclean's* [*Canada: Portrait of a Country*] have both arrived. Thanks. However, lost them on the tube yesterday. Thk the best solution wd be for you to send me

off copies of both bks every wk. Hope to have largest collection in Eng.

2. Want you to be the first to know. I've made it! I'm going to be published by Ryerson. Prof.? Desmond Pacey[1] wrote me a smarmy letter, asking for a story for some collection he has coming out with Ryerson, and I offered him my dirtiest one, and quickly. Richler has arrived.

3. *Their Canada, and Mine* (or *Canada Paid Me*) will be coming your way late this month. A warning. It reads less and less like a bk abt Canada, and more and more like an autobiog. with spleen. Built-in spleen[2]

4. A further warning:
Contrary to yr usual practice I expect you to *read* this bk before undertaking to publish same. This is known in the trade as "publisher's responsibility." André Deutsch[3] has traded in his bicycle (a two-wheeler, actually) for a motorbike as he expects you to order 20,000 copies.

Am going to Israel end of Jan. for *Maclean's*. America, America come April. [Brian] Moore will get us a house by the sea in Amagansett.
Florence sends her best.

Mordecai

What sort of advance did you pay Norman [Levine] for his stories, goddamn it! He's got a shoeshine box out on Trafalgar Square and wears a sweatshirt with McCLELLAND & STEWART printed on the back.

1. Desmond Pacey (1917–1975): New Zealand-born literary critic and professor of English literature at the University of New Brunswick. Pacey was an early champion of Canadian literature and Canadian studies. His books include *Ten*

Canadian Poets (1958) and the once-influential *Creative Writing in Canada: A Short History of English Canadian Literature* (1952).

2. The allusion is to Levine's *Canada Made Me.*

3. Richler's English publisher.

TO MORDECAI RICHLER

September 8, 1961
Mr. Mordecai Richler
11b Parkhill Road
London, England

Dear Mordecai:

1. Re Davies and *Maclean's.* I'm shipping 500 copies of each to you herewith. Hope the supply will last. If you run short of *Maclean's,* there are 1500 copies sitting in a warehouse dock somewhere— due to a horrible catastrophe—and we are trying to get rid of them. Perhaps you can draw on these if you run short.

2. Congratulations. Pacey is great as a critic. I always say, how can we lose in this country when we have Pacey and Fulford, and of course, Bill Deacon.

3. Thanks for warning me [about the] manuscript. You sound more and more like Norman. Perhaps we can box your book with his. I understand the English publisher still has sheets in his warehouse.

4. Re my reading your manuscript, don't be a fool. I read Levine's and you know what happened there. Or is it the publicity you're after?

Amagansett sounds terrific, wherever the hell it may be. Hope you get back before the atomic bombs start to fall. It seems strange—or maybe it doesn't—but people are beginning to believe here that this may really happen. I am having an air-raid shelter built on our property here out of unsold books from our spring list. If it survives the first blast, I will have solved the remainder problem for the book trade. We will go into the air-raid-shelter business, become wealthy and retire.

Re Norman's advance, tell him to drop the shoeshine box, get out a pad and paper in Trafalgar Square and write a book that we can sell. Short stories ain't the easiest thing in the world to peddle, my boy. Even *Ten for Wednesday Night*, which includes the work of so many great masters, is finding no ready market.[1] How, then, are we to sell Norman?

Cheers!

Jack

1. *Ten for Wednesday Night*: The full title is *Ten for Wednesday Night: A Collection of Short Stories Presented for Broadcast by CBC Wednesday Night* (M&S, 1961). It was edited by Robert Weaver.

FROM PHYLLIS WEBB

Phyllis Webb (b. 1927): an underrated West Coast poet who worked in publishing and radio (she conceived the CBC program "Ideas"). Her books include *Naked Poems* (1965) and *Wilson's Bowl* (1980). *The Sea Is Also a Garden*, the manuscript discussed in the next two letters, was published in 1962 by Ryerson Press.

4566 West 10th Avenue
Apt. B
Vancouver, B.C.
August 28, 1961

Dear Jack:
I will certainly be glad to withdraw my manuscript [*The Sea Is Also a Garden*] not only for a year but totally from M&S. I was in

fact thinking of withdrawing it myself, though not for the reasons your critics (I use the term loosely!) suggest, and for reasons that would probably be of no interest to you. I will now withdraw it because I am shocked at the reports and their low critical level. May I illustrate?

I will number the critiques for brief reference:

Critic One: letter beginning "I can understand why your readers have been baffled ..."

Critic Two: letter beginning "There are some genuinely clever areas ..."

Critic Three: letter beginning "Here are 40 poems in much the same mood ..."

Critic One: Take this sentence: "It has some good things in it and some that I find dense, obtuse and obvious." A rather brilliant combination you must admit. I would like to know, too, what is meant by the reflection this "critic" finds in the MS of "her own mental collapse ..." Does this mean the poems are intellectually insignificant—or just plain crazy?

If you compare this "critic's" checklist with that of Critic Two, you will notice that seven of Critic One's "No's" cancel with the "Yes's" of Critic Two. Further cancellations occur by comparing checklist of Critic Three. It is also interesting to see the Haiku being highly praised by Critics Two and Three and damned by One.

However, one always finds disagreement on individual poems among readers. What disturbs me more in these critiques is the idiocy of some of the comments.

"'Trial' is quite obviously the Eichmann trial.'" Obviously! That's why I didn't call it "Eichmann Trial"—and, pray tell me, what does such a comment add to your understanding of the poem or its place in the book or in my thinking? And look at that list of symbols—wowee! How clever to detect the "sea" and the "garden" as important in a book called *The Sea Is Also a Garden*.

But what is revealed of any understanding of these symbols? What is the importance of the central theme? Did anyone stop to think?

My students could do better than this. Also, my students would never be such poor stylists:

"On the other hand, *the likes of* her first poem ..."

This "critic" (Critic Two) is unable to understand my "lavish metaphor" in that strictest of poems, "Mad Gardener to the Sea." I cannot find any lavish metaphor hanging around this particular poem, which, incidentally, is going to be published soon in *The Massachusetts Review* and which is, I believe, one of the best poems in the collection. "Critic" then blames me for my "contrived symbolism" (nonsense!) and weakly admits that this poem and another were "lost entirely on me." If your critics can't do better than that, you'd better get rid of them. Critic Two is the most offensive and stupid of them all. "For the life of me (get that style again!) I don't understand why women have decided that their poetry must be *nice*, not offensive to anyone." What the hell is nice about "The Effigy," "Beachcomber," "To Friends Who Have Also Considered Suicide," "Grey Day" (the only shit in the book, I know, but I tried), "Trial," "A Pardon to My Bones," etc. etc.? And then the further comments in the checklist "A Tall Tale": "This girl has actual genius! I would consider this the best poem in the book." What rot! If I have "genius" (I, modestly, would not agree), how is it then that "the selections which I consider to be outstanding are far outnumbered by those which were inconsequential." And of "Love Story": "it was simple but *completely shattering* for me." How can anyone believe such a person has a taste for poetry if they use such lousy English in their own writing and reveal such an abysmally low IQ? Have any of these people, I wonder, studied any of the theories of criticism? Not one gives me any indication that they have seen the overall structure of the book, the connection between ideas, images, symbols and form.

No! Send the book back, love. Let's call it quits.

Cheers to you,

Phyllis Webb

P.S.: Several people here whose opinions I respect have read the MS and been excited by it.

P.P.S.: That the book could do with more poems, I agree; that I will write more and better poems is possible, though unlikely within the next eight months.

TO PHYLLIS WEBB

September 1, 1961
Miss Phyllis Webb
Apt. B
4566 West 10th Avenue
Vancouver, B.C.

Dear Phyllis:
I anticipated a sharp reaction but nothing quite as devastating—not the right word—as this. I have some comments that I want to make re your criticism of the critics, but let's first deal with the main issue. Phyllis, if you want to withdraw the manuscript, that's clearly your prerogative and there's not a damn thing I can do about it except tell you how I feel.

First, on personal grounds the withdrawal of the manuscript would make me extremely unhappy. Although it has nothing to do with publishing, the fact of our friendship has been important to me—and I hope this apparent nasty turn of events hasn't marred that too greatly—and this makes it seem more or less logical that we should publish your books. I would not like to see it otherwise.

From the publishing point of view, I feel somewhat less aggrieved about the whole thing. As you well know, poetry is not a personal interest of mine and therefore I don't care too greatly what we publish in the field. We publish it because we consider it an essential part of our function that we do so. As long as we're going to do it, we feel we should do the best poetry available. Yours certainly fits into that category and therefore we want to publish it. But leaving aside the personal element, from the publishing viewpoint my attitude is, very simply, that you can't publish everything, and if you want to withdraw the manuscript, that's too bad and it's very much your affair.

The thing that upsets me more than anything else, though, is your suggestion that your other reasons for wanting to withdraw the manuscript would be of no interest to me. What, in God's name, do you mean by that? You can be very certain that the reasons, whatever they are, would be of considerable interest to me. Leave us not play guessing games. What are the reasons?

Now let's take a look at your criticism of the critics. I have no doubt it is entirely valid. But surely to God, Phyllis, knowing what you know about the book business and knowing what you know about the state of poetry criticism in this country, the report didn't surprise you. I didn't include with my letter the most favourable reports we have had on the manuscript, nor did I include the most critical. What I did send you was a selected group of reports that, in my opinion—and I think after fifteen years I have some ability at evaluating reports—best represented the critical response that the manuscript received here. The reports that we have had, as I said in my last letter, represent outside readers and readers on our staff. But whether you like it or not, and whether I like it or not, you have to believe, Phyllis, that when this manuscript goes out in book form, this is the level on which the manuscript is going to be judged. When it comes to evaluating your manuscript they may be bloody fools, but it is true that at least three of the reports that I have had on the script are from people whose opinion you and others in the field value, and in those three cases are people known to you personally and people who admire your work.

Certainly the reports read badly. They were not prepared for publication, nor were they prepared for the author's eye. I've probably had manuscript reports from you too that didn't read well and that would have sent the author screaming to the nearest bar if I had sent them on to the author. But I thought you understood all this.

I'm not saying these critics are right. I can have no opinion on that. I can tell you this—if I fired the whole lot of them, including the external readers, I might just as easily fire the whole critical apparatus in Canada, because if these people don't know what they are talking about, then nobody knows what they are talking about in this country. The only thing that they are saying, as far as I am concerned, and the only point that has any significance to me in any of the reports that I have seen of your manuscript is that the script is uneven, that you could improve it by weeding out the weaker poems and substituting better poems as they occur. If you don't agree with that criticism—and I'm not concerned with specifics, because if a poet doesn't know which are the weak poems in his or her own collection he shouldn't be a poet—that is your prerogative. I suspect that the general criticism is probably sound. That is, that you would do yourself a disservice by rushing this into print. The overall reaction was extremely favourable. You are close to having a very good book indeed, but we think you haven't quite reached it yet.

You know too from talks we have had what I think of the report that [several of your friends] have been excited by the manuscript. Probably they are right. Why shouldn't they be? It's a damn good manuscript. But unless they are a very different breed from the majority of the people that I come in contact with in the writing field, and the academic field, and in fact any field you want to name, the reports that they give to the author are a very different thing from the reports that they will give to a publishing house that's paying for their report. This doesn't make them dishonest. It makes them human. It just happens to be the way things are. Your friends may be different, of course, but they'd have to be a hell of a lot different.

Well, that's just about all I've got to say. I wish I could take the manuscript home and read it tonight and send you an ecstatic report, but you know as well as I do that that would be bloody foolish. If you want the script back, say so in your next letter and I'll airmail it to you the day your letter arrives. But I do wish you would think it over very seriously. The sensible course would be to sit on the manuscript and make whatever possible improvements you can in it over the next eight to ten months, but maybe there comes a time when one doesn't want to be sensible, or maybe too we are the ones that are not being sensible and the manuscript is right as it stands. The decision is yours either way; regardless of the outcome, I still love you dearly!

Cheers!

J. G. McClelland

TO IRVING LAYTON

Irving Layton (b. 1912): The books of poetry that Layton published with M&S in the late fifties and through the sixties, as well as his public championing of poetry, constitute a major episode in our cultural history. He was a one-man delegation for poetry and, as his letters indicate, for Irving Layton. His M&S books, designed by Frank Newfeld (see note to Leonard Cohen letter, September 2, 1964), were among the most attractive to appear in the country up to that time. Layton's letters are as expressive of his character and personality as, in their different way, are Margaret Laurence's of hers. Layton was the editor of the volume of Canadian love poems discussed below.

July 6, 1962
Mr. Irving Layton
c/o R. Cousens
R.R. 1
Eastman, Quebec

Dear Irving:
Harold Town¹ and other male readers who have looked at the collection [*Love Where the Nights Are Long*] agree with me that we still need a stronger injection of sex if you can find it. This would mean substitution but the general feeling is that while the poetry is good, the overall effect is not yet sufficiently provocative to ensure us the market we want. I'll write you further about this, but I wish you'd think about it. There must be some more sexy poetry around.

Sincerely,

J. G. McClelland

1. Harold Town (1924–1990): Toronto-based painter and a member of Painters Eleven, a group of abstract-expressionist painters in the fifties. He did the cover drawing for Leonard Cohen's *Beautiful Losers*, and wrote the text for *Albert Franck: Keeper of the Lanes* (1974), a selection of works by the Toronto artist, and, with David Silcox, *Tom Thomson: The Silence and the Storm* (1977). J.M. seems to have shared Town's conviction that he, Town, was a genius, even though Town engaged him in controversies of varying degrees of intensity with Silcox, Irving Layton and Al Purdy, all of whom were involved in projects with the painter. Layton collaborated with Town as illustrator on the anthology of *Love Where the Nights Are Long: Canadian Love Poems* (1962), while Purdy's projected anthology foundered in a clash of egos when the poet and the painter couldn't agree on royalties (see the sequence of letters beginning May 1, 1972).

TO IRVING LAYTON

This letter was dictated but finally not mailed.

July 19, 1962
Mr. Irving Layton
c/o R. Cousens
R.R. 1
Eastman, Quebec

Dear Irving:
Believe me, the bloom is really off the rose. What you need is a
goddamn wet-nurse. Some weeks ago a mutual friend suggested
to me that you were editing the Ryerson anthology. I replied that
even though you had no contractual obligation to us, I
presumed that you were neither that hard up nor that thick-
skulled. So I was wrong! So thanks very much! Congratulations!
You've really arrived. Migod. You've been selected to edit a
volume of poetry by the United Church Publishing House. If we
kept our fingers crossed, I might just be able to arrange for you
to write a monthly column for the *Red Cross Junior*. Or, failing
that, I might get some of your poems published in the *Western
Druggist*.

If you judge by the foregoing that I am irritated by the fact
that you have undertaken this project, I will not have failed to
communicate with you. But let me make it clear that my
criticism is directed at you, not the Ryerson Press. I have only
the greatest respect for them. I was raised in the United Church.
My father was employed by the Ryerson Press (then the
Methodist Book Room) before he started his own firm. I think
they have done more for Canadian literature than any other
single publishing house through the years. But if you don't
understand why—at this stage in your career—I would prefer to
have you arrested for relieving yourself at the corner of Pool and
St. Catherine than being exposed as the editor of an anthology
of new poetry published by the United Church Publishing

House, then you are a goddamn blockhead, and it ain't kosher. It's like Dylan Thomas writing for the *Reader's Digest*, only less respectable because it's at least commercial. As I say, you don't need a publisher; you need a wet-nurse.

So much for that. We'll have it out eventually, I suppose—I mean this insecurity problem—but it can wait until we meet. Meanwhile, I like the sound of what you're going to do with the book, considering the fact that there is no virile poetry around any more. The title—we'll call it *Love in a Cold Country*. I'm tempted to call it *Love Poems for Women Under 35*,[1] but we might be promising too much. So get cracking. You can still redeem yourself. And my love to Aviva and cordially.

Sincerely,

J. G. McClelland

1. The book was published as *Love Where the Nights Are Long: Canadian Love Poems.*

FROM PHYLLIS WEBB

4566 West 10th Avenue
Apt. B
Vancouver, B.C.
September 29, 1961

Dear Jack:
I can just hear you saying, "I hate authors!"

Actually, my silence has not been as wilful as you might think; it began as an attempt to calm down. Then it just slipped into the mood of whatthehell. Now I don't care if I never publish again. Why bother? So I'd like the MS back, please—no contract, no nothing. I want to feel free to eat it or send it out again or revise it, should my present mood change. (And as you know my moods *change*.) (I am now taking anti-depressants, and though I feel better about lots of things, no pills will make me agree with your assessment of the critical structure of Canada.)

Am back at work and fairly busy. As for beachcombing, there's a little driftwood here and there but not much else.

I hate publishers—though, to reassure you on this score, I still love you too.

Cheers, tra-la

Phyllis

TO MORDECAI RICHLER

October 23, 1962
Mr. Mordecai Richler
11b Parkhill Rd.
London, England

Dear Mordecai:

I have now had a chance to go through *You Bet Your Life* [*The Incomparable Atuk*] on a more leisurely basis and I want to upgrade my opinion. I really think it's quite terrific now. It's been sharpened in every way. I would honestly not have thought it possible to improve it so much without altering it far more than you have found necessary.

I haven't a clue how it will hit Simon and Schuster. Presumably they liked it to a considerable degree in the first place. It is still very local. I am by no means sure that the local knowledge is necessary for enjoyment of it. In any case, congratulations! I am prepared to raise our sales estimates considerably, but I'll wait to see what my associates think on that score.

On going through it, I found that there weren't nearly as many of the spelling mistakes (local) as I had thought. It's a small list but we'll send it off to you next week. There are one or two minor points that I would mention. First, you misspelled "Eglinton." This may have been deliberate, but I think it would be better to use the correct spelling rather than your

"Eglington." It's an awkward-looking word, and even if you spelled it this way deliberately I think it's more likely to jar a local reader and make him think it's carelessness or ignorance.

The only other point that I would like to mention is that I would prefer to see you drop some of the references to the toilet and bodily functions relating to same. Believe me, this is not prudery or any form of censorship—and it's only a suggestion anyway—because we're now publishing books freely with all the four-letter words. Nothing is sacred. My point here, though, is that this book potentially could reach a very wide market. I don't think it's going to be helped by these references. I don't think they are necessary and I think they could hurt. I think they could prevent some people from recommending the book. Maybe it's a deep-seated aversion on my part personally—who knows? It probably is. But even so, I would recommend dropping as unnecessary the references to the wiping of the behind, and so on. And even the use of a particular four-letter word which, as I recall, appears only twice.

One final point. You have a lot of fun in the book with the RCMP, and I think that's fair enough. The reference on page 73, "Among the RCMP it is commonplace ..." is, I think, a little on the vicious side and could be inviting trouble. If I were the commissioner of the RCMP and this were brought to my attention, I would very quickly and very efficiently have the book banned and removed from sale in Canada. Believe me, Mordecai, this is the simplest procedure in the world and could never be traced, and while we talk of the commercial effect of censorship, it's not going to do you or anybody else any good if we were simply prevented from selling the book. Certainly we would win out eventually in an appeal—maybe $50,000 later—but what's the point?

To recap then, I think it's a hilarious book. I think we'll do well with it. We'll be making an offer within the next few days.

All the best!

Sincerely,

J. G. McClelland

TO MORDECAI RICHLER

January 22, 1963
Mr. Mordecai Richler
11b Parkhill Road
London, England

Dear Mordecai:
O.K. So I'll get around to answering your letter of December 22. Don't get so snotty! It didn't arrive here until after Christmas. That's the drinking season, boy. One doesn't have time to write letters.

I don't honestly know what to say about the whole financial potential here. It's fairly tough, I think, unless you are prepared to take a lot of time away from your serious work. I think Brian Moore has a pretty tough time financially, for example. He gets the odd windfall. I understand he is now working on a book for [the publishers of] *Life* magazine—$10,000 for a 35,000-word book on Canada. I think he may eventually feel that he's earned this money the hard way. But who knows?

As I think I said to you before, were I in your position I would try and sign up for one film a year. If you can get $15,000 for three months' work, would you not spend part, at least, of that three months in Canada? In other words, live here, do one film a year, and spend six weeks out of the year in England, and leave your family here.

Your second-best bet is to get a regular TV or radio job here. TV particularly, as you know, pays well.

I know of no jobs part-time in the publishing business that pay well enough to make it worthwhile. (Why do I say part-time—they don't pay well enough full-time.)

I think you're right in coming back to Canada. I think it's what you should do, but until you really hit it big on the commercial level with one of your novels—and you will sooner or later—I think you're going to have to face the necessity of really scrambling here or going back to England every year. But as I have said, what could be better than that? Hell, at $15,000 for three months, you could afford to fly back and forth three or four times in each period for script conferences. The expense would be deductible. You couldn't lose! I think that's the best suggestion I can make.

One thing you can do for me. One of my favourite writers, a gal by the name of Margaret Laurence, is now living in London. Her husband is off in deepest Africa or some such, and she's there with her children. I don't know whether you know her writing. She's won several University of Western Ontario President's Medals for her short stories, which have been published in *Tamarack, Prism*, etc., and also *Saturday Evening Post*. She's had one novel published, and I have sent a copy of it to you, under separate cover. Her address is 35 Heath Hurst Road, London, N.W.3. I'd be grateful if you and Florence would have her over some evening and introduce her to a few people. She's extremely intelligent and a lot of fun. I think you'd like her.

Cheers!

J. G. McClelland

TO MORDECAI RICHLER

February 28, 1963
Mr. Mordecai Richler
11B Parkhill Road
London, England

Dear Mordecai:
If you insist on accepting bad advice from your English and American publishers in the matter of titles, there is not a hell of

a lot I can do about it. I think there is one thing to be said for *Stick Your Neck Out* [*The Incomparable Atuk*]. It will probably win an award as the worst book title of the year or at least get a mention in the *New Yorker*.

I'm serious about this, Mordecai. I plead with you, as a friend and a publisher. If you accept that title, you're accepting stupid advice. It's a bad title. It's not witty. It's not imaginative. It has nothing to recommend it. No one is going to be able to remember it. And I honestly think it's going to set the wrong tone for the reception the book is going to get.

I presume, if you use this title, that you change the name of the TV show to conform. Well, surely to God, if you think about it, and it's worth thinking about, you can come up with a better title for your TV show than this. Think about it, man. You've got to do better than that. Can't you get a little bit of the Charles Addams[1] into it? Something like *Stop! You're Killing Me* or *This One Will Kill You*, or maybe *Don't be Half Safe*, or maybe something from Jack Paar, like *I Kill You Not* or *Heads You Lose*. Actually if they did it on American television they'd probably call it something like *Meet Your Maker* or *The Last Supper*, or *That Was Your Life* or *Bet an Eskimo*. Well, it's your problem.

Cheers!

Jack

1. Charles Addams (b. 1912): American cartoonist and creator of the Addams Family. His books include *My Crowd* (1970) and *Chas Addams Favorite Haunts (1976)*.

TO WILLIAM ARTHUR DEACON

William Arthur Deacon (1890–1977): essayist and reviewer with *Saturday Night* and the *Globe and Mail* (1936–60). Author of *My Vision of Canada* (1933) and the pamphlet *Sh-h-h ... Here Comes the Censor* (1940). J.M. responds in this letter to Deacon's request for an interview about the state of Canadian publishing.

March 21, 1963
Mr. William A. Deacon
48 Killdeer Crescent
Toronto, Ontario

Dear Bill:
For many weeks now it has been in my mind that you must feel
that I am either extremely rude or very inefficient and forgetful.
I hope you will forgive me. The fact is that the matter has been
very much in my mind, but I haven't quite known—and still
don't—just how to explain my reluctance. I'll do the best I can
to explain myself. I do so in confidence and as an old friend.

To be very candid, Bill, I have in the last six months or so
become quite disenchanted with the Canadian publishing
business. I am glad to say that I am beginning to recover from
my gloom—although not entirely—but during this period I
have been disinclined to say anything on the subject that I
would want to read in public print. I felt it would be unfair to
you and to myself to attempt an interview during which most of
my comments would be not for quotation.

What's behind all this—well, frankly, Bill, a lot of things. I
have become increasingly discouraged by Canadian authors. So
few of them produce anything that's really worth publishing. I've
become discouraged by Canadian book pages. I think it's fair to
say that the three Toronto newspapers have reached their lowest
level in twenty years, as far as their book pages are concerned.
I've become discouraged by the Canadian booksellers and their
apathetic promotion effort. I've become discouraged by our
own activities. As a matter of fact, it's only been in the last few
weeks that I have finally decided against selling the firm and
seeking greener fields.

As I have said, I tell you all this in confidence as an old friend.
I'm not yet ready to discuss the book business with you. When I
am I'll let you know and I hope you'll still be interested.

Yours sincerely,

J. G. McClelland

FROM ROBERTSON DAVIES

Robertson Davies (1913–1995): one of Canada's most distinguished men of letters, Davies was a newspaper publisher (Peterborough *Examiner*), playwright, critic, university professor and novelist. Although he published eleven novels, the best are probably the three novels of the Deptford trilogy, *Fifth Business* (1970), *The Manticore* (1972) and *World of Wonders* (1975). He received his only Governor General's Award for *The Manticore*, although there is a general consensus that *Fifth Business* is the finer work. *The Cunning Man* (1994) was his last novel.

400 Water Street
Peterborough, Ontario
April 16, 1963

Dear Mr. McClelland:
Next year *Holiday* magazine is publishing an issue devoted to Canada and has asked me to write an article on Canadian writing. I am going to tackle it from the point of view that Canada, without having produced any writer of towering world stature, has a very sound literature, fully comparable with that, for instance, of Australia. I intend to base a great deal of what I say on the evidence provided by the New Canadian Library, which is the most comprehensive collection of good Canadian books that is available. I am writing to you to ask what additions you intend to make to the library within the next year so that I can be up-to-date in what I say. I have the library pretty well complete up to volume 27, but beyond that I have not a direct knowledge of it. If you could tell me what follows that volume, and what lies in the future, I shall be very greatly obliged, and of course I should be glad to know of any personal opinions you have about Canadian literature, its development and possible future.

With good wishes, I am
Yours sincerely,

Robertson Davies

P.S.: Though the "Canada" issue appears next year, the deadline
for the article is July 1, 1963!

TO ROBERTSON DAVIES

April 19, 1963
Mr. Robertson Davies
400 Water Street
Peterborough, Ontario

Dear Mr. Davies:
I was delighted to have your letter of the 16th and to learn of
your plans for an article on Canadian writing. The *Holiday*
magazine people seem to be fairly well organized when they can
work to deadlines so far in advance.

I agree with you that the New Canadian Library gives a fairly
impressive picture of the writing that has been done in this
country. I wish that we had a comparable series on the non-
fiction side because I think much of the best Canadian writing
has been in that form. It is possible that we will change our
policy and begin to include non-fiction, although we have no
definite plans at this time. You may be interested to learn,
however, that we are launching the first five titles in a new
Canadian paperback series next month in conjunction with
Carleton University. It will be called the Carleton Library. The
selection of titles is based on a survey carried out by their
Institute of Canadian Studies and the institute itself forms the
editorial and selection committee. They have surveyed the need
at the Canadian college (and to a lesser degree high school) level
as far as out-of-print Canadian works are concerned, and so the
series will be a combination of reprint and new compilations.

The New Canadian Library itself has been moderately
successful. Most of the early titles in the series have been
reprinted more than once, in some cases five and six times. We
are running into difficulty with the new titles, I think largely

because of generally increased competition in the paperback field, and for this reason we have slowed down our publication program slightly, but I expect we will continue to issue at least five or six titles a year for the next five years, providing we can continue to secure rights.

I am enclosing a list of the titles that have been published since number 27, the titles that have been published this year, and a tentative list for 1964. I have also arranged to send to you separately copies of the books that have been published from 27 on.

As to general comments on Canadian writing and Canadian literature generally, I find that my attitude changes from day to day, and I am not certain that anything I would want to say today would still be applicable a year from now. I think it is true that there are now more good young writers developing in this country than ever before and, generally speaking, they are finding a good market. Although it seems to be a truism, we are finding more and more that in most categories, the better the book—from the standpoint of the quality of writing—the better the sales. This was not always true in Canada. We went through a long grey period when the most successful books from the sales point of view were likely to be the very worst from the critical point of view. The audience has improved, and this of course is the result of increased educational levels, as well as immigration. A good example of what I am trying to say is that we are in a period when we can publish a book such as Sheila Watson's *Double Hook*. This is a difficult novel, and it's one that we should have had to decline on commercial grounds ten or fifteen years ago. Today it is more likely to meet with success than the run-of-the-mill novel in the more popular tradition.

Although I think it's fair to say that Canada, on a relative basis, has always supported its poets well, the market for contemporary poetry in Canada is very good indeed. Leonard Cohen, Irving Layton, Birney, Gustafson, Jay Macpherson, Reaney,' etc.—to mention only a few—sell rather better today than the run-of-the mill novelists. We have sold, for example, more than 7,000 copies of Irving Layton's *Red Carpet for the Sun*, and Leonard Cohen's *Spice-Box of Earth* has sold about 3,000 copies and is now out of print.

One interesting fact is that we don't seem to have much luck with novels in the currently popular European tradition—that's worded rather imprecisely, but I'm thinking of Marie-Claire Blais, Diane Giguère,[2] to mention only a few—and this is a situation that seems to reflect North American tastes rather than just Canadian. It's the era of the "thing" novel, to borrow a term used by an American editor. North American readers seem to want to pick up factual information as a by-product of their recreational reading. So, to sum up, I would say that Canadian readers today favour non-fiction, poetry, big novels of an almost documentary nature and, to a lesser degree, experimental literary work. But they don't seem to want run-of-the-mill fiction or even the more serious novel of ideas in the short European tradition.

Again, in summary, the overall situation is good both from the writing and publishing point of view. More and more authors are producing worthwhile material. More and more authors are finding it possible to support themselves by writing books in Canada. We will publish more than eighty new Canadian books in 1963. The market is still too small to make publishing a profitable enterprise, but thus far at least we seem able to survive, and indeed to expand our program. I hope some of these thoughts are of use to you.

With all good wishes,

Sincerely,

J. G. McClelland

1. Ralph Gustafson (1909–1996): long-time M&S poet and author of numerous volumes of poetry, including *Rocky Mountain Poems* (1960) and *Fire on Stone* (1974), for which he received a Governor General's Award. He also edited the historically important *Anthology of Canadian Poetry* (1942) for Penguin. Jay Macpherson (b. 1931): Toronto poet best known for *The Boatman* (1957), which won the Governor

General's Award. James Reaney (b. 1926): poet and playwright who has won the
Governor General's Award for poetry on three occasions. His poems were
collected in *Selected Shorter Poems* (1975) and *Selected Longer Poems* (1976).

2. Marie-Claire Blais (b. 1939): novelist and major figure in contemporary
Québécois literature. Her novels include *La Belle Bête* (1959), *Une Saison dans la vie
d'Emmanuel* (1965), *Les Manuscrits de Pauline Archange* (1968) and *Le Sourd dans la ville*
(1980). Almost all her poetry and prose have been translated into English, and the
fiction has been awarded the Prix France-Canada, the Prix Médicis of France, and
two Governor General's Awards. Many of her novels were published in English by
M&S. Diane Giguère (b. 1937): Québécois novelist. Author of *Le Temps de jeu* (1961),
L'Eau est profonde (1965), *Dans les Ailes du vent* (1976). The English translations were
published by M&S.

TO PHYLLIS WEBB

April 24, 1963
Miss Phyllis Webb
1126 Cypress Street
Vancouver, B.C.

Dear Phyllis:
Migod, I should have written long before this to thank you for
sending me a copy of your book [*The Sea Is Also a Garden*]. Since it
took you a long time to send me a copy—and even that after
prompting—perhaps it's only appropriate that I should be slow
in responding. I think it's a delightful book in every way. And yes,
you bitch, I have noted the reviews. They've been impressive. I
have even noted somewhere a comparative review with one of
our books (I can't remember which one). This, of course,
offended me greatly since you came out miles ahead. But that's
the way these things go. You'll remember, my dear Miss Webb,
that we didn't reject your book. It was all a matter of timing.

Layton is as ebullient as ever, drawing crowds to speaking
engagements, autographing parties, etc. I like his new book
[*Balls for a One-Armed Juggler*] very much, although there are at

least half a dozen poems that should have been omitted.

Sorry you're not coming East. I'm still trying to organize a trip in your direction, but God knows when. The workload seems worse than ever. I don't feel that I'm winning or even gaining ground. Maybe what I need is some exciting new book to reawaken my interest in this crazy business. Why don't you write a novel? A good way to spend the summer.

Cheers!

J. G. McClelland

TO WALTER GORDON

Walter Gordon (1906–1987): minister of Finance from 1963 to 1965 in the Pearson government. Gordon was an economic nationalist who published in 1966 *A Choice for Canada: Independence or Colonial Status*. His later books include *Storm Signals* (1975) and *What Is Happening to Canada?* (1978). The title of Denys Smith's biography *Gentle Patriot* gives a sense of Gordon's nationalism.

July 3, 1963
Hon. Walter L. Gordon
Minister of Finance
House of Commons
Ottawa, Ontario

Dear Walter:
I hate to join the pack of hounds snapping at your heels, but I think a brief note on the effect of the 11 per cent sales tax on production machinery and equipment, etc. as it affects the book industry from the inside may be of interest to you. I would make the following points:

1. After a series of representations by librarians, authors, booksellers, publishers, and repeated pronouncements from

UNESCO and others, it was a Liberal administration (Mr. Abbott was the minister, I think) that removed the sales tax from books. It seems a pity that such a tax on the principal tool of learning, and one that has no advertising support, should be introduced by another Liberal administration.

2.The proposed tax as we read it is discriminatory as far as Canadian book publication is concerned. Imported books we presume will of necessity escape this tax. It is already difficult enough in this country with its small reading public to publish Canadian books and to keep our prices within a reaching distance of the imported counterpart without this additional tax.

3.There is no question but that this tax will hit Canadian book production severely. A representative case in point: We had just made arrangements to import a set of plates from the U.S.A. of Farley Mowat's new book [*Never Cry Wolf*], which we will be publishing in Canada this fall. Actually it would have been about 4¢ a copy cheaper for us to import finished books from the U.S.A. We were prepared to pay the 4¢ because we prefer to manufacture Canadian books here for a variety of reasons, not the least of which is the nationalistic feeling that we should (incidentally this is a two-way street; his last book was set in Canada and plates were exported to the U.S.A.). But the effect of this 11 per cent tax on imported plates will tip the scales and we shall be forced to import finished books from the U.S.A. This is one isolated example of a fact that is going to hit the Canadian printer and the Canadian public, who will be paying higher prices for Canadian books. Since books are otherwise sales-tax exempt and since the total amount of the money that will go into the treasury as the result of the 11 per cent tax on plates and engravings is so slight (despite its importance in the overall pricing structure of the book business), it seems to me that it should not be pursued.

On a more personal note, I would like to congratulate you

on refusing to give in to the artificial pressures imposed on you by the Opposition in the House. Certainly there were aspects of the budget as originally presented that were untenable and for which you and your associates are responsible. On the other hand, had you given in to these pressures, the certain effect would have been to discourage other men of good will and intelligence from entering politics in the years ahead. You have my admiration.

Yours sincerely,

J. G. McClelland

TO HAROLD TOWN

J.M. responds here to Town's proposal that M&S publish a reference work by the art historian J. Russell Harper guaranteed to lose money.

July 9, 1963
Mr. Harold Town
9 Castle Frank Crescent
Toronto, Ontario

Dear Harold:
Your Independence Day letter received and contents noted. There's something I don't understand. Why do you hate me? I've never done you any favours. I've never loaned you any money. I've never praised your work extravagantly. I don't even publish Arthur Hailey. Why, then, should you hate me? Why, then, do you want to see me with an alms box at Bay and King? Surely to God I'm getting there fast enough on my own without publishing a "Dictionary of Painters, Sculptors, Wood Carvers and Engravers ... born before 1867."

I realize that you would like to have such a book in your private library and that this is a brilliant, even ingenious, way to arrange for it to be published so that you can demand your free copies. I can see it all now. There will be one copy in the National Gallery, one copy in the Toronto Public Library, and one copy in the H. Town Archives. The remainder of the first edition would look well in our warehouse.

But I'll go along with the gag. We'll get in touch with Russell Harper[1] and see how it looks. Speaking of how it looks, how does your own book[2] look? Have you been doing any writing? I shall be calling you in a week or two (when I return from one of my extensive vacations) and will expect to have a vast sheaf of manuscript pages delivered into my eager hands.

Cheers!

J. G. McClelland

1. J. Russell Harper (1914–1983): curator and art historian. His major works are *Painting in Canada: A History* (1966) and *Krieghoff* (1979).
2. *Enigmas, Enigmas, Enigmas* was published in a limited edition in 1964.

TO PETER NEWMAN

Peter Newman (b. 1929): editor (with the *Toronto Star* and *Maclean's*), journalist and author whose books have focused on politics and business. They include *Renegade in Power: The Diefenbaker Years* (1963), *The Canadian Establishment* (1975), *The Bronfman Dynasty* (1978), *Canada 1892: Portrait of a Promised Land* (1992), and, most recently, *Defining Moments* (1997). Most of his books during the fifties, sixties and seventies were published by M&S.

July 30, 1963
Mr. Peter Newman
Apt. 105
85 Range Road
Ottawa, Ontario

Dear Peter:

From the reports I have had, I judge that all is proceeding according to schedule and that we will have the completed manuscript on Friday. We have taken all possible precautions to insure that we shall have the book [*Renegade in Power*] on the market as quickly as possible. We can't give a specific firm date yet, as I guess you realize, and won't be able to until after typesetting is complete.

I had a call this morning from one of Diefenbaker's associates (who also happens to be a friend of mine) expressing his concern, and I imagine Diefenbaker's concern, that you had not interviewed Dief in connection with the book. I pointed out that in my opinion this was a considerable exaggeration and that you had had all sorts of opportunity to watch the great man at close range, but I have the very definite impression that they plan to use the fact that you have not called on him recently as a means of attempting to undermine the book.

I see no reason why this should cause you any concern, and I am well aware why you haven't seen him—and apart from the fact that it's not really my business—but it does occur to me that if you could find time to see him for an hour and could take along a list of questions (dummy) that you want to check out or confirm, it might be an effective way of spiking this particular gun. At worst it would make it less easy for him to come up with a snappy comment, and at best he might refuse to see you. They don't really know the state of things and apparently were under the impression that the book was due to appear within the next several weeks.

I hope you are in reasonably good spirits. I judge you have been working around the clock. You have my unbounded admiration for completing on schedule. I look forward to seeing you here before too long.

All the best,

Sincerely,

J. G. McClelland

FROM MARGARET LAURENCE

The novel discussed as *Hagar* in this letter was eventually published as *The Stone Angel*, voted the best Canadian novel at the 1978 Calgary Conference on Canadian fiction. Revealing a puckish sense of humour, Laurence alludes in the letter—"a film about animals running away from home"—to J.M's rejection of Sheila Burnford's *Incredible Journey*, a book with $23 million in sales worldwide.

35 Heath Hurst Road
London, England
August 26, 1963

Dear Jack:

Many thanks for your letters of August 12 and August 21. As a matter of fact, I only received the August 12 one today, as it had been sent sea mail—don't tell me times are getting that hard! I hope the enclosed card may cheer you up, if you need cheering up.

Seriously, I was extremely glad to have your reactions to *Hagar* at last, although when you say you think at least it'll have a fine critical reception, this sounds to me as though you suspect that it may sell about six copies, probably all to members of my family. Nevertheless, I am greatly relieved that you did find something in it, and now that Knopf has taken it, the sales picture may not be so bleak as we both feared. By the way, in reference to your August 21 letter, I have a feeling that it will be some considerable time before the "vast wealth" starts rolling in. But you never know. If Walt Disney can make a film about animals running away from home, why not a film about an old lady running away from home? (Was that a low blow, Jack? If so, I'm sorry!)

Re the question of title—I do hope you will not begin to feel that I am becoming awkward and difficult to deal with in editorial questions. I don't want to be difficult—quite the contrary. But the fact is that when Macmillan took the novel here, the question of title arose, as some people at Macmillan also had the feeling that *Hagar* gave the impression of a historical or biblical kind of novel. At that time, I knocked my brains out for about a fortnight, trying to dream up another title. Titles are not usually a problem for me, but once I've got the title, I find it difficult to change. Anyway, I suggested *Rage Against the Dying*, from the Dylan Thomas lines at the beginning of the novel. I felt, myself, that it sounded like an imitation of an O'Hara¹ title. I then began rereading all the Psalms, as a great deal of the spirit of Presbyterianism in a way of Hagar herself is to be found there. I came up with *Sword in My Bones*—"As with a sword in my bones, mine enemies reproach me, while they say daily unto me, Where is thy God? Why art thou cast down, O my soul? And why art thou disquieted within me?" Et cetera. After a few days this title seemed to me to suggest either a whodunnit by Mickey Spillane or some kind of blood-and-thunder story, piracy on the high seas or something. At this point, it became clear to me that the title of the book was really *Hagar*, and that I couldn't think of it in any other way, try as I might. And I did try, Jack, honestly. My feeling was that most people do not know who the hell Hagar in the Bible was, anyway, and that the kind of title I wanted was something exceedingly sparse, plain, unfancy, kind of Canadian gothic, if you know what I mean. I also felt that the book was in a sense a one-character novel—I mean, she *is* the story. As far as the

American and Canadian markets are concerned, it might be advisable to have another title, and I am perfectly willing to consider any suggestions, if anyone has any to make. I am very reluctant to have it brought out with different titles in North America and England, but I don't think it would be too late to change it here. I must say, however, that I am not very enthusiastic about changing it, for reasons which I have explained. Personally, I think the "image" of the book would depend, in this case, to a large extent upon the jacket design— i.e., if it were quite clear from the jacket that it was *not* a biblical or historical tale, then people would not get the wrong idea. At least *Hagar* is simple and easy to remember. Also, I think I am getting kind of tired of these twenty-four-word titles—"Stretch My Soul Upon a Rack of Clouds" and that sort of nonsense. Anyway, if both you and Knopf feel very strongly about this question, do you have any good idea man who might make any worthwhile suggestions? I don't think I can. I'm really sorry, Jack, as I feel I have been so much trouble to you of late. Maybe someday it will all be seen to have been worth it—I hope so.

 All the best.

Sincerely,

Margaret Laurence

1. John O'Hara (1905–1970): popular American short-story writer and novelist (*Appointment in Samara*, 1934; *Butterfield 8*, 1935). Many of his stories were first published in the *New Yorker*.

FROM PETER NEWMAN

August 29, 1963
Apt. 105
85 Range Road
Ottawa, Ontario

Dear Jack:
Thank you for your nice comments about the book; I was
particularly pleased that you consider it to be a fair
presentation. Actually, it's understated all the way—I used only a
quarter of the anti-Diefenbaker material I had, because I
realized that to overplay and overdramatize would destroy both
my case and my integrity.

1. I'm anxious to hear the verdict from your lawyer. With
regard to Coyne,[1] I do not think it would be a good idea to show
him the galleys. He is not, in my opinion, a rational judge of his
own behaviour. One problem is that he believes his theories are
economically justified, though Walter Gordon's fate clearly
proves that they are not. I portray him as something of a hero in
this chapter, and I don't think he can have any grounds for suing.
The reason I suggested that I had doubts about him was not
anything contained in my chapter, but his own strange psyche.
If, however, either you or the lawyer feel strongly about this, I'd
be happy to have the chapter submitted to him.

2. I've had one long interview ($2\frac{1}{2}$ hours) with Diefenbaker,
and he wants to see me tomorrow morning again. He's been
very nice to me, and has answered all my questions with
surprising frankness. I am incorporating his replies in the
galleys. He questioned me about the book only to the extent of
ascertaining whether it was a biography. When I replied that I
would not have the presumption to write a biography without
his consent and that while there was a chapter on his early life,
the book was, in effect, a review of his time in power, he seemed
quite satisfied. (I understand Richardson's[2] after you to publish

some of Dief's speeches in book form, but I understand it won't be for this fall.)

There is some behind-the-scenes manoeuvring going on to get Diefenbaker on a TV program with me (probably on November 18 on "Inquiry") to discuss the book. Diefenbaker has tentatively agreed, and, of course, so have I. (Please keep this confidential.)

With best wishes,

Peter

1. James Coyne (1910–1983): governor of the Bank of Canada from 1955 to 1961. His support of tight money and a low rate of inflation brought him in conflict with the Diefenbaker government. For a full account, see Denys Smith's *Rogue Tory: The Life and Legend of John G. Diefenbaker*, p. 394 ff.

2. B. T. Richardson was special assistant to John G. Diefenbaker.

TO HUGH GARNER

Hugh Garner (1913–1979): short-story writer and novelist (*Cabbagetown*, 1950) who received a Governor General's Award for *Hugh Garner's Best Stories* (1963).

August 30, 1963
Mr. Hugh Garner
51 Parkwoods Village Drive
Don Mills, Ontario

Dear Hugh:
Believe it or not as you choose, I am delighted that Ryerson is doing the short stories. I would be even more delighted if the next novel turned out to be a great one.

But for Christ's sake, let's end the business relationship. Certainly I don't want to read any further documentation of our sin.' Meanwhile, you can feel happy and secure in the certain knowledge that every time I walk past a stack of unsold copies of *The Silence on the Shore* in the warehouse, I'll have the feeling of real satisfaction as I think to myself, Thank God I was right, even though I used all my Machiavellian cunning to prove my point.

So we'll see you in church—the United Church. No, that's unfair and I don't really mean it. Seriously, though, what I don't understand is that a guy came in here the other day to see me with a manuscript, and he said he came at your suggestion. He also said he was a friend of yours. Do you really hate that guy? No, don't tell me, I'll decide for myself after I see the editorial reports on the manuscript.

For God's sake don't reply. It ain't worth it!

Cheers.

J. G. McClelland

1. Owing to a stevedores' strike, the finished copies of *The Silence on the Shore*, which was manufactured in the U.K., were held up on the docks of Montreal for weeks. Garner held J.M. responsible for this, believing that the momentum lost through this stalemate damaged both the book's sales and its critical reception.

TO HUGH GARNER

September 4, 1963
Mr. Hugh Garner
51 Parkwoods Village Drive
Don Mills, Ontario

Dear Hugh:
Your reason for sending your Canadian authors to us is marvellous, and I agree with it completely. As a matter of fact, I have drafted a form letter that will go out with all our contracts in the future. It explains very clearly that in all probability we will do a lousy job—that the book in all probability will be late, that we probably won't sell it very well and that we certainly are unlikely to promote or advertise it well. Some contracts will go

unsigned because of this, but in most cases the authors will think I'm kidding, and when they find out later, to their horror, that I really wasn't, they won't be able to say they weren't warned. Really, I have a nasty streak, but I don't like spending all my time apologizing.

Cheers!

Sincerely,

J. G. McClelland

FROM LEONARD COHEN

Leonard Cohen (b. 1934): poet, novelist and singer who, as they often say, needs no introduction. Though the two men often disagreed about various details of the production and promotion of Cohen's books, J.M. always supported Cohen's work, even when, as was the case with *Beautiful Losers*, he didn't claim to understand it. M&S also published Cohen's poetry from *The Spice-Box of Earth* (1961) on.

Hydra, Greece
September 9, 1963

Jack good boy. Me like Jack.

I got your letter today. I really wouldn't like you to publish the book [*Flowers for Hitler*] feeling as you do, so cautiously honouring my place in Canadian letters. I want you to love me and my work. Then you will push the sales and make me rich and famous.

I didn't send you the whole manuscript. I have about ten more long rather important poems that I hadn't written or finished then. I have a rather fine verse play. I'd like to have a look at your readers' reports. As long as my favourites aren't despised, I'm quite willing to make a number of substitutions. I want to give you a book that you can go all-out for. I'm not worried about the poems I might withdraw. They will find their life somewhere. Will you let me sound off for a second? I know this book is a masterpiece, a hundred times better than *The Spice-Box of Earth*. I also know that there is no one in the country who can evaluate these poems. My sounds are too new, so people will say, This is derivative; this is slight; his power has failed. Jack, there has never been a book like this, prose or poetry, written in Canada. The peers of "The Hearth," "Police Gazette," "On the Death of an Uncharted Planet," "I Wanted to Be a Doctor," "What I'm Doing Here," "Style," "It Uses Us!," "My Teacher Is Dying," "Hitler the Brain-Mole," "Alexander Trocchi," "Cruel Baby," "The Failure of a Secular Life," "THR Project," "The New Leader," "The Glass Dog," "A Migrating Dialogue," "The Bus," "Destiny," "Baudelaire," "For Anyone Dressed in Marble" simply are not to be found in our country's writing. That's a lot of important poems for one book. Believe me, I could produce another *Spice-Box* and everyone would be happy. I know the formula. But I'm moving into new territory. I'm quite willing to junk a few of the pretensions in the MS I sent, such as the dedication, but I will never again produce another *Spice-Box*. "A writer is a man who conducts his education in public." I do want you to like my book, Jack. I want you to follow my education with enthusiasm. I would like that to be your house's policy to every serious writer. But please don't publish me for the libraries. As always, both with *Spice-Box* and the novel, I'm willing to work with you until we get something we both like. I'm in one of my most fertile phases and I've got a lot of poems. I don't mind saving a few for my *Collected Poems*. As long as the basic structure of *Flowers for Hitler* isn't altered, I'm willing to take a hard, long look at it. Let me see the reports. If there are any good ideas, I'll follow them up. If they merely express a nostalgia for the poet I was three years ago, then I'll forget about them. Incidentally, a few good minds have seen the book and approve heartily. John Knowles (*A Separate Peace*) raved about it. Kenneth Koch. And what I like most: many young writers have read it, writers in the game for real, working with the new language— and they've been staggered, and they don't pull punches in their criticism. This book moves me from the world of the golden-boy poet into the dung pile of the front-line writer. I didn't plan it this way. I loved the tender notices *Spice-Box* got, but they embarrassed me a little. *Flowers for Hitler* won't get the same hospitality from the papers, but if you get behind it, produce it in a cheap edition, put it in the hands of my generation, I guarantee a best-seller. And that's what you want, isn't it? It's what I want. Otherwise, I'll circulate the MS in private, as I do with a lot of my work. So send me back the MS and the opinions of your pros. I'll carve a little here and there, as long as I don't touch the bone, and maybe I'll give you back something you can feel a little better about. (Would you do everything by registered mail? The system is breaking down on this side.) And thanks for not getting angry at my impatience and for sending the cable and even for the strange flattery of the acceptance letter. I hope we can work together.

All good things,

Leonard

I'm enclosing two new poems so you can get the idea.

1. John Knowles (b. 1926): American novelist (*Morning in Antibes*, 1962; *A Separate Peace*, 1960). Kenneth Koch (b. 1925): American poet, often associated with the New York school of poetry of John Ashbery, Frank O'Hara. His *Collected Poems* appeared in 1996.

FROM MARGARET LAURENCE

35 Heath Hurst Road
London, England
September 16, 1963

Dear Jack:
Thanks for your letter of August 30. I have now heard from Knopf about the question of the title *Hagar*. They have made two suggestions for titles, neither of which seem suitable at all

to me. These are *Mrs. Shipley*, which seems merely dull, and *Old Lady Shipley*, which seems out of character with Hagar. However, do not despair. As I was brooding about this question, another title occurred to me, and now it seems to me that it was so clearly meant to be the title of this novel that I am astonished I did not think of it before. It is *The Stone Angel*. I wonder what you think of it? I have written to Willis Wing, asking him to contact Knopf and see if they will agree to the use of this title. I have been in touch with Macmillan here, and they all agree that this is a good title. Although it will mean that they will have to have a new jacket design, and also that changes will have to be made in title page, etc., they have agreed to use this new title, provided Knopf and yourself are in agreement, for they feel, as I do, that it would be a mistake to have the novel published with two different titles, in England and North America. I wonder if you would let me know as soon as possible your opinion about this title?

Perhaps I should explain some of my reasons for liking *The Stone Angel* as a title. The figure of the stone angel recurs throughout the novel, and Hagar associates it with her father's stern pride and devotion to outward appearances. It also has associations with her ineffectual mother and hence with Hagar's own locked-in womanhood. Only gradually does she come to see the figure of the stone angel as herself, dogmatically pointing what she feels to be the proper way to her family, without really knowing who they are at all. In the end, she sees her son Marvin as Jacob, demanding the angel's blessing. She has been a figure of rigid authority in the lives of her family. Her adherence to the conventional proprieties and her withholding of love have damaged all the people most closely associated with her. She has always wanted for herself an independence which she has been unwilling to grant to others. The stone angel, as Hagar ultimately sees, will someday topple entirely and no one will set her upright again. But Hagar's strength and tenacity, as well as being damaging, have also been admirable. She is a fighter right to the end, and in this way she is, as Marvin says of her, "a holy terror." This, in very brief terms, is why I think *The Stone Angel* would make a good title. In strictly practical terms, also, I think it is interesting and would lend itself to a good jacket design. Please let me know what you think. I could kick myself for not having thought of this title six months ago, especially as it was there, staring me in the face all along. All this difficulty might have been avoided, but I suppose there is no use in thinking about that now.

If Knopf and yourself are not keen on this title, I would like the title to remain *Hagar*, or else to be *Hagar Shipley*, which at least relates to the title of the English edition. But if you think *The Stone Angel* is okay, I would now feel happier about the book appearing under this title in all three countries. I am sorry about all this business.

All the best.

Sincerely,

Margaret Laurence

1. Laurence's New York-based agent.

TO DOUGLAS LEPAN

Douglas LePan (b. 1914): though best known as a poet (*Weathering It*, 1987), LePan also received a Governor General's Award for his novel *The Deserter* (1964). Before becoming a university professor (first at Queen's, then at Toronto), he had a distinguished career with the Department of External Affairs.

November 26, 1963
Professor D. V. LePan
Department of English
Queen's University
Kingston, Ontario

Dear Professor LePan:
I think your reaction to *Naked Lunch*¹ is interesting. If you are
serious that you mean it was a relief to find a book even more
brutal than [*The Deserter*], let me say that this clinches the matter.
You must publish with us. If there is one thing that we want to
do more than anything else at the present time, it is to have an
all-out battle with the forces of censorship in this country on a
book written by a Canadian, published in Canada and in which
we have faith. I don't know whether you are serious on this
point or not. If you are, then let's waste no more time. Revise the
manuscript and let's have it. What Canadian publishing needs
and what we need is a strong book. I hope yours is it and I hope
you will send it to us. I promise you one thing. We'll support
your right to say what you want to say the way you want to say
it, and on that score I mean it as an absolutely firm
commitment.

> Yours sincerely,

> *J. G. McClelland*

1. *Naked Lunch* (1959): William Burroughs's influential experimental novel about the
life of a drug addict, recently given the Cronenberg treatment on the screen.

FROM PETER NEWMAN

December 5, 1963

Dear Jack:
I'm writing this from deep in Diefenbaker country, about

halfway in my journey across this large land.

I thought I should tell you that I have discovered that Ottawa-Toronto-Montreal are not the areas limited to the almost constant discussion of my book. I'll go into details when I see you, but I've been utterly astonished at the interest in the book everywhere I've gone, and I think I can guarantee that you can sell at least two more printings and probably more before Christmas. I exaggerate not.

For my next book, I'll gladly set fire to myself in front of Hollinger House if you think that'll help sales, but the one thing I will not do is speak to the Canadian Authors Association. After my impassioned oration on democracy and literature, one little old lady in Winnipeg got up and said, "Mr. Newman, do you write in long hand or by typewriter?" Never again.

With best wishes,

Peter C. Newman

TO PETER NEWMAN

December 12, 1963
Mr. Peter Newman
Parliamentary Press Gallery
Ottawa, Ontario

Dear Peter:
I think you saw the story in the *Globe and Mail* with the picture of Lester Pearson signing copies of *Renegade in Power*. Apparently, according to the news story, he signed five copies of the book at Victoria College when he was speaking there. I don't suppose one should bite the hand that feeds one, but on the other hand, it occurred to me that if you could surreptitiously arrange for a friend in the Press Gallery to suggest to Conservative or NDP members that it's hardly proper for the prime minister of the country to sign copies of a book about the leader of the

Opposition, it might lead to an interesting interchange in the House that would be reported across the country. It may be difficult for you to act on this, but I leave it with you just as an idea.

Sincerely,

J. G. McClelland

TO ROLAND MICHENER

Roland Michener (1900–1991): Speaker of the House of Commons (1957–62) and popular Governor General of Canada (1967–74), probably remembered as much for his encouragement of jogging as for his official functions.

December 20, 1963
Mr. Roland Michener, Q.C.
50 King Street West
Toronto, Ontario

Dear Mr. Michener:
According to a report in the *Globe and Mail* of December 18, you and your associates have under consideration the preparation of a uniform history textbook for Canadian schools. As a Canadian book publisher of some experience, I would like to say to you that of many worthwhile centennial projects that could be undertaken, I think it is unfortunate that a member of the committee has hit on this particular idea. It is my considered opinion that this would be a backward step, not only from the standpoint of Canadian writers but from the standpoint of Canadian education and Canadian children generally. There are always people who are willing to suggest this sort of idea for a centennial, but I hope that after you have given this matter some consideration, you will realize that this is not a very sensible idea.

There can be no such thing as an official history. History is an interpretative matter. Some of the great minds in Canada through the years have devoted their time to the proper interpretation of history, but to have anything considered as a standard and even semi-official history of Canada is to compose something artificial, and it will almost certainly have a stultifying effect on Canadian historical research and on Canadian writing as well.

I am sure that mine is one of many letters that you will receive on this subject. Even if it should turn out to be the only complaint that you receive, I hope it will steer you and your associates away from such a disastrous course. If you need a further argument on the subject, let me say only that there may be a need for a standard history in Communist countries, but there is no need for such an article here. I would go further and say that even if we as Canada's leading general book publishing firm were offered a contract to publish a standard history for use in all Canadian schools, we would reject the idea out of hand as undesirable and in opposition to the general principles of free thought to which we hold firmly.

I recognize that you may have been, and probably were, misreported. However, I find the whole concept sufficiently upsetting at this stage to write you a letter in these strong terms.

Yours sincerely,

J. G. McClelland

FROM LEONARD COHEN

Hydra, Greece
September 2, 1964

Dear Jack:
It's a historic Greek morning. Your peevish letter [about *Flowers for Hitler*] delighted me. Shiva is dancing. Does it matter to my

chickens that I happen to draw better than Frank Newfeld?[1] The summer has been cool and bright.

It is clear that you want to punish me for insisting on my title. If I had known that the price I would have to pay was Newfeld's second cover, I would have called the book *Lyrical Poems*. It is unacceptable. My Buddha Nature accepts it, of course, along with flies and garbage. We are all very interesting and beautiful. I love fighting in my detached Samurai manner. Newfeld's second cover, besides being devoid of taste and meaning, is a successful attempt to humiliate the author of the book it pretends to advertise. From the corner of my eye which concerns itself with such mosquitoes, I must consider his second cover a personal affront (unconscious, no doubt, and based on a complicated Jewish gestalt). Needless to say, I forgive him. I forgive you for your joylessness. Nevertheless, I am fascinated by the mechanics of your world, and so I persist in this curious struggle.

Nobody is going to buy a book the cover of which is a female body with my face for tits. You couldn't give that picture away. It doesn't matter what the title is now because the picture is simply offensive. It is dirty in the worst sense. It hasn't the sincerity of a stag movie or the imagination of a filthy postcard or the energy of real surrealist humour. It is dirty in the brain. It is not Art or even Illustration because it is an Insult, and operates with the psychology of the insult: disguise and contempt. The first cover was a masterpiece of the totalitarian sledgehammer poster cliché, based merely on a misunderstanding of the book, and I'll take this anytime over the second, which is a confused degenerate attack on the book's contents, and a vicious annihilation of the writer. Naturally, and with a great deal of happy disinterest, I am moved to resist this assault.

You invite me to sue you. You don't know how much just such an irrelevant battle tempts me. Our legal positions are interesting, since there is no contract between us. What is more pleasant than a match between comrades?

You write that your agreeing to the title was a concession, and that now you find that your concession has resulted directly in "all that damn trouble with the design." This is because you accepted the concession in such a mean-spirited manner, and attempted to reverse it by disguising the words of the title in every possible way. And whether the title is obscure or not, or to how many poems it relates, is not at all "the fact of the matter." It has been my experience in dealing with your "shop" that as far as literary estimations go, I do far better to depend on my own judgements.

Incidentally, Jack, you really don't expect me to travel all the way back to Canada to preside over the distribution of that crude hermaphroditic distortion of the image of my person. I'd really be ashamed to stand beside a stack of them at a cocktail party. I'd be in danger of losing my high. So why don't we forget about the whole thing? You never liked the book very much. Publish Layton and the two others—that's enough verse for one Canadian season. I sense an underground will in your firm to murder *Flowers for Hitler*: for instance, half the changes I made in the galleys, changes which I marked, put in letters, and discussed with Claire Pratt[2] over the phone, have simply been ignored. I find the Dachau dedication which I removed months ago, and for which I substituted For Marianne, staring at me in the bold type which the whole book should be printed in. I find no mention of my previous books. Poems are badly chopped.

Here the Swedish girls are suntanned. The dragonflies have wings that would break your heart. My new novel *Plastic Birchbark* [*Beautiful Losers*] is deep into its asylum. We had some good drinks together. I'm not very close to anything except facts. Your official male business language is part of a perfect morning. We will all do what we want. The cover is unacceptable. I will consider its publication an act of hostility (with the part of my mind dedicated to mosquitoes). It will be fun to slosh around in the mud. Let's be two good soldiers with different uniforms.

All good things,

Leonard

1. Frank Newfeld (b. 1927): an artist and book designer with M&S during the sixties and seventies. He also designed and illustrated Dennis Lee's collections of children's poems, *Alligator Pie* (1974) and *Garbage Delight* (1977).

2. Daughter of E. J. Pratt and editor at M&S. The cover was changed, though M&S did not use any of the six cover designs submitted by Cohen.

TO MORDECAI RICHLER

October 8, 1964
Mr. Mordecai Richler
Hillcrest
Kingston Hill
Surrey, England

Dear Mordecai:
I have come to two conclusions about you. The first is that you are absolutely out of your mind. Why in hell anybody would turn down an offer of $7,000 to go to Africa to write a film script, I'm damned if I know. You must have more money than brains. Here I am, Canada's great white publishing father—and leading Jewish publisher—and I'd go to Africa and write a film script for half that sum. I think being a father has gone to your head and has probably addled your brains. I am shipping a ten-year supply of Enovid pills to Florence. She is to take one pill a day with the compliments of your Canadian publisher until you are over the hill.

Second, I have decided that you are a real son of a bitch in the figurative sense. For years you send me at least a letter a month saying when in hell are you going to publish *Son of a Smaller Hero* in paperback. Finally, not because I believe we should publish *Son of a Smaller Hero*, but simply to cut off the flood of letters, I agree. I plead with our editors. I say, "Please publish *Son of a Smaller Hero*," but they say, "We want to publish *Maria Chapdelaine*."¹ I say, "No. Publish *Son of a Smaller Hero*." Finally, they say, "Yes." We hire an eminent man of letters to write an introduction. We set the goddamn book in type. We're about to go to press and then a letter comes in from the goddamn author saying, "Please, Jack, don't publish *Son of a Smaller Hero*. Some despicable Yankee firm has offered me $1,500." Some firm I've never heard of—Paperback Books, USA yet—all I can say is, "Thanks very much."

Then you tell me that the English publisher wants to flood the Canadian market with his edition of *Son of a Smaller Hero*. Everybody wants to sell *Son of a Smaller Hero* in Canada but me. So who got screwed—poor little old me.

In view of all this, your new novel should be not only long and dirty but very, very good. In the meantime, I suggest that you contact Ted Allan.[2] He knows of an extremely good psychiatrist in London. Anyone who turns down a $7,000 offer needs a psychiatrist.

Mazeltov,

J. G. McClelland

1. *Maria Chapdelaine*: a classic Canadian novel written by Louis Hémon (1880–1913) and published as *Maria Chapdelaine: récit du Canada français* in serial form in France in *Le Temps* (1914) and in Canada in 1916.
2. Ted Allan (1916–1995): novelist, biographer and scriptwriter. His books include *The Scalpel, The Sword: The Story of Dr. Norman Bethune* (1952, 1973), the play *Lies My Father Told Me* (1975) and the novel *Love Is a Longshot* (1985). He also wrote under the name William Maxwell.

TO IRVING LAYTON

December 22, 1964
Mr. Irving Layton
5731 Somerled Avenue
Apt. 6
Montreal, Quebec

Dear Irving:
Some years ago we reached an agreement on one point. I agreed not to tell you how to write your poetry, not to criticize your

poetry, and in fact not even to read it. Can we now reach an agreement on the other side of the coin? Please leave the publishing to us. You are a great poet, but you know nothing about book manufacturing; you know nothing about publishing, and goddamn little, if your figures are to be believed, about marketing. That's our side of the problem.

It would be absolutely impossible to run the two books at the same time. The only saving would be on the cost of composition. Without going into laborious explanations, you can take that as fact, so let's forget it.

We will proceed as planned to publish the *Collected Layton 1945–1965* next fall. The *Selected* edition, if the *Collected* edition has done well enough, will appear in the fall of 1966. As I said in my last letter, we'd be quite happy about doing the reverse, but it's neither practical nor sensible to attempt to do both at the same time. To say that they won't compete with each other is meaningless. As to the proposal that you assume half the financial cost of the *Selected* edition, I would point out first that we are not in the cooperative publishing business, and second, if we were going to do it, I would ask you to assume half the cost of the *Collected*, not the *Selected*. You must think I'm some kind of nut.

So that's the story, Irving. You have the story plus my earnest plea that you concern yourself with your responsibilities and I'll worry about mine.

Cheers!

J. G. McClelland

TO MARGARET LAURENCE

May 4, 1965
Mrs. Margaret Laurence
Elm Cottage, Beacon Hill
Penn, Bucks., England

Dear Margaret:
I have owed you a letter for a very long time. Forgive me.
Actually I wrote several weeks ago—a beautiful letter it was—
and it seems my dictaphone machine had stuck on one spot,
and so at least a dozen great masterpieces were never recorded. I
am only now beginning to recover.

I'm sorry in the one sense but glad in the other to hear of the
separation. By that I mean these things are always sad, but the
real point is that since you have finally made the decision, it is
undoubtedly the right one and will turn out well in the long
run.

Silly though it may seem, I'm beginning to think that there
may be some correlation between intelligence and marital
problems. It would be too pat to conclude that intelligent and
creative people don't stay married, but there seems to be some
sort of pattern. Three of our most gifted authors have been
involved in separations in the last twelve months, and I know at
least three others who have seriously contemplated it during
the same period. If misery loves company, then you've certainly
got it. On the other hand, it does rather strip one of the
originality of the thing. But damn it, there must be some sort of
pattern in this thing. I expect someone has already investigated
it at great length. Unless one is extremely fortunate, and even if
one is, I think marriage probably requires an extraordinarily
unimaginative type of complacency.

I don't really know what one wants to hear when they have
just recently decided to separate. Probably they don't want to
hear anything, but for what it is worth, let me say to you that
you have something that is more important than any marriage

I've ever heard about. By which I mean your career, which I say in all humility should make you one of the great international writers in the next decade or so. I don't think you can afford to concern yourself about the dissolution of a marriage, no matter how serious a jolt it may seem at the time. So forget it. It's of relatively no importance.

Although I can't imagine that it has even crossed your mind, I am mad as hell about the fact that you didn't receive the Governor General's Award for Fiction. A number of the critics across the country have been irate about this and rightly so. It's a question of principle. As it happens, we published Douglas LePan's book [*The Fugitive*] which won the award, but even though we did, I have no hesitation in saying that it doesn't belong in the same category as *The Stone Angel*. I can't imagine what the committee was thinking about. It's not untypical of judgements that Governor General's Awards committees have made in the past. It's a goddamn disgrace.

Cheers!

Jack

TO LEONARD COHEN

J.M.'s excited, baffled and ambivalent response to the manuscript of *Beautiful Losers* foreshadowed the reactions of many readers and reviewers. The novel is still in print in a New Canadian Library edition.

June 15, 1965
Mr. Leonard Cohen
Hydra, Greece

Dear Leonard:
When I talked to Irving, I had only had a chance to read the first thirty-odd pages. I've now finished it. Migod, it's a fantastic book.

It astounds me and baffles me and I don't really know what to say about it. It's wild and incredible and marvellously well written, and at the same time appalling, shocking, revolting, disgusting, sick and just maybe it's a great novel. I'm damned if I know. I have no way of knowing. It's the majority view at Viking that it's a very superior piece of work. All I can say is that I think it is an amazing book. I'm not going to pretend that I dig it, because I don't. So leave us not pretend. I enjoyed reading it. I would like to reread it and will when I have a chance.

Are we going to publish? At the moment I don't know. My guess would be yes, but I'd better wait and see what sort of reaction I get from some of my associates. They could scream, although I don't really anticipate that they will. I'm a little apprehensive about the reaction of the Catholic Church. It's either pretty damn sacrilegious or it isn't. Certainly it is in extract, but whether it is in total is for the author to say. You could fool me. The odds are, though, that we will make a publishing offer and I'll let you know as quickly as possible. Let me be truthful about this. If it were being published in the U.S.A. by Grove, I'd be very apprehensive. When it is published by Viking, I think we have a fighting chance. I'm sure it will end up in the courts here, but that might be worth trying.

You are a nice chap, Leonard, and it's lovely knowing you. All I have to decide now is whether I love you enough to want to spend the rest of my days in jail because of you, and even though I can't pretend to understand the goddamn book, I do congratulate you. It's a wild and incredible effort.

Cheers!

J. G. McClelland

TO MORDECAI RICHLER

March 10, 1966
Mr. Mordecai Richler
Hillcrest
Kingston Hill
Surrey, England

Dear Mordecai:

Thanks for your note. Yes, my normal commission on Canada Council grants is 50 per cent. You may think this is high, but we have to be realistic about these things. The awarding of the grant had little to do with your distinguished writing career. It's a well-accepted fact that when I say the word, the Canada Council jumps. However, I do have a special rate for a select list of impecunious authors—I think immediately of yourself, Norman Levine and Stan Obodiac[1]—so if you send me 40 per cent that will be fine. *Son of a Smaller Hero* has gone off and will probably arrive ahead of this letter. I'm sorry about the fact that they put Paul Anka on the cover instead of you, but these mistakes occasionally occur. Okay, so get cracking and get the novel done.

Cheers!

J. G. McClelland

1. Stan Obodiac (1922–1984) was the publicity director of Maple Leaf Gardens and the author of *The Leafs—The First 50 Years* (1976).

TO LEONARD COHEN

May 9, 1966
Mr. Leonard Cohen
599 Belmont
Westmount, Quebec

Dear Leonard:
I made a number of attempts to try to reach you by phone on
Friday and Saturday but had no success. Since I will be away
most of this week again, I thought it might be useful for me to
record my reaction to the various complaints that you have
made and criticisms that have been reported to me.

I presume that you are serious about this. I am prepared to
treat your complaints seriously. In the process of publishing a
great many books over a period of years, we have made a great
many errors. Mistakes have been made in editing; in design; in
production; in promotion; in advertising, and in sales
promotion and sales coverage. When mistakes have been made,
I have usually been the first to admit it and done what I can to
rectify it. I have done so both because I have no particular
interest in the sensibilities of people working for this firm, and
because it has always been my basic publishing philosophy that
it is our responsibility to do the very best that we can for any
author who we agree to publish.

We are extremely sensitive about author criticism because
our interest is something more than commercial. Because each
individual book is more important to the author than it can be
to the publisher, it is a truly sensitive area. The only authors who
can be sure not to complain are those whose books sell well.
Because few books sell well in this country, it follows that we
can be subjected to a reasonable amount of abuse. That's fair
enough. It is not often, thank God, that we receive complaints
and criticism that I consider to be not only unjustified but
wildly irresponsible. From the reports that have been reaching
me indirectly—and I have the impression that you have no great

wish to discuss this with me directly because you have not responded to my phone messages—I judge that we are dealing with just that situation in your case. Perhaps it is time that you looked at a few truths. I gather that your catalogue of complaints is a lengthy one. Let's look at a few of them.

I understand that you are bitching because *Beautiful Losers* is not available in all stores. Certainly this is frustrating, but just what in hell did you expect? You may be naive, but you are certainly not stupid. Booksellers have a perfect right to decide what they will sell and what they will not sell. Many stores have decided that they don't want to take the risk of handling this book. That's their prerogative, but why complain to us about it. We have told them that we are prepared to defend the book to the Supreme Court if the need arises. Our people have presented the book with enthusiasm. Our sales coverage has been thorough. There is nothing more that can be done about the stores.

I enclose copies of correspondence with the head of W. H. Smith and Son, who, as you know, have a chain of important bookstores. Although the reply to my letter is inconclusive, I am told that they subsequently, on their lawyer's advice, decided not to handle the book. Simpson's, I believe, has taken the same attitude and they are not alone. You have a right to write the book. We have a right to publish it. We don't have the right to ram it down anyone's throat. To make an issue of this matter would, in my opinion, be downright idiocy. Freedom of choice has to work both ways. The surest way to end up in court, which I don't think would be either to your advantage or to ours, is to be petulant on this point.

Second, I understand that you are complaining about the price. Apparently you feel that we should not only publish it but subsidize it. The fact of the matter is that we are. Even at the $6.50 price, we are making less than our normal margin. The price in the United States is $5.95. The book, as you know, was imported in sheets and bound here. On the importation of sheets we have paid a 10 per cent duty, 8 per cent exchange on the American dollar to which has been added a reasonably good binding and, for a relatively small run, an expensive jacket. It is the reaction of most people that I have talked to that this is one of the most beautiful jackets they have ever seen on a book.

I understand that you are whining about lack of promotion. I am delighted to look at that one too. What has been done? We have sent out, given away, or distributed about three hundred copies of the book covering all publicity media across Canada. We have sent out three different printed promotion pieces, plus press releases, biographical data, specially printed coasters, a substantial number of posters to which we added a large and rather expensive promotion party (the value of which was almost totally lost because you didn't think it suited your image or were unwilling to put yourself out). Now all that adds up to one helluva lot of promotion, and I dare say rather more direct promotional effort than any other book has ever received. The book has had radio publicity from coast to coast; television coverage from coast to coast; it has been written about in *Time*, *Maclean's*, and the majority of major newspapers and the reviews in the little magazines will follow. Having just returned from the West, I can tell you that the book is being discussed and talked about across the country. It is beginning to sell moderately well in some stores. If it is not a raging best-seller, it is not because the book hasn't been promoted. It is not because the book isn't known. It may have something to do with the fact that the reviews have not been all that one could hope for.

I recognize at once that since you have suddenly become an authority on all subjects, you will point out that although we have spent a lot of money, it's been badly spent. Well, I can't do very much about your opinion in these things. In my personal view, it has been a superb promotion and publicity campaign. The only part of it that misfired, in my opinion, was the failure to con more people into liking the book in advance at the party.

I understand, too, that you are complaining about lack of advertising. Surely to God, Leonard, we don't have to go into that. You have been around the book business long enough to know the facts of life. There are young, inexperienced authors who can be forgiven for thinking that advertising sells books, but there is almost no one in the book business who hasn't had to recognize the fact that almost no book can be sold on a commercial or economical basis through advertising. Retail stores continue to advertise of course, because although they pinpoint specific books, they are advertising their store. Your book has appeared in our group ads in major papers across the country. It will be appearing in a separate ad next Saturday (which I may say I thought was scheduled to appear on publication date but was replaced by the group ad), so I suggest you make a little test for yourself. Check with the key Montreal stores; find out how many copies they each sold the week preceding the ad and the week following the ad. To pay for itself that particular ad would have to sell, on a conservative basis, about two hundred books. It is much more likely, based on hundreds of such tests, to sell fourteen copies. But try it yourself and let me know. The fact of the matter is that one good recommendation by a columnist will sell many more books than a string of ads.

Finally, I understand that you want a party in Montreal. I can't imagine what conceivable purpose that would serve at this stage. You are not prepared to talk about the book at such a party. I can't believe that there is anybody in the Montreal book trade or, indeed, any serious buyers in Montreal who don't, by now, know of the existence of the book. Sure, we'll be telling them in the ad that a few American critics think the book is very good and it may, or may not, help, but at this stage I can't see any sense in a party except as a means of wasting money.

From this point on, I think the only effective way of promoting the book is through radio and television appearances. Your last word to me on this subject was really that the strain is too much. If you have changed your mind, we'll try to arrange more of that sort in both Montreal and Toronto. I think the interview on "Seven Days" was absolutely superb, as already reported to you. The more radio and TV appearances you can make, the better, as far as the sales of the book are concerned. I would make some effort to avoid calling it a pornographic book yourself, though. People have been hanged for less.

And now a final message on the whole situation. I realize that the book is very important to you. I realize the total personal involvement and that you are particularly sensitive to everything relating to the book. That is understood and I think the importance of the book is accepted and appreciated in the few important places where such can be understood and appreciated. But migod, Leonard, it is a bonehead time for you to lose your cool head on this thing. For God's sake, relax. Even though you wouldn't accept my saying so in advance, it was completely predictable that almost no critics or reviewers were going to understand or identify with the book. If the reviewers and the critics don't dig it, you can be certain that it takes a long time for any substantial segment of the public to react. It takes nothing away from the book to say that there is no way that it's going to get through to the masses at this stage. If the book did become a best-seller in a major sense, it could only be for all the wrong reasons. There is sound evidence for believing that the value of the book and the importance of the book have been recognized, and that the recognition will ultimately spread by degrees. There is no other way. People can't, and won't, be bludgeoned by it. My sincere recommendation to you as a friend is that you relax. Let the achievement of this book speak for itself. Don't expect any goddamn miracles and forget your new self-appointed and somewhat unbecoming role as an authority on typography, design, art, promotion and publicity, advertising and market analysis. I have long felt that one of your greatest personal attributes is the fact that you are sincerely modest about your accomplishments and that you don't take yourself seriously. On the basis of our last meeting and the reports that have been coming to me lately, I am beginning to

think that the National Film Board did you no favour.[1] So as a
friend, not as a publisher, I say to you relax a little.
Sincerely,

J. G. McClelland

1. The film *Ladies and Gentlemen ... Mr. Leonard Cohen* was a 1965 National Film Board
documentary directed by Donald Brittain. It began as a film about the 1964
reading tour organized by Jack McClelland for Irving Layton, Earle Birney, Phyllis
Gottlieb and Cohen but was reshot and re-edited with a focus on Cohen. Cohen's
letter (March 1, 1965) to McClelland records his response to the tour: "The
reading-tour made me an enemy of the whole country and ruined my Canadian
life. This was not due solely to my obnoxious personality. It also resulted in the
minimum attention for the book it proposed to promote. And worst of all, it
doesn't look like we're going to get any money out of it. Yankel, Yankel, why did
you lie to us?" (See Ira Nadel's *Various Positions: A Life of Leonard Cohen*, 1996, for the
whole story.)

TO N. GLAURI

Mrs. N. Glauri, who wrote J.M. to complain about the language
and content of Irving Layton's poems, has not been traced.

July 26, 1966
Mrs. N. Glauri, R.N.
137 McVey Place
Lasalle, Quebec

Dear Mrs. Glauri:
Thank you for your letter of July 21. I think I can set out our
point of view on this matter precisely. We do not feel that it is
necessary for us to justify the publication of a work by Irving
Layton. His poetry speaks for itself. It has established his
reputation among critics, scholars and students of English as
one of the finest poets that this country has yet produced. I

think that no further justification is needed.

This opinion of Layton's book is clearly not shared by you. Certainly there are others who would agree with you. The evaluation of an artist is, to some degree, a subjective matter. It is not an exact science. You are entitled to your opinion, just as I feel entitled to mine.

As to your suggestion that we or anybody else should censor Layton, I must categorically disagree. I have not met, nor do I ever expect to meet, an informed, intelligent person who believes in censorship. Many people believe in partial censorship. They believe that objective evaluations of obscenity can be made. I do not. Your own point of view with regard to Layton is a classic example. Are you in a position to censor or deprive people of the right to read and enjoy Layton? I don't ask you to read and enjoy Layton; I ask merely that you give others the right to do so. I don't propose to argue the pros and cons of censorship here. I have neither the time nor the energy. The fact is that John Milton treated the subject exhaustively in the seventeenth century and no further argument should have been necessary. I urge you to consider his views.[1]

Yours sincerely,

J. G. McClelland

1. See Milton's *Areopagitica* (1644), written in part to protest the attempt by Parliament to suppress his pamphlet on divorce, *The Doctrine and Discipline of Divorce* (1643).

FROM JOHN FISHER

John Fisher has not been traced.

271 Truman Road
Willowdale, Ontario
August 22, 1966

Dear Mr. McClelland:

Writing this letter was a difficult decision for me, but one that I felt must be done even though I suppose my voice will be the lonely one in the wilderness of a society that does not seem to care.

I am writing to vigorously protest at the recent publishing of the book *Beautiful Losers*. It saddens me to see the leading Canadian publisher stooping to such filth, such obscenities, all the creation of a sick mind.

I wonder, Mr. McClelland, do you ever stop to think of the tremendous responsibilities you publishers have? The current trend to more and more depraved literature, sicker plots ranging from the exploits of lesbians to the odd spot of incest all helps to drag our society down further into the muck of its own degeneration—all in the name of art and free expression.

Beautiful Losers contains no literature that even vaguely resembles art. There is no real reason to drag in every foul word that would never be aired in *your* living room. Sex is dragged even lower into the gutter, and any pretence at plot or narrative is abandoned in an orgy of filth. I read several pages, threw the book on the floor in disgust, then skim-read the remainder before writing this letter.

I don't know who Mr. Cohen is, I wish him no harm, but he must be a sick man to write such garbage—and you made a grave error of judgement when you allowed his writings to bear the stamp of McClelland and Stewart Ltd.

Mr. McClelland, I don't know what plain citizens like myself can do to halt this terrible headlong rush to degradation in publishing. I suppose most of us are afraid to say anything for fear of being accused of Victorianism, scorned as "queers," unnatural—not "hip." At thirty-nine, Mr. McClelland, I'm not old-fashioned, nor am I repressed or "queer," but something snapped inside me when I started to read that library book and I decided to do *something*.

I must tell you that I intend to write to the Chief of the Morality Squad (or whatever department is responsible) and lodge a formal citizen's complaint and request that the book be withdrawn as obscene. I realize sadly that this is probably just what would help to increase its sales—but unless someone cares, Mr. McClelland, I don't know what is to become of our society.

There must be hundreds of Canadian authors with good, exciting and acceptable novels waiting to be published—give them the break, Mr. McClelland—leave the sick-minded avant-garde crowd where they belong ... in the gutter.

Sadly—very sadly yours,

John Fisher

TO JOHN FISHER

August 26, 1966
Mr. John Fisher
271 Truman Road
Willowdale, Ontario

Dear Mr. Fisher:
Thank you for your letter of August 22. I am sorry that you have been upset by Mr. Cohen's book. I am interested to learn of your point of view as a reader. I am only too pleased to have the opportunity to give you my point of view as a publisher.

Let me start by referring to Leonard Cohen. You say you don't know who he is. Cohen is a poet. I think it is no exaggeration to say that in the opinion of the majority of responsible critics, he is one of Canada's most gifted and accomplished poets. Many would say he is our best. His poetry and his fiction have been published not only in Canada but in the U.S.A. and the United Kingdom. His work has been acclaimed internationally. He is without question a gifted artist.

You ask if I ever stop to think of the tremendous

responsibility I have as a publisher. I think about this a good deal. Ours is a serious publishing house. We think it is one of our prime responsibilities to publish the works of our serious and gifted creative artists. By contemporary standards, Leonard Cohen is a serious and gifted creative artist. *Beautiful Losers* is a serious work. Undoubtedly it may offend some people, but I cannot feel that this is sufficient justification for suppressing such a work. I think it is no exaggeration to say that a large proportion of great artworks have at one time or another offended many people. It will be for future generations to judge whether or not Cohen's work can be classed as a major contribution. At this point in time, I think we can be certain only of his intent and his integrity. I can assure you that Mr. Cohen is a very serious and very thoughtful young man.

I do not believe in censorship. I think there is abundant evidence available to thoughtful people that the evils of censorship are far greater than whatever evils the censors might attempt to correct. However, I do respect the right of any citizen to care, and I do respect the right of any citizen to endeavour to do something about any matter on which they feel strongly. However, Mr. Fisher, if you do feel that you must make a stand, if you do care, and if you do feel that you must do something about it, I suggest that you might find a far more worthwhile starting point by looking at the "pulps" on the local newsstand instead of attacking the work of a serious writer.

Yours sincerely,

J. G. McClelland

TO MORDECAI RICHLER

November 22, 1966
Mr. Mordecai Richler
Hillcrest
Kingston Hill
Surrey, England

Dear Mordecai:

Migod, it's good to hear from you. Your letter sort of surprised me. I ran into Bob Weaver last week. He said that he had heard from you and that you were gloomy, dispirited and God knows what else, but you don't seem so in this letter except that it's awfully bloody commercial.

So come back to Canada and visit us. It's been a long time. I don't see any hope of my getting to England in the near future, but you never know. All sorts of shuffling, reorganization, etc. are taking place in the firm. I will write you a full report one of these days, when time ain't at such a premium.

Re *Son of a Smaller Hero*, what in God's name do you expect? It's already been available at $4.50 or whatever; then it was available at 75¢. Our edition is purely for prestige purposes— our prestige and yours. Don't you love prestige?

Okay, so make your [new] book sexy. You can't shake me. We publish Leonard Cohen. We are dedicated to sex. What more can we do?

My best to you and your lovely, lovely wife.
Cheers!

J. G. McClelland

TO ALFRED A. KNOPF

Alfred A. Knopf (1892–1984): founder and head of the distinguished New York publishing house that carried his name. Thomas Mann and Wallace Stevens were among his authors, and in 1964 he published three books by Margaret Laurence on the same day.

January 10, 1967
Mr. Alfred A. Knopf
Alfred A. Knopf Inc.
501 Madison Avenue
New York, N.Y.

Dear Alfred:

Thanks for your letter. Perhaps mine was a bit misleading because you seem shocked. I certainly have no thought of selling the firm to Seagram's. I am hopeful of obtaining some funds from them on a debenture issue. As you probably know, Canadians have no great reputation for putting up venture capital. This characteristic is more than evident in this tight-money period. I'm hoping that Seagram's will prove to be the exception to the rule, and my feeling is, provided that the conditions are satisfactory, one dollar is about the same as another.

I like your analogy re the brewer and the French vineyard, but I would quarrel with the premise that book publishing houses are worthy per se. I would have to concede that I have somewhat more confidence in the consistent quality standard at Seagram's than I have in the quality standard at McClelland and Stewart. I rather like their product. I am less certain of many of ours. Canada has reached the stage where one can publish here with moderate success, but I am afraid we are many years away from being able to take much pride in many of the books we produce.

Perhaps I am just despondent because it is January and we have about sixty titles on our Spring list. I wish we had ten. We

couldn't live with ten, but I'm not certain we can live with sixty.
   With all good wishes.
                               Sincerely,

                               J. G. McClelland

TO ALFRED A. KNOPF

May 30, 1967
Mr. Alfred A. Knopf
Alfred A. Knopf Inc.
501 Madison Avenue
New York, N.Y.

Dear Alfred:
Thanks for your letter and your comment about our catalogue.
The fact is, you are right. We can't keep track of the titles and
authors. We'd be far better off with a much smaller list, except
that my current philosophy is that we can't survive in the
Canadian market without a lot of titles.
   I appreciate your point re doing new fiction in either
paperback or cloth but never both and preferably the latter. I
think the sad truth is that in the Canadian market we should
publish almost no new fiction. The market is getting worse,
except for the odd person like Margaret Laurence.
   Re the Robertson Davies book [*Marchbanks' Almanac*], I can't
honestly feel that it would be of interest, but I am arranging to
send about one-third of the manuscript down to you so that you
can get the flavour of it. Perhaps you could find a small market
for it. It's a thoughtful book, but with a very limited appeal, and
our only real hope on it is that he is so well respected in Canada.
We think a lot of his students and former students will buy it
along with a segment of readers of his earlier books.
   All the best.
                               Sincerely,

                               J. G. McClelland

TO JOHN DIEFENBAKER

John George Diefenbaker (1895–1979): prime minister from 1957 to 1963, and, if Peter Newman's *Renegade in Power* and Denys Smith's *Rogue Tory* are to be believed, one of the strangest men ever to hold public office in Canada. Despite J.M.'s efforts, M&S didn't publish any of his books. Macmillan brought out *One Canada: Memoirs of the Right Honourable John G. Diefenbaker* in 1975.

September 13, 1967
The Rt. Hon. John Diefenbaker
House of Commons
Ottawa, Ontario

Dear Mr. Diefenbaker:
You may recall that several years ago we had some correspondence with [your special assistant] B. T. Richardson about the possibility of publishing a collection or selection of your speeches. We were interested and ready to proceed, and indeed at one time it was my understanding that we were definitely going ahead. The manuscript itself, however, was never completed, and my understanding at the time, or at least my recollection of it, is that you had personally decided that it was not an appropriate time to proceed. It may have been that simple, or there may have been other factors that I was unaware of at the time. I would like now to re-express our interest in such a book. It would form an important part of the Canadian historical record, and it's my opinion, as a book publisher, that such a volume should appear either now or in the not too distant future.

At the same time, it is my hope that you will soon give serious consideration to the preparation of your memoirs. I have noted several references in the press recently to such a possibility, and I have been told further that several universities have expressed interest not only in your papers but in the possibility of having you spend some time in residence in order to advance the compilation of your memoirs.

I am certain that it will occasion no surprise when I say as a book publisher that such a volume or volumes would have widespread interest for many Canadians. Our interest in such a book is very considerable and very real and would include making available a substantial sum for whatever editorial or secretarial assistance you might wish to have.

I would, therefore, like to put our interest on record in a formal manner. I think I have already done so informally on a number of occasions when I had the opportunity to present you with copies of George Grant's book *Lament for a Nation, The Canadian Dictionary* and others that were of special interest from time to time. I have no doubt that you have already been approached and will be approached by other publishers, and would like to have the opportunity to convince you that we could probably handle the matter for you better than anyone else. I would be glad to meet with you at your convenience at any time or date that you might designate to discuss the matter.

Yours sincerely,

J. G. McClelland

TO MORDECAI RICHLER

January 17, 1968
Mr. Mordecai Richler
Hillcrest, Kingston Hill
Surrey, England

Dear Mordecai:
This letter is to inform you officially that I have just accepted the appointment as Editor-in-Chief of the Ryerson Press. There were several conditions attached. I told them that a few of our important authors (Richler, Norman Levine and Eddie Shack) would move with me and this is part of the contract. That's fair enough, but now I must tell you that it will mean some change in your writing style. All four-letter words must be omitted, and

in future please no references to screwing, buggery or to any perverted acts. I admit that won't leave you much to write about, but that's the price of loyalty.

Please purchase a bicycle for Norman Levine and charge it to my advance account.

Okay, so put us down in *Star Weekly*. We are so big in *Time* (where it really counts) that it doesn't matter. We're still trying to find out whose picture they used, and incidentally if you're such a big deal with *SW*, ask Gzowski why they're not using your name in the radio promo. I've heard it a few times. Never have so many distinguished writers been gathered together in a single magazine—just think of it. Nathan Cohen, Robert Fulford, Sylvia Fraser, Walter Stewart, Joe Snarf, Eddie Shack,[1] but not a single mention of Mordecai Richler. As a matter of fact, I suspect that there is prejudice at work here. Am I correct in thinking that you are Jewish? *The Star* is well known for its racist attitude, and I guess poor Gzowski has been forced to go along with it.

No, I hadn't heard about Gottlieb in control of Knopf, etc.[2] I'd like to know more. I was supposed to have lunch with Alfred in New York on Thursday but had to bow out. Unless he's retiring, though, I would doubt that Gottlieb is going to assume "control" in any real sense. It's a fascinating development. Although *Cocksure* is not involved, from my personal experience with Alfred Knopf, I would say that it would not be exactly his cup of tea. As a matter of fact, I would go so far as to say that Gottlieb's tenure at Knopf would be very short-lived if he proposed many books of the *Cocksure* nature.

Please stop writing letters. It is clear that they are all written with a view to a collection of letters at some future date in book form and our maximum advance for such a volume is $10. Furthermore, I don't have time to answer them.

Yours from THE SMUG MINORITY.

Cheers!

J. G. McClelland

1. Nathan Cohen (1923–1971): influential drama critic, first with the CBC and then, from 1959 to 1971, with the *Toronto Star*. He is the subject of Rick Salutin's *Nathan Cohen: A Review* (1981). Eddie Shack: a colourful hockey player for the Toronto Maple Leafs during the 1960s. Robert Fulford (b. 1932): Toronto-based journalist best known for his columns in *Saturday Night* (which he edited), the Toronto *Globe and Mail* and *Toronto Star*. He's a cultural critic and a political commentator with a wide range of interests and a broadly liberal approach. His books include *Crisis at the Victory Burlesk* (1968) and the memoir *Best Seat in the House: Memoirs of a Lucky Man* (1988). For Sylvia Fraser, see the letter of February 16, 1976. For Walter Stewart, see the letter of June 26, 1979. Joe Snarf has remained elusive.

2. Robert Gottlieb (b. 1931): editor and publisher, who was editor-in-chief at Knopf from 1968 to 1987.

TO SCOTT SYMONS

Scott Symons (b. 1933): controversial novelist and passionate social critic whose fiction manages to reconcile what could be called Red Tory values with a sexual polemic that owes much to André Gide, D. H. Lawrence, Wilhelm Reich and gay liberation. He has written three novels (*Helmet of Flesh*, 1986, is the most recent) and an original study of Canadian furniture, *Heritage—A Romantic Look at Early Canadian Furniture* (1972). *Civic Square* (1969), an attack on what Symons calls Toronto's "Blandmen" who control the country, ran into problems because much of its material was clearly autobiographical and it sometimes read like a *roman à clef*. It was published in manuscript format in a blue box resembling the trademark packaging of Birks jewellers, the Toronto firm traditionally patronized by the city's elite.

March 12, 1968
Mr. Scott Symons
c/o Mr. Vince Kelly
Suite 701
85 Richmond Street West
Toronto, Ontario

Dear Scott:
Hello, wherever you are. I am sorry to say that I am the bearer of

some uncheerful news. We have had to postpone publication of *Civic Square*. Nothing serious and we'll still be going ahead, but it looks as though this delay will mean holding it off until fall because there ain't much purpose in publishing in mid-summer. The problem, Scott, is legal. Among other things, you made a tactical error in sending a chapter of the manuscript to a friend at Trinity College School. I don't know who this was or why you sent it, but it created problems that I simply have not been able to deal with. Our lawyer is reviewing the manuscript; I'm reviewing the manuscript; John Colombo¹ has done his job and we have his recommendation, but there are problems in this material that we just cannot take lightly. Elimination of specific names doesn't solve anything. The identification is too clear. We don't want to screw around with the manuscript without your approval. By the same token, I am not prepared to go ahead until we know exactly what is going to have to be done. You'll just have to live with it.

The best guess is publication in September. This may be a good thing, in any case, because you will be back by then and I really think you should be in evidence when it comes out to field criticism or applause—whichever is forthcoming.

I'm truly sorry about the delay, but if I had more time and if our lawyer had more time it would have been possible to deal with the matter more quickly. But it is a lengthy manuscript and it's a delicate decision area.

While I am writing, one other thing you should know. An old Navy friend of mine who is now a magistrate in Kitchener has been bugging me on behalf of the parents of some teenagers reputed to be in your entourage. They are all apparently very upset. I have explained that we have no information about your whereabouts or anything else. All of which is true, but I thought you should know about the static.

Hope all goes well wherever you are.

Cheers!

J. G. McClelland

1. John Robert Colombo (b. 1936): a jack of all trades in Canadian letters, Colombo was managing editor of *The Tamarack Review*, has edited several anthologies as well as *Colombo's Canadian Quotations* (1974), and has published several volumes of "found poems" (*The Great Wall of China*, 1966).

TO DAVID MACLELLAN

May 7, 1968
Mr. David Maclellan
General Manager
Graphic Arts Industries Association
75 Albert Street
Ottawa, Ontario

Dear Mr. Maclellan:
Thank you for your letter of May 3. I have had previous complaints on this point, including at least one from a union, so I am well aware of the problems.

I have said before and I'll say again that we do not like to print in Italy. In terms of Canadian nationalism, I take second place to no one, but it has boiled down to a simple matter of economics. Either we do the books in Italy or we won't do the books at all. The difference in quoted price is substantial, particularly when the price is related to quality, but even without the quality consideration, it is substantial.

It may be true that there are a number of printing firms in this country who haven't been asked to quote. If you will give me the names of these firms, we'll be delighted to get in touch with them. If they have satisfactory equipment and are hungry enough, they can certainly do business with us. Because of the convenience and the time factor, it would be to our advantage to pay a little more for Canadian manufacture than we can afford to pay in Italy, but of all the figures I have seen thus far, the Canadian prices have been beyond the practical range.

I would be glad to discuss this whole matter with you when

you are in Toronto, or if an opportunity affords when I am in Ottawa. I suspect that Canadian printers are not being entirely realistic about the problems of Canadian book publishing. Certainly we are prepared to pay more for a Canadian product. As you have noted, we do so in almost every field. Even when we manufacture a Canadian book outside this country, the price for the product in Canada is higher than the price of a comparable book in the U.S.A. or the U.K., and this relates to the size of the printing run. But there is a limit. We have to sell in competition with British and American books. Our product has to look something like theirs in terms of price. It's not an easy problem.

If you can find a book manufacturer here that can help us, though, I assure you that we are more than ready to listen to them.

With all good wishes.

Yours sincerely,

J. G. McClelland

TO MARGARET LAURENCE

June 24, 1968
Mrs. Margaret Laurence
Elm Cottage
Beacon Hill
Penn, Bucks., England

Dear Margaret:
As I tried to indicate in my cable, I think *The Fire-Dwellers* is superb. I have said to you several times before, and I can say it again now in all sincerity, that you are the only writer I know who improves with each successive manuscript, and you are still doing it. A lot of critics didn't think that *A Jest of God* was an advance on *The Stone Angel*, but this was not an opinion I shared,

as you know. One was a critics' book; the other was a readers' book.

I'm confident that this one is going to satisfy both the critics and the readers. It's a gutsy novel. The intuition, insight, the incredible power that you have for allowing the reader to identify with what you are saying—it's a fantastic achievement. I read it at one sitting (and incidentally the only other person here who has had a chance to look at it is my eldest daughter, whom I think you have met, and who shares my enthusiasm). It's a great book.

I am not going to attempt to play editor. That's not my particular bag, and to be honest about it, you obviously know so much more than anybody else about what is right and what is wrong about a novel that it would be presumptuous of me to do much more than give a judgement, and my judgement is that you have done it again. It's a great success, and I haven't the slightest doubt that it will do very well.

Having said that, I can tell you that there is only one chunk of the novel that didn't grab me particularly, and that is Luke's lengthy description of his science-fiction novel. I won't pretend to be enough of a critic to have any sense of its significance in relation to the whole, but that may be largely because I skimmed that section. It slowed the pace. It didn't interest me, and no matter how relevant it may be in actual fact, I suspect its relevance may be artificial in the sense that I, at least as one reader, felt I really didn't give a goddamn what his science-fiction novel was about.

Obviously I don't think it is vitally important whether or not you leave that part as is; eliminate it or cut it, but I mention this one particularly because the novel as a whole, while it is full and rich in detail, seems to me to be virtually devoid of irrelevancies or artificialities. A skilled editor might want to suggest the odd minor cut in other parts of the script, but I hope any such treatment would be fairly light. Stacey comes through superbly (and by the way will be a superb character for stage and for films), but I think you have been successful with many of the others—Mac, Thor and Katie particularly—and it may be that because Luke didn't grab me quite as much as some of the others I didn't really give too much of a damn about his novel.

But it is a fine novel, Margaret. It can do nothing but enhance your reputation and enlarge your market. I presume that Macmillan, Knopf and ourselves will all want to do it in the early spring, and I don't anticipate any difficulty in working out a simultaneous date that will please everyone. This one is going to make you wealthy, baby, and you deserve it. My advice on the film rights would be to play it very cool and wait until they at least triple their initial offer whatever that initial offer might be.

Cheers!

Jack

TO MARGARET LAURENCE

July 23, 1968
Mrs. Margaret Laurence
Elm Cottage, Beacon Hill
Penn, Bucks., England

Dear Margaret:
First, my apologies for not having written before. It was a wonderful visit and I enjoyed it very much. I only wish we had had more time. I may say that goddamn bus got me to the station about two minutes after the train had left, so I spent a full hour examining the beautiful posters. Actually it wasn't that bad. After about fifteen minutes, several ravishing creatures in mini-skirts came along, and I spent the remainder of my time examining them. Fortunately the train arrived before I was arrested.

On the way back to London I gave further thought to the title [*The Fire-Dwellers*] and I have capitulated. By no stretch of the imagination do I think it is a great title, but if you like it and you want it, then I think you should have it. Actually it is not a bad title (nor is it, I think, particularly good) but it shouldn't do the book any harm, and if it is well handled from the design point of view, it could after the fact become an effective title.

I think the point here, as we discussed it, is that authors tend to think in terms of book titles that sum up or reflect the message or meaning of the book, whereas publishers tend to think of book titles in terms of something that is going to sell the book in advance. I can understand that the author takes pleasure in thinking of the reader reacting to the aptness of a title after reading a novel. A publisher, on the other hand, is more inclined to say, "I want a title to get them to buy the book. I don't really care whether or not the title has anything to do with the book itself as long as it sells."

In any case, Margaret, as far as I'm concerned it's the end of the argument. If you want to call it *The Fire-Dwellers*, then that's what it should be, and I would, as you say you intend to do, stand firm. And who knows a year from now we may be saying, "Migod, that was wise of us to let Margaret choose her own title."

All the best.

Sincerely,

J. G. McClelland

TO MALCOLM ROSS

This letter is one of a series between J.M. and Ross over whether to include *Beautiful Losers* in the New Canadian Library. J.M., always one of Leonard Cohen's biggest champions (even though he himself was baffled by *Beautiful Losers*), thought the book was a significant piece of work worthy of inclusion; Ross felt equally strongly that the book was artistically unsuccessful and should not go in. Ross won out in the end, and *Beautiful Losers* did not appear in NCL until 1991, after his retirement.

September 9, 1968
Dr. Malcolm Ross
Department of English
Dalhousie University
Halifax, N.S.

Dear Malcolm:
Thanks for your letter. It's a strong letter and it is obviously a matter that you feel very deeply about. It leads to some very serious problems at this end.

Let me start by saying that I have never questioned and do not now question your right of veto over the inclusion of any title in the New Canadian Library. It is your prerogative and your function. On the other hand, we are dealing with a difficult case here. It doesn't fit into the normal pattern. I will list the problems that it poses for me—not necessarily in order of importance—in hopes that some sort of satisfactory resolution can be found. Our problems are the following:

1. Cohen has already been told that his book [*Beautiful Losers*] is to be included in this series. This was, of course, necessary in order to clear the rights.

2. Cohen is a friend for whom I have a great deal of admiration and, indeed, affection. Although he is an individual with an astounding range of moods, he is also an extremely sensitive person.

3. Although I don't like to write this in proximity to item #2 for obvious reasons, it just happens that he is now one of a half dozen most important authors on our list commercially. This wasn't true a couple of years ago. It is true today. He is the best-selling poet in Canada, even including Layton, by a considerable margin. In fact, he may be close to the best-selling poet in North America. Viking has sold over 25,000 copies of his new *Selected* volume, and Bantam is about to publish *The Spice-Box of Earth* as a mass-market paperback in the U.S.A., which is

virtually unprecedented.

4. Bantam has offered us $3,000 as a second advance for the right to extend their contract for the paperback of *Beautiful Losers* in Canada. We have never been offered a second advance before on any book, and this second advance is the largest figure we have ever been offered for Canadian paperback rights except for Winston Churchill.

5. You did agree to the inclusion of the book. I am quite prepared to admit that it was a hasty decision made under abnormal circumstances and perhaps under pressure, but you nevertheless did agree. I think there is some distinction between right of veto and right to second-guess your own decision.

6. I suspect that you are inadvertently being subjective rather than objective. I say that as an old friend and admirer. I've never known you to do that before, and I don't know why you should start now. My justification for the statement? Your letter of September 2. You state, for example, that we are in a period of anti-morality and anti-art to a point of disintegration and decline. While I am taking those statements slightly out of context (you used them to support the Cohen book as a psychological or sociological case study), it seems to me that it does indicate a point of view and a point of view that you are applying subjectively to your evaluation of the Cohen book. Decline, as far as our values are concerned, there certainly is. Decline, as far as real value, is another matter, and one that is surely open to serious debate. I truly don't know whether *Beautiful Losers* is or is not a great novel or a great work of art. I think that might be known in about twenty-five years. I am quite prepared to admit that you are far better qualified to make such a judgement than I am at this point in time, but I don't think you are in a position to judge Cohen's intent, his motivation or his justification. You have judged that he did not

succeed at whatever the hell he was trying to do, and that's fair enough. But you are making assumptions and delving into areas that trouble the hell out of me. Cohen is pretty unhappy with our values, and in that he represents most of the younger generation throughout the world. I think his chief message is traditional enough but maybe of particular contemporary importance is [the idea] that liberation comes only through debasement.

Assuming for a minute that this is what he is trying to say, what I truly don't understand is why his book succeeds only in offending you and the vast majority of our generation, but at the same time sells in vast quantities to the younger generation. They are not buying it as pornography because it sure as hell isn't pornographic. Are they buying it because they revel in obscenity? Surely not. There are lots of books around that are much more obscene than this one.

I am not arguing that a book is great or even important because it sells very well. A book like Terry Southern's *Candy* becomes a best-seller. One can understand why. It is an extremely erotic book. A book like Jacqueline Susann's *Valley of the Dolls* becomes a best-seller.[1] One can understand why. It was because it was widely promoted, and although it is a bad book it is some sort of sex substitute. But tell me why the younger generation and the younger critics are buying, discussing and promoting *Beautiful Losers*.

Out of the foregoing you will see that there are essentially two problems. The first is that we are put in a difficult position as publishers. The second is that I think you are being subjective and that you are dead wrong about the significance of this book. We have published some pretty bad novels in the New Canadian Library because of their historical significance. On the grounds of historical significance alone, I think that *Beautiful Losers* must be included. Whether it is a great artistic creation or not remains to be seen, and no one can be absolutely certain at this point, but there can be no doubt about its importance in terms of Canadian letters. That is a pretty good argument for inclusion.

The resolution I suggest is that we put it up to arbitration. We used this technique once before and it didn't work, but that may have been because we picked only one individual. In this case, I suggest that we have a panel of three. You pick one, I'll pick one and the two we pick will pick the third. If they can't pick a third, then they will each pick another one and the four of them will pick a fifth, etc.

The issue fascinates me. It is much more important to me than a difference of opinion between Jack McClelland and Malcolm Ross. Much more important than whether or not *Beautiful Losers* should be included in the New Canadian Library. That is our key problem, but what I would really like to learn from this is whether or not there is any literary significance in the argument. Is it just this specific novel of Cohen's that is not an artistic success? Why is it that most of the new fiction that reaches us today is closer to Cohen than, say, Callaghan? What is going on in the world? I think that is the real point. Needless to say I look forward to your reaction with great interest.

Sincerely,

J. G. McClelland

1. Terry Southern (1924–1995): American writer best known for his screenplays for *Dr. Strangelove* (1964) and *Easy Rider* (1969), and the novel *Candy* (1958, 1964). Jacqueline Susann (1918–1974), an American, had her more than fifteen minutes of fame with the best-selling novel *Valley of the Dolls* (1966).

TO MORDECAI RICHLER

December 18, 1968
Mr. Mordecai Richler
1 Malcolm Road
Westmount, Montreal, Quebec

Dear Mordecai:
Thanks for your note. Those are great pictures. I'll let you have
them back in due course. In the meantime, we'll give some
thought to using one or the other on the back of the jacket [of
The Street]. There may be some delay, the main problem being
that I can't decide which of the snapshots would be more
effective in killing the sale of the book completely. Who in hell
would want to buy a book written by a snot-nose little brat who
looked like that?

    Elizabeth didn't mind your taking the glass from the party. I
am still trying to find out who took several cases of booze. We
couldn't possibly have consumed that much. One of these days
I'm going to learn not to drink at my own party so that I'll have
some idea afterwards what took place. Truthfully, I can
remember almost nothing. I went to bed at seven and am told
that the party officially ended at seven-thirty when a taxi came
to remove Harold Town from the premises. I hope as one of the
guests of honour, you felt it incumbent on you to remain until
at least seven o'clock.

    Incidentally, Layton's *Selected* has just been turned down by
Cape. I have suggested to Irving that he might ask you about the
current London scene. In case he doesn't, I may ask you directly.
Which would be the most likely house to be interested in
Layton? I realize that the answer will probably be none, but if
you have any suggestions I'd appreciate them.
                             Cheers!

        J. G. McClelland

FROM MARGARET LAURENCE

Elm Cottage
April 4, 1969

LINES OF ENCOURAGEMENT TO J. G. McCLELLAND

roses are red
violets are blue
one of your authors
has faith in McStew.

violets are blue
roses are red
i don't believe
you've got rocks in your head

violets are blue
roses are pink
let nobody say
as a bookman you stink

violets are mauve
or purple or worse
in two hundred years
who'll give a curse?

roses are crimson
and green is the chive
whatever your troubles
i know you'll survive

roses are red
violets are blue
be heartened old buddy
i'm betting on you

With love from your slightly mannish but not unmotherly,[1]
Aunt Margaret

1. For an explanation of "mannish but not unmotherly" see the next letter.

TO MARGARET LAURENCE

Margaret Laurence had been appointed writer-in-residence at the
University of Toronto for 1969–70. Despite J.M's anticipation that
her duties would be light (the position involved holding office
hours once a week to meet young writers, occasional visits to
classrooms and a spring reading), Laurence probably worked
harder than any writer who ever held the post, and complained in
later years that she had been unable to do any of her own work.

April 11, 1969
Mrs. Margaret Laurence
Elm Cottage, Beacon Hill
Penn, Bucks., England

Dear Margaret:
First, how does one reply to a poem? It's great. It's much
appreciated and I'll also promise not to publish it.
   I enjoyed your letter. I ran into the local *Time* magazine rep a
week or so ago, and I told him that I wasn't overly delighted with
their piece and I didn't think you would be, and he was quite
upset. They have their own particular problems at *Time*, but as I
have said, it does no harm.[1]
   Glad you've got a house, and we are going to look forward to
having you here. If Jack Ludwig's experience [as writer-in-
residence] is any criterion, you'll have a marvellous time. No
duties, obligations or anything of that sort. He has actually
completed a novel since his arrival, and as he's taken at least six
years for each of his previous novels, it's some real indication of
the demands they have made on his time. Actually, that's not fair.

His reason for writing so feverishly is that he is sick as hell, and I think basically suspects he won't be around too much longer or able to write too much longer. I may be overdramatizing the situation, but he has fantastic physical problems.

So you'll love it at the U. of T., and actually I understand you are going to be the first woman with an office or apartment or whatever the hell you call it in Massey College. This has great possibilities. If I do actually ever solve all my problems and can become a book publisher again, I'll revert to my real character and arrange a series of wine festivals with you in your digs at Massey so that you will be thrown out of the university in great disgrace, which will sell hundreds of thousands of copies of your books, which is, after all, what publishers are supposed to do.

Cheers!

J. G. McClelland

1. The piece referred to is a "Letters" column in *Time* (Canada Edition, March 28, 1969, p. 13). It combines a favourable review of *The Fire-Dwellers* and a personality piece on Margaret Laurence. The writer comments that the novel is "a deft exploration of the menopausal landscape," while Laurence is described as "Chunky, with short brown hair pulled into a bun behind her head" and "as slightly mannish without being unmotherly." One suspects that it wasn't the review portion of the column that unsettled the forty-two-year-old Laurence.

TO NORMAN LEVINE

July 29, 1969
Mr. Norman Levine
45 Bedford Road
St. Ives
Cornwall, England

Dear Norman:
It's been a long time, and it is good to hear from you again. Your letter is a difficult one to answer. It reminds me somewhat of

the old bit about "when did you stop beating your wife?" I presume you still harbour the notion that we attempted to suppress *Canada Made Me*. It wasn't true at the time, and the passage of years hasn't changed that fact. I wasn't able to commend the book personally, but that is a different matter. We have published many books through the years—some successful, some not—that I haven't been very enthusiastic about personally. We do try to operate as a book publishing house, not as a platform.

I think the answer here, Norman, is that there is no reason why we should not put our whole weight behind your stuff. Maybe it is one of those things we can't win. If you are convinced in advance that we don't do so, then you probably should look for another publisher. If you are not, then you should publish with us. It's that simple.

I should warn you in advance, I suppose, that the fiction market in Canada is abominably bad at the present time for the serious writer. Fine novels by Brian Moore, Mordecai Richler, Leonard Cohen and Margaret Laurence are selling very poorly indeed (except in paperback reprints). Depressing as it may seem, in North America it is clearly the age of the Arthur Haileys, Harold Robbinses, Jacqueline Susanns, etc. So whether you publish with us or with someone else, you should reconcile yourself to this in advance. Promotion helps, of course, but the results remain as depressing as hell for author and publisher. The financial results are, of course, far better than they ever were, if one is lucky in things like paperback rights, movie options, etc., but income from royalties on hardbound book sales is depressing. We would like to have a crack at the new novel [*From a Seaside Town*], but I ain't about to make any wild promises to publish it. It's up to you whether you want us to have a look at it.

All the best.

Sincerely,

J. G. McClelland

TO DAVID GODFREY

From 1968 to 1972 **Dave Godfrey** edited M&S's *Canadian Writers* series of critical monographs. The following letter deals with the editing of the manuscript for Michael Ondaatje's *Leonard Cohen* (1970).

April 23, 1969
Professor David Godfrey
"Les Camus"
13 Puyricard, France

Dear Dave:
Predictably [Michael] Ondaatje has reacted somewhat strenuously to the suggestion that certain words and phrases be deleted from his Cohen manuscript. I don't blame him. Ultimately the decision is yours as the editor of the [*Canadian Writers*] series. Ondaatje chooses to consider it censorship, which may be unfair but is nonetheless a fact. Our policy at M&S is diametrically opposed to censorship of any sort when the author feels that censorship is at issue. In short, we will make suggestions on grounds of taste or market, but policy precludes us from insisting, unless the author agrees with us. We'd be glad to know your views.
    With best regards.
                        Sincerely,

                    J. G. McClelland

THE SEVENTIES:
The Publisher
as Phoenix

The financial instability of the late sixties became the norm for
the rest of Jack McClelland's career. If the 1945–60 period had
hinted at the possibility of a strong Canadian publishing
industry, the sixties brought everyone back to earth with the
arrival of American branch plants in Canada. By 1969, not only
were 80 per cent of all imports American in origin, but 59 per
cent of all books published in Canada originated from
American branch plants. Only 20 per cent were Canadian. And
in the vital paperback market, the Canadian presence was
ghostly, almost non-existent. Surveying the situation, the
secretary of state, Gérard Pelletier, warned that Canadian
publishers would not survive and that "before the last resistance
to the foreign flood collapses, the government will have to step
in with permanent long-term programs to support this sector of
Canadian culture." Paul Audley, writing for the Committee for
an Independent Canada, went so far as to argue that "we will
ultimately have to ensure complete control of the industry or
[have] virtually none."

It was in this context that M&S continued to publish nearly a
hundred books a year as McClelland practised his version of
chaos theory. Among the new projects were the *Illustrated Natural
History of Canada*, the Canadian Nature Classics, the Generations
series with a multicultural emphasis, and the paperback reprint
series Canadian Children's Favourites. A more important move
into the paperback field took place in 1977, when M&S joined
Bantam Books to form M&S–Bantam Ltd. with the Seal Books
imprint. This began life as an annual competition with a $50,000
prize for the best first novel by a Canadian. Aritha van Herk was
the first winner, for *Judith*.

Though McClelland was rarely out of the public spotlight
because of the company's finances (1971 and 1976 were
particularly bad years), he was especially prominent on two

occasions. In 1975 Coles bookstores began selling or clearing, at a lower price, American editions of books by Canadian authors, books that were still selling locally at full price in their Canadian editions. Letters to cabinet ministers, threats of legal action, letters to newspapers, even the picketing of Coles by prominent authors were used to publicize the issue and to gain support for changes in copyright law. A different whiff of controversy attended the 1978 conference at the University of Calgary, where Canadian academics were summoned to name the one hundred greatest Canadian novels. As the correspondence reveals, McClelland hoped to use the conference to honour Malcolm Ross's very real contribution to Canadian literature and letters, and to gain some publicity for Canadian writing and the New Canadian Library. There was also some discussion of publishing a new paperback series of classic Canadian novels as an offshoot of NCL. What he hadn't anticipated was that the academics, doing their best to imitate Swift's intellectuals in Laputa and Lagado, would stumble and grumble every step of the way before issuing a list that left almost everyone dissatisfied. On the positive side, it remains the only conference on Canadian literature that ever generated any significant disagreement and controversy.

Among the major books of the decade were Berton's *Great Railway 1871–1881* (1970), *The Collected Poems of Irving Layton* (1971), Atwood's *Surfacing* (1972), Laurence's *Diviners* (1974), Ken Adachi's *Enemy That Never Was* (1976), Newman's *Canadian Establishment* (1977) and Michael Ondaatje's *There's a Trick with a Knife I'm Learning to Do* (1979).

TO PIERRE BERTON

Pierre Berton (b. 1920): editor, journalist, television personality and author. One of Canada's all-time best-selling authors, Berton has been a prominent figure on the national scene for nearly half a century, both as a popular broadcaster and as the writer of books such as *The Comfortable Pew* (1965), *The National Dream* (1970), *The Last Spike* (1971), *The Dionne Years* (1977), and *The Invasion of Canada 1812–13* (1980), all published by M&S. During this period, he also hosted "The Pierre Berton Show" (1962–73) and was a panellist on "Front Page Challenge." His later television shows included "The Great Debate" and "My Country." Though there are more files devoted to Berton and his books than to any other M&S author, the letters are disappointing because they deal primarily with matters of design, contracts, promotion and royalties.

February 11, 1970
Mr. Pierre Berton
Screen Gems
72 Carlton Street
Toronto, Ontario

Dear Pierre:
I have read the report [on *The National Dream*] from your historian¹ with great interest. There is much of value in it, and unquestionably parts of the manuscript can be pruned and sharpened to advantage.

I hope you will give very careful consideration to the nationalism issue before reaching a final conclusion. You have already told me that you believe him to be right. I wish I could be as certain.

His report, intelligent as it is, is so typically that of a frustrated academic that it really troubles me. I think you should take care not to be too confined by the inhibitions of the academic historian. He says, "Yet no historian under 55 would dare follow Creighton all the way in his portrait of Macdonald."² Partly true, but it's precisely because Creighton had more guts than most of our historians that his Macdonald book was important and useful and widely accepted. He goes on to say that by far the best parts of the manuscript are those describing the struggle of man against nature, such as the surveyors in the Rockies and the construction crews west of Lake Superior. These, he says, "at least are the parts that emotionally involve me, both as a reader and an historian." To that I say horseshit. It's all very well for a historian to tell an amateur historian that his most important contribution is "the first good account of the role of the people who really did the physical work" so that you will be known as the man who glorified the working man, but migod, Pierre, this is arrant nonsense. This material is valuable. It gives depth to the book and it is interesting (although it is my opinion that there is too much of it; that it is too similar and that if anything this is where the book should be cut), but it is like saying the interesting aspect of the pipeline is how they laid it, not the scandal attached to it.

Your book is important because it is well structured, well organized, readable and interesting and because you have assembled a vast amount of little-known historical data into a cohesive whole. It is my instinct that you could hurt the book very considerably by watering down its theme and unity. I ask you, before you swerve too far, to consider this quote from his report: "the narrow, simplistic, nationalist theme only interferes with this 'gut' story of the CPR—hacking a railroad out of a wilderness. This was the essential theme of the Canadian experience, as it is of virtually all pre-industrial human experience, long before a generation of insecure nationalists began to rewrite our history to provide themselves with an emotionally satisfying past." Or perhaps I shouldn't finish the quote there. Perhaps I should go on: "Moreover, it's a theme that stresses the real achievements of the ordinary Canadians, the workingmen, who essayed far more than politicians ever did." I don't know what a psychologist would make out of that statement, but I for one would be very reluctant to heed the advice of a man who could write such tripe. He may be a sound, academic historian, but I think he is somewhat lacking in practical judgement.

Cheers!

Jack

1. The historian was Michael Bliss (b. 1941), a professor at the University of Toronto and author of, among other books, *Banting: A Biography* (1984).

2. Donald Creighton (1902–1979): perhaps Canada's greatest historian. In the fifties he published a two-volume biography of John A. Macdonald: *The Young Politician* (1952), and *The Old Chieftain* (1955). Both received Governor General's Awards.

TO WALTER GORDON

June 3, 1970
The Hon. Walter Gordon
22 Chestnut Park
Toronto, Ontario

Dear Walter:
For some reason it has been on my mind for the last few weeks that the reading public is being deprived of a very good book. Have you given the matter any further thought? It may be that I was reminded of this by the realization a few weeks ago (following Kent State and Cambodia) that I am no longer just a mere Canadian nationalist; I am now actively anti-American. I enclose a copy of a recent piece by Jim Eayrs[1] which makes a lot of sense to me. Do let's think again about your book.[2]

Sincerely,

J. G. McClelland

1. James Eayrs (b. 1926): political scientist at the University of Toronto, newspaper

columnist and prolific writer on international relations. His books include *The Art of the Possible: Government and Foreign Policy in Canada* (1961), *In Defence of Canada* (1964, 1965, 1972) and *Greenpeace and Her Enemies* (1973).

2. M&S didn't publish a book by Gordon until 1975, when *Storm Signals: New Economic Policies for Canada* appeared.

TO BRIAN MOORE

June 10, 1970
Mr. Brian Moore
33958 Pacific Coast Highway
Malibu, California

Dear Brian:
I should have written to you long before this about *Fergus*. *Fergus* is a fine piece of writing and I think one of your great characterizations. It's alarmingly real and perceptive and right for the time, and maybe for me this is the most significant thing about it. By this I mean—and someday I am going to take a short course in how to express these things properly—that it has the all-too-rare validity of the artist dealing precisely with his own times, with his particular own skills and idioms. I guess I mean by that there is no faking, no compromising, no concession—it is a piece of art and craftsmanship by Brian Moore, at his best.

A couple of points that might interest you. I decided to test out two audience reactions. To find out what the critics might think, I turned to Bob Fulford. He thinks it is a great book and says that the critics as a group are going to love it. [The] comparison [would be] with *I am Mary Dunne*, although he doesn't think it has as much appeal for the general reader as *Mary Dunne*; he thinks it has rather more for the critics. That will give you something to think about. The other reaction that I wanted to test was that of the young reader so I tried it on a young McClelland. She is twenty-two, just out of university, spent four summers working in bookstores, is a good reader, will never be a publisher—thank God, I'm reserving that fate for my worst enemies, not for my children. In any case, she digs the book. She thinks it may be large on the campuses in paperback, and I think she may be right.

All the best.

Sincerely,

J. G. McClelland

TO ROBIN MATHEWS

Robin Mathews (b. 1931): poet, critic and professor of English. Mathews's criticism (*Canadian Literature: Surrender or Revolution*, 1978) is nationalistic and neo-Marxist in its orientation.

November 9, 1970
Professor Robin Mathews
82 Fourth Avenue
Ottawa, Ontario

Dear Robin:
Thanks for your note. I, too, was sorry that we didn't travel back together. I would have enjoyed continuing our conversation. The Ryerson takeover is a bit sickening, I agree. I don't, however, agree with much that has been said about it. The firm had to be sold. It was sick, sick, sick, and in my view it lacked the personnel and resources to pull out of it. To say nothing of money. What I don't understand is how the United Church of Canada would sell to McGraw when they could have sold to Maclean-Hunter. I guess the dollar is still a very effective weapon even with the Church.

All the best.

Sincerely,

J. G. McClelland

TO WALTER GORDON

M&S published *A Political Memoir* by Gordon in 1977. J.M. is
probably discussing an early draft of it in this letter.

December 7, 1970
The Hon. Walter Gordon
50 King Street West
Toronto, Ontario

Dear Walter:
I'm returning to you herewith the copy of your manuscript as
edited by John Colombo. In reading it, I noticed a few minor
errors here and there that could be picked up in a normal
copyedit. Because my impressions of it are fresh in my mind, I'd
like to record some of the thoughts I had while reading it.

First, I don't really think that you should hold back
publication now because of [the critical] comments about
Lester Pearson. It is perfectly clear in the manuscript that he let
you down as he let down a few others in different ways—
Cardin, LaMarsh, Lamontagne'—but on the whole this is pretty
mild criticism and he comes through not too badly. If I had any
criticism on this score, it would be that you soften the punch
too much, protest too much in the sense of pleading his
accomplishments. On that score, as the manuscript now stands,
at least one critic is quite likely to say that the accomplishments
he made during his first administration were largely engineered
by you, and that it was his failure to heed your advice, and your
absence, that led to his failure in the second period.

On the whole, though, I can't really think that the criticism
of Pearson is sufficient to justify holding back what is a very
useful, indeed valuable, book. It is highly critical of Mitchell
Sharp, of course, but I would think you have no concern about

that. Publication may have the effect of performing a real
service for Trudeau, Benson, etc.[2]
  With best personal regards.
                                    Sincerely,

                        J. G. McClelland

1. Lucien Cardin (1919–1988): Liberal politician who served during the sixties as
associate minister of National Defence, minister of Public Works and minister of
Justice and Attorney General (1965–67). He is probably best remembered for
breaking the Gerda Munsinger scandal, his handling of which has been described
by the historian John English as "one of the lowest moments in Canadian
parliamentary history, and the nadir of Mike Pearson's public career" (*The Worldly
Years: The Life of Lester Pearson 1949–1972*, 355). Judy LaMarsh (1924–1980): Liberal
politician during the sixties, minister of Health and Welfare (1963–65), secretary of
state (1965–68). M&S published her political memoirs, *Memoir of a Bird in a Gilded
Cage* (1968). Maurice Lamontagne (1917–1983): economist and Liberal politician,
appointed to the Senate in 1967.
2. Mitchell W. Sharp (b. 1911): Liberal politician prominent in the Pearson and
Trudeau governments, minister of Trade and Commerce (1963–65), minister of
Finance (1965–68) and secretary of state for External Affairs (1968–74). Edgar
Benson (b. 1923): Liberal politician, minister of National Revenue (1964–68).

TO EARLE BIRNEY

January 11, 1971
Dr. Earle Birney
The Park Plaza Hotel
Bloor Street West
Toronto, Ontario

Dear Earle:
At the end of a long day I just had the pleasure of reading a copy
of your most recent letter to John Newlove.[1] The content of the

letter doesn't surprise me any more than one is surprised by the sound from a broken phonograph record, but it suddenly occurred to me that you could do us both a favour by asking yourself why you wrote this letter to John.

Are you trying to turn him against me? Are you trying to endear yourself to him? I mean, what is the purpose of the exercise? You complain about our sales people, about our promotion people, our editorial people, our design people, our accounting people, about [my secretary] Mrs. Hodgeman, about me. Okay, we've heard all that. Are you trying to get cooperation from John Newlove or are you trying to turn him against you? I haven't discussed the letter with him and I don't intend to (although he will have a copy of this one), but what in hell are you trying to do? My guess is that his only conclusion will be that you are a real horse's ass. Has it not occurred to you that John, even though he has only been here a few months, might have developed a little loyalty towards me? Has it not occurred to you that Marge Hodgeman might have a little loyalty towards me, or Anna Porter,[2] or our sales people, or our promotion people? We are in the publishing business, you know. They know what we are trying to do and they know something about the difficulty, and you, after Christ knows how many years, remain blissfully ignorant of everything but your own paranoia. Do you really expect to get better results from M&S with all this shit? If you do, then I urge you to stop and think about it a bit.

On the record, I don't get mad all that easily, but you are beginning to get to me. Maybe that's what you want to do. My impression now is that if I gave you a list of the employees at M&S, each one of them within two months would receive the same fucking hysterical diatribe. If there is a purpose in all this shit, then why don't you say so. If there isn't, then I'd be grateful if you would find a more constructive hobby.

Cheers!

J. G. McClelland

P.S. What! There were no flowers or no fruit in your room when you arrived. That goddamn Catherine Wilson[3] has fucked things up again. I'll speak to her.

1. John Newlove (b. 1938): poet who worked as editor at M&S. His collections of poetry include *Moving in Alone* (1965), *Black Night Window* (1968), *The Fatman: Selected Poems 1962–72* (1977), *Apology for Absence: Selected Poems, 1962–92* (1993).
2. For Anna Porter, see the memo for August 19, 1975.
3. Publicist for M&S.

TO EARLE BIRNEY

January 15, 1971
Dr. Earle Birney
The Park Plaza Hotel
Bloor Street West
Toronto, Ontario

Dear Earle:
I received your message from John Newlove. I am prepared to apologize in the sense that in retrospect I would certainly not have worded my letter in that offensive fashion. On the other hand, I can hardly withdraw the message or the intent of the letter, which was to ask you to consider the purpose and the effect of your own attitude.

I should add—because I am getting at least as prickly as you—that my apology is sent because of an old friendship that I value, not because of concern about libel. You see, the libel file would only be useful after a review of your own letters. I think your lawyer might be disenchanted by continuing references to incompetent promotion types, drunken editors and other professional slurs. I will concede that a court action on all these matters might obviate the need for a Royal Commission on publishing and save the government some money, but I am not overly keen.

In any case, I admit that we have been responsible for many errors and inefficiencies; I admit that I wish you would stop your repetitive complaining; I apologize for my intemperate language; and although I am fond of you, have great admiration and respect for you, I admit that I still think you are a shit.

Cheers!

J. G. McClelland

TO EARLE BIRNEY

February 12, 1971
Dr. Earle Birney
Apt. 406
2030 Barclay Street
Vancouver, B.C.

Dear Earle:
Paranoia or paranoii. I guess a fair assessment is that we both have some of it in this whole matter. I was surprised by your reaction to my letter of January 15. It was intended as an apology—as a hatchet-burying letter. And strangely enough, the warmest part of the letter was, I thought, the last sentence. Of course there was a smile on my face when I dictated it. Of course I feel entitled to call you a shit if I think the circumstances warrant calling you a shit. Had I thought you would take offence at that, I wouldn't have said it. I guess it wasn't the right time to expect you to be reading between the lines.

Perhaps not too surprisingly, one of a multitude of considerations that have influenced my recent decision to try to get the hell out of book publishing is the fact that I wrote that first letter to you. Through the years I have often felt like writing such letters to a great many people but have usually refrained from doing so. I don't think a sensible publisher has any business writing such letters at any time, and when he does start writing such letters, it is time for him to look for something else new. That was not the major motivating factor, of course, but it was one.

So let's meet halfway and forget the whole damn thing. Please don't send me copies of letters to the staff. Not only is it unnecessary but I don't really want to read them. I do appreciate the more kindly tone that has been recently apparent.

I'll even see what I can do about getting the errata slip inserted in the *Selected*. Of course I agree that this should have been done a long time ago. I expect to be in Vancouver on March 3—although very briefly—and if possible will try to get together over a drink.

Cheers!

J. G. McClelland

TO PETER NEWMAN

May 13, 1971
Mr. Peter Newman
Editor
Maclean's Magazine
481 University Avenue
Toronto, Ontario

Dear Peter:
God help us. I don't really have time to answer this sort of questionnaire but if you really want the information, I'd better dig in and get it done right now, because if I put it in my backlog, I'll never get it to you by the 21st.

On the newspaper side, I read the *Globe and Mail*, the *Telegram*, the *Star*, the *New York Review of Books*, the *Financial Post*, the *Financial Times*.

On the magazine side, I read *Maclean's, Saturday Night, Weekend*, the *Canadian,* the *United Church Observer, Time,* the *Atlantic Monthly, Canadian Business, Executive, Beautiful British Columbia, ArtsCanada, Canadian Geographical Journal, Campus, Imperial Oil Review, Canadian Journal of Political Science, Scholarly Publications, Tamarack, Prism, Canadian Literature,* the *Business Quarterly, National Geographic, Publishers Weekly, Quill and Quire, Board of Trade Journal,* the *Structurist, Canadian Forum, Avant Garde, Good Housekeeping, Ladies Home Journal, Chatelaine, Playboy* occasionally, the *Mysterious East, Canadian Author and Bookman,* a number of small literary magazines, a number of dirty magazines such as *F.U.C.K.* and others when I can get my hands on them, and I have probably left a few out. It would have been a help if you had supplied a list of magazines. Of all of them, I guess I look forward most eagerly to the *Atlantic Monthly.*

As far as books are concerned, I read the majority of the books we publish, a fair sprinkling of the best-sellers we don't publish, and a helluva lot of books that we don't publish and that somebody else might publish someday.

As far as radio is concerned, I seldom listen to it except when I am in my car. Then I am usually tuned to CHUM or CFRB. Occasionally CKEY and CHFI. My kids invariably turn the car radio to CHUM when they borrow it and I am usually too lazy to change it.

On the TV side, I watch football, I watch hockey, I watch special programs like "Telescope," "The Morning After" and other programs such as "The Pierre Berton Show" when our authors are involved or when time permits. Very infrequently I watch a late movie. I even admit to enjoying the "FBI" and "Mannix." I used to enjoy "The Dean Martin Show" until he started copying "Laugh-In," which I consider to be the single worst continuing television show ever perpetrated on the public. It is even worse than "Lassie" or "Tom Charrington" or whatever the hell his name is. I also watch "Under Attack" from time to time, and I think it can be very good, although I am partial to the Berton show.

I almost never go to the theatre, legitimate or otherwise. I manage to see a fair number of the most-talked-about films usually on out-of-town trips and, of course, like any red-blooded old man, I've seen a few of the skin flicks when in New York. I don't, by the way, consider them pornographic. I think they have developed an entirely new form of humour inadvertently, and these so-called sexy pornographic films have developed, unintentionally, an entirely new mother lode (what an expression) of humour. Despite the foregoing, I find the best way of keeping in touch with what is going on both in Canada and in the world at large is to meet frequently with Canadian writers, editors, TV and film producers, artists, musicians, and the young people who visit my children.

My personal conclusions about all the foregoing:

I feel that I am incredibly well informed about Canada, not so well informed about the rest of the world. What am I doing to try to keep even better informed? I can only think of a favourite line from Betty MacDonald's *Egg and I*. She said, "I had so much culture I could hardly walk." I feel that I have so much information I can hardly walk. I don't read *Reader's Digest*, but I would welcome a digest of all the information I am exposed to. I have one great advantage over Pierre Berton. He remembers everything he reads. I have complete non-attention and remember nothing. This gives me the advantage of having an open mind—essential to a book publisher. The worst book publisher I ever knew was so well organized that his wife actually got up several hours before he did, went through all the newspapers (this was in New York) and clipped out anything that he would want to read. Every time he sat down to a meal at home, he would save time by having a pile of clippings from newspapers and magazines in front of him. From that contact I developed the theory that a book publisher should not be orderly. Because of my own nature, I have rationalized the theory that a book publisher should have a very poor memory.

All the best.

Sincerely,

J. G. McClelland

1. Betty MacDonald's *The Egg and I* was published in 1945 in New York by Lippincott. It was made into a film that starred Claudette Colbert and Marjorie Main.

TO AL PURDY

Al Purdy (b. 1918): one of the major Canadian writers, he published volumes of poetry (*Wild Grape Wine*, 1968), anthologies (*Storm Warning: The New Canadian Poets*, 1971), a collection of prose (*No Other Country*, 1977) and a novel (*A Splinter in the Heart*, 1990) with M&S.

May 31, 1971
Mr. Al Purdy
R.R. 1
Ameliasburgh, Ontario

Dear Al:
I have your letter. That sounds fine for next year. The only thing that bothers me about the *Selected* is that I am not all that enthusiastic about an introduction by George Woodcock. I have no objection to George personally, but I do feel that you denigrate yourself by having an introduction attached to your *Selected* by someone else. It is a point of view that I have always maintained. I think that you, for example, are much more important than George Woodcock, so why should he be introducing your book to the public?[1]

I recognize, however, that you probably invited him to do it, and we can't do anything about it now, so we'll just have to accept it, but I wish you would remember that again in principle. This is the reason that we don't have outside introductions for Birney or Layton and really as a matter of principle try to avoid it. If it is a new poet, that's one thing. He perhaps needs an introduction, but you don't.
Cheers!

Jack

1. Purdy's *Selected Poems* appeared in 1972 with a perceptive introduction by Woodcock.

TO MARGARET ATWOOD

Margaret Atwood (b. 1939): best-selling poet and novelist, all of whose novels have been published by M&S. Her influence on Canadian poetry, fiction and criticism (through *Survival*, 1972) has been enormous.

October 22, 1971
Mrs. Margaret Atwood
27 Hilton Avenue
Toronto, Ontario

Dear Peggy:
I had a report yesterday from Doug Raynor, one of our college representatives, which I found very disturbing. He told me of a recent meeting with you in which you reviewed a series of complaints that you had about Jack McClelland and McClelland and Stewart. The report from Raynor may have been exaggerated. If that is so, I would be glad to be reassured. If it is not so, I feel that I would like to set the record straight, because I think that you have either been deliberately misled or simply misinformed by a number of people on a number of subjects.

I have been under the impression that you and I had a reasonably friendly relationship which had not developed beyond that point simply because we've seldom had the opportunity to meet. Beyond that point, I have had the impression that you have a good rapport with Pamela Fry, your M&S editor, and that's the way it should be.

Let's review, then, some of the points that Raynor reported to me. I don't know the order of importance, but let's start with your agent [Phoebe Larmore]. I understand you are angry because I didn't see her. Hell, Peggy, I not only did not know that she was coming to Toronto, I didn't even know that she was in our office until after she had left. Apparently I was in a meeting while she was at the office. My secretary would certainly have got me out of that meeting had you or another important author arrived and asked to see me urgently, but what the hell gives with your agent? I understand she spent a long time with Pamela and I believe had lunch with her, but I do have a fairly rough schedule, and the next time your agent wants to see me, I suggest that she phone in advance and make an appointment. If it is unreasonable of me to expect that, then I guess I am unreasonable.

After she left, I received a note from her—to be truthful I had to ask who the note was from—in which she asked about our reaction to the novel [Surfacing]. Well, I am sure that Pamela Fry told her our reaction to the novel. Our editors are extremely enthusiastic. I read it at least a month ago. I said, "Yes, we will publish. Let's proceed as soon as we can." My personal reaction to the novel is somewhat less enthusiastic than that of our editors but for a specific reason. I think it is superbly well written. I dig the subject matter, or background if you like, because surprisingly enough—maybe—I spent a good part of my life canoe tripping, fishing, etc. My reservation is simply that I don't think the book is going to be as easy to sell as The Edible Woman. That is purely a publishing notion based on the belief that not as many people will identify with this one as with The Edible Woman. From the standpoint of sales, this may well be offset by the fact that your stature has continued to increase, so maybe in fact the book will do better. In any case, I thought it had been understood for weeks that we were going to publish. Is this not your understanding? And if it is your understanding, is it not your agent's understanding? I'm baffled.

The next point. I am told that we lost a manuscript of yours for two years. Is this true? If it is, it is the first time that it has ever been drawn to my attention. What manuscript? When? And to whom did you complain?

Finally, I am told that we didn't promote The Edible Woman. Do you really feel this? My impression was that we promoted it rather effectively. I am asking our promotion department to tell me exactly what was done, how much it cost, and I'll be glad to supply you full details if you want them.

Why am I writing you at such length? There is only one reason. I am upset. One of our college representatives happens to see you because you are now teaching at York. He comes back and reports that you are very bitter about McClelland and Stewart. Well, how in hell have communications deteriorated to this degree? Do you ever talk to Pamela about such matters? Have you any reason to believe that I am disinterested? Has it never been indicated to you that we consider you one of a handful of major authors that we publish? Ours is an incredibly sloppy, inefficient organization. So is every other publishing house that I have ever had any dealings with. That's the way it is. The one point on which we differ with many houses, however, is that it has always been our active policy that the author is the most important person we deal with, and that the author's interests are more important than ours. Although I can think of several notable exceptions, most of the authors we publish are at least moderately happy with what we do. Until this point, I have had the impression that you felt that way. Perhaps we can do something about it. Perhaps we can't. If you can tell me, I'd really like to know how things reached this state.

Sincerely,

J. G. McClelland

FROM MARGARET ATWOOD

27 Hilton Avenue
Toronto, Ontario
October 25, 1971

Dear Jack:
Thank you for your letter. I shall try to answer it point by point. I certainly don't wish you to be upset, at least not to the extent you seem to be.

Yes, I get on great with Pam. No, I'm not angry that you didn't see Phoebe [Larmore]. I think it might have been helpful if you had, and people at M&S certainly knew she was coming. But she had very little time in Toronto; however, she'll be back and you shall see her then, no doubt. In fact, she did try to set up an appointment with you, no result.

Yes, of course I knew you were going to publish. I also knew you weren't as keen on the book as others were. I also knew you didn't like the title. None of those things bother me in the least. *I* like the title. Phoebe likes the title. If you want to talk about the title, I'd be perfectly happy to have a conversation with you about it. Anytime.

The MS of mine you lost for two years was that of *The Edible Woman*, as you'll recall. I sent it in fall '65, got an initial letter back, then silence. I wrote several letters in spring '67 asking where it was; again silence. It turns out the lady in charge had got pregnant and left the company, or something, and my MS was in a drawer somewhere, along with those of my letters that had not been lost. I was about to request return of the MS when I heard from you—you'd written me a long letter based on some newspaper interview, asking me whether I had an unpublished novel, then discovered you'd had the thing since '65. Surely you remember that. I complained, as I recall, to you, and you apologized. I'm not mad at you for that, though it does make a good story.

No, you didn't promote *The Edible Woman*, certainly not initially; there was that poster, but that was a bit of an afterthought. I think most of the real promotion came through the movie thing (Yorkville Book Cellar tells me they can hardly keep it in stock, and such a sudden resurgence in sales could only be attributed to that, with perhaps a bit of spillover from *Power Politics*) or through readings, etc. And I know there was a distribution problem too. I just don't want the same things to happen with this one, especially as I think it's a much better book and has (and here I disagree with you) a much greater sales potential—especially should you be astute enough to issue it in paperback. But such are really matters to be discussed with Phoebe.

I'm not "bitter" about M&S. No one in Canada is bitter about them, because they have been a major publishing force, and I'm in favour of seeing that continue. But they are notorious in certain areas, and one discusses their failings as one discusses the failings of an eccentric aunt to whom one is, inevitably, related and committed. I feel you would be much better and do a much more splendid job if you could get the books to the stores in time for the reviews and keep things in stock (especially NCL, whose big sales time is the fall) and publish certain things in paperback and be more aware of the market and a few things like that. I don't think a Canadian house up against strong American competition can *afford* to be inefficient in those areas.

Your informant seems to have become overly excited, or to have misinterpreted my manner (which often happens). The only point of any importance in all this is the royalty thing, which we should get cleared up as soon as possible.

As for you and me, dear Jack, my major concern is that you be as stunning a publisher as possible. Far be it from me to wish to upset you except in ways conducive to that end. I know that my kind of thing is not exactly your favourite cup of tea, but I don't care about that as long as it doesn't affect how well you publish the book. *Compris?*

Sincerely,

Peggy Atwood

1. *Power Politics* (1971) is a collection of nearly aphoristic lyrics which, as a group, suggest that romantic love is really power politics.

TO MARGARET ATWOOD

October 28, 1971
Mrs. Margaret Atwood
27 Hilton Avenue
Toronto, Ontario

Dear Peggy:
That's a nice letter. I am glad that things are not as bad as they seemed. It doesn't surprise me that my informant had over-reported. He has that tendency. I guess, too, Pamela has a tendency to under-report to me but there are a number of reasons for that, not the least of them being that I am not easy to get at and she doesn't like to bug me.

I guess you are right about *The Edible Woman*. I remember now that you did tell me about it, but it had gone completely out of my mind, mainly because I was not aware of it at the time. On the promotion, well, I am waiting for the report which I will send to you. If we under-promoted I can assure you that it was not deliberate. It was my view at the time that the book could be very successful if properly promoted. If we failed to do that, then I will have learned something.

You are right, of course, about NCLs being out of stock and all those things, but the truth of the matter is that that has been largely an end product of our financial difficulties. That's behind us now, and now that we have the money we still can't keep up with the NCLs and some other titles simply because Canadian manufacturing resources are tragically overloaded at the present time. But to hell with that. Those are problems that we will solve before long.

Someday soon we'll have a long talk about publishing and favourite cups of tea and things, and sometime soon, hopefully very soon, we'll talk about the title. We will publish the new book well. I am, however, getting a little bit concerned about timing. We certainly want to get the book out before the late spring publishing doldrums arrive.

Cheers!

J. G. McClelland

TO THE *GLOBE AND MAIL*

Alan Wheatcroft had written to complain that although M&S had recently received "a loan of close to $1 million from the Ontario Government," the publisher was "using our (yours and mine) tax dollars to have books printed outside Canada—a recent book called *Heritage* which sells for $25 was printed in Italy." The full title of the book is *Heritage: A Romantic Look at Early Canadian Furniture* (1971), and it is by Scott Symons.

October 29, 1971
The Editor
The Globe and Mail
140 King Street West
Toronto, Ontario

Dear Sir:
In response to the letter from Mr. Wheatcroft (October 27) I should like to point out that the Ontario government had already anticipated the point. One of the conditions of our government loan is that 80 per cent of our books must not only be manufactured in Canada but in the province of Ontario.

We cheerfully agreed to this condition because it has always been our practice to do most of our manufacturing here and well over 90 per cent of our Canadian titles have always been manufactured right here.

At McClelland and Stewart we take second place to no one

in terms of our nationalism. At the same time, we recognize that not everything can be done in Canada, and not everything need be done in Canada. International trade is a two-way street. We should do in Canada what we can do best here; we should recognize that some things can be done better and much more economically elsewhere.

Mr. Wheatcroft refers specifically to a book called *Heritage*. With all modesty, I would say that this book on classic Canadian furniture is one of the most beautiful Canadian books ever published. It was written in Canada. The photographs were taken in Canada. It was edited and designed in Canada and the type was set in Canada. The investment to that point was close to $30,000. The book was manufactured in Italy. The retail price is $22.50. Had we manufactured locally, the retail price would have been $32.50 for a book of comparable quality. It was our publishing judgement that not enough Canadians would pay $32.50 to permit us to dispose of our first printing of 10,000 copies, which was the minimum economical run.

We have to compete with foreign books in this market, and competitively speaking this book would have seemed outrageously priced at $32.50. Occasionally, then, our choice is to manufacture elsewhere or not publish. The creative work was done in Canada, the mechanical work in Italy. If that doesn't make the book Canadian enough for you, then we can only hope that the large Italian community in Toronto may feel differently and learn about the heritage of their new country in this beautiful book, which is a fine example of great cooperation between Canada and Italy.

Yours very truly,

J. G. McClelland

TO BRIAN MOORE

The exchange in the next three letters over Brian Moore's
novella *Catholics* is a good example of the attention J.M. paid to
novels, even though he wasn't directly involved in their editing.
Despite J.M.'s enthusiasm over the novel, it did not become "a
runaway international best-seller," nor is it a favourite among
Moore's critics.

March 13, 1972
Mr. Brian Moore
33958 Pacific Coast Highway
Malibu, California

Dear Brian:
What you so casually refer to as a long short story also just
happens to be one of the finest pieces of writing that I have seen
in a long, long time. Hasn't anybody told you that almost no one
in the world writes this well any more? I mean, like having
characters that live and breathe that the reader can almost hear
and touch. Like having a setting that is totally credible and when
the weather changes the reader can feel it change. Migod, Brian,
it is an incredible work of art. A masterpiece, and you know
what—and I may be awfully wrong about this one—I had some
feeling that this little novel may be a runaway international best-
seller. It's beautifully written. Thematically it deals with one of
the major issues of our age. The only thing that will prevent it
from becoming an international best-seller of staggering
proportions is luck and timing—and behind this proper stage
management, word of mouth and all the supposedly hidden
craftsmanship of the book trade.

Having said all that, I have one editorial quibble. It may be
because I am not a Catholic. It may be that I am obtuse. It may
totally destroy all the nice things I have said. The quibble—I
don't really dig the last page. I've read it and reread it and I don't
understand it. In maybe not understanding it, I do understand it

or maybe it is too subtle for me. I guess what I am really saying is that I think the last page needs some more shading. The climactic build-up in the story is very powerful, and I concede that I don't really know what I want you to do except maybe look it over again.

All the best.

Sincerely,

J. G. McClelland

FROM BRIAN MOORE

33958 Pacific Coast Highway
Malibu, California
March 18, 1972

Dear Jack:

As always, I value your opinion and am very very pleased that you liked *Catholics* so much and that you think it has a chance at a large audience.

On the ending. Nobody else has mentioned your worry, but still ...

What I am trying to say on the last page is this. The Abbot, ever since his experience in Lourdes (described on pages 82–84 in MS) has found that when he tries to really pray to God, he is plunged into an almost clinical depression because his prayers are mere words in his mind and he realises his life as a religious is meaningless because he no longer believes in God, in the Church, in the host, in the tabernacle, and so enters a sort of depressive hell which he calls "null," a state which has sometimes lasted for months; i.e., a depression. So he avoids prayer, goes about his work much as a farm manager would. However, at the very end of the story he realises that in this instance, where the faith of his community of monks is threatened, he must do something exceptional to strengthen their resolves and calm their terrible fear. So on page 103, bottom of page, he makes the decision to do that which he has feared to do ever since his visit to Lourdes which produced his first depression. He must really try to pray, even if, as he knows, it will bring on in him yet another terrible clinical depression.

And so on the last page, he kneels and prays. In so doing he produces the trembling (described earlier on page 82–84), which precedes depression. The monks kneel. He wins back their faith, but himself is plunged, as he feared, into a depression from which he may never emerge. For as always, his prayers are meaningless to him, mere words, bringing him not hope but despair. But, at his own expense, he saves the faith of the others.

Maybe you would read it again, or have some other people on your staff read it, and let me know if this obscurity still persists. As I said, it was not brought up by other readers or editors and the novella is marching elsewhere towards publication. But as I value your opinion, I'd be grateful for another look at it on your part.

Best, as ever,

Brian Moore

P.S. If we can get comment from people like Graham Greene, we will be launched. The other thing I don't know if I told you is that I haven't had such a uniformly optimistic advance reaction since *Judith Hearne*.

TO BRIAN MOORE

March 23, 1972
Mr. Brian Moore
33958 Pacific Coast Highway
Malibu, California

Dear Brian:

Thanks for your letter. The explanation is clear and tends to confirm my sense of minor clarification being useful. What is nagging at me is that while the Abbot's act of prayer (and sacrifice) is fully meaningful to him and to the reader, it is not necessarily so to the monks. How does he win back their faith and settle the problem? Would the act of prayer be that meaningful to them? Would *they* be aware that he was really a farm manager and had been avoiding prayer? (Or more likely to me, he had been a skilful fake.) Or is it his words—that prayer is the only miracle—that win them back? Or is trembling the clue they need?

My problem as a reader, then, is not in understanding the Abbot, it is in accepting their awareness of his sacrifice. Can we through some shading know that they know what he is doing? Or is it the duty thing or his words about the importance of prayer?

I feel that I am being obtuse, but there are lots of us dumb ones, and I sense that a line, a phrase (not obvious direction), would strengthen the climax for me. [1]

Sincerely,

Jack

1. The ending of the published version seems to indicate that Moore made no changes. His letter of March 18 offers an accurate summary of it.

FROM AL PURDY

This letter marks the beginning of a lengthy disagreement, carried on primarily through the mails, over an anthology of Canadian poems and portraits of Canadian writers that Purdy and Harold Town were supposed to co-edit. The main and perhaps only reason for the failure of the project, though it's worth noting that the two did not get along, was a disagreement over how the royalties were to be divided: Town wanted 75 per cent for himself, while Purdy wanted an equal division. Purdy's autobiography, *Reaching for the Beaufort Sea* (1993), offers another account of the incident (pp. 245–7). J.M., while trying to placate Purdy, supported Town's position.

R.R. 1
Ameliasburgh, Ontario
May 1, 1972

Dear Jack:

Thank you for taking the time to set out your position on the TOWN/purdy book at some length.

Recently a friend passed thru Toronto on his return from Florida. Ron Everson,¹ whom Town had portrayed some months before. He phoned Town, as he had apparently been invited to do previously. Town said on the phone: "It's my book, not Purdy's." Now Town knew Everson was a friend of mine and would repeat this to me, so obviously it's a message to me. His attitude, as yours, is pretty clear.

However, friendless as I am in the places of power, I must reiterate one or two things, even add a point or two. In the first place, no contract has been offered me, and this three years (since the summer of '69) after the book's inception. After the said three years, a financial arrangement is proposed that is definitely to my disadvantage. I feel this is an injustice, and feel wounded that my own publisher, who has always had first refusal of any books I've written, should now be asking me to accept an unfair arrangement.

You mention that for a time Town felt strongly that an anthologist should not include his own work in his own book, but that you explained the matter to him. I've only one comment on that: it was and is none of his business who goes into that book. He is the artist, and I the editor. Of course it is obvious to me that he wants to be more than artist as per his comments to Ron Everson.

You say we're dealing with a black-and-white situation, and that Town is inflexible. So, it appears to me, are you.

What Town does and says really doesn't concern me a great deal. I remain indifferent to his opinions in every respect. What you say and do concerns me a great deal. I had not expected this attitude on your part, and it leaves me with a depressed feeling.

Best wishes,

Al Purdy

1. Ronald Gilmour Everson (1903–1992): Canadian poet who practised law and also worked in public relations. Among his many collections of poems are *A Lattice for Momos* (1958) and *Selected Poems 1920–1970* (1970).

TO AL PURDY

May 5, 1972
Mr. Al Purdy
R.R. 1
Ameliasburgh, Ontario

Dear Al:
Your letter is one that I can't really deal with. You say that mine "leaves you with a depressed feeling." I am sorry about that, of course, but you have not really come to grips with what I said in my letter. Let me restate the position.

Town's position is inflexible. The right or wrong of that position is totally irrelevant. He is inflexible, and based on my knowledge of him, there is no possibility of his changing his view. My attitude towards his position is also totally irrelevant. I can't change his view. I can't force his view. You have no contract—well, neither does he. Contracts, as it happens, are to me one of the least important aspects of book publishing. I deal in good faith. I stand by any commitment I make. I simply don't feel that contracts are any more than a necessary evil. Admittedly, had we had one in this case, no problem would exist now. There would be no book. But such an occurrence is so rare that it's not worth talking about.

You seem to resent my black-and-white attitude but damn it, Al, it is a black-and-white situation. All the talk in the world, all the opinions in the world, are not going to change this one. What I am saying is—you can talk to Harold Town, if you wish, or I will meet with you and Harold, if you wish, but I don't think it will change anything or help.

I am truly sorry about it, but that's the scene. The options I set out are all open, but if they don't appeal, then there is no book.

Sincerely,

J. G. McClelland

FROM AL PURDY

R.R. 1
Ameliasburgh, Ontario
May 8, 1972

Dear Jack:
You say I have not really come to grips with the situation, said situation being that Town is inflexible. You also say that Town has no contract, which seems to be unimportant in his case, and that you deal in good faith.

Well, cast back your mind to the time when this book was conceived, when it was suggested that I edit the book and Town do the portraits. In good faith I accepted; in good faith I took it for granted that the eventual contract would call for a fifty/fifty division of whatever money derived from the book. It never occurred to me that suddenly—after three years—Town would suddenly—no, not suddenly, but after three years—say he wanted most of the money. I don't think your good faith is involved in this situation at all, since there is no contract: my good faith is, for exactly the same reason. I have worked on the book, off and on, for three years, without a contract, which surely calls for a modicum of "good faith" on my part. I had to have good faith in the absence of a contract.

Yes, I have a very depressed feeling about this whole business. Principally because of your attitude. Town's doesn't surprise me at all. Even tho it was unexpected. I think that Town's ego demands that he be the whole show with this book, and that you support him in this. Which is why I say your attitude is depressing to me.

You say you are contending with a situation "in being" so to speak, things as they are, rather than harking back to a contract that should have existed but does not. Surely you must be aware that I took this book on the aforementioned "good faith," are you not? If it had occurred to me that such a situation would arise, then I would have asked for a contract at the book's inception. Isn't that *good faith* on my part?

Isn't it also good faith that you have had first shot at any book I've ever written? You have not been interested in any book I edited—with the exception of *Storm Warning*, for obvious reasons—only in those I wrote directly. My point here is that a contract would have been handy as well as good faith in this instance, the latter being insufficient.

So all right, Town is inflexible. I don't feel very flexible myself either. I think you ought to arbitrate with Town on my behalf. But you don't think I have any case, other than the fact there should have been a contract in the first instance. You don't feel that my own *good faith* has been in any way betrayed by Town. You don't believe that in a case like this, where there is no contract, that I am justified in thinking all along that the fifty/fifty split was natural and inevitable.

I don't want to meet Town any longer. Re taking this demeaning and unjustified short end (very short) of whatever there is from the book, I won't. This in all good faith.

Best wishes,

Al Purdy

TO AL PURDY

June 16, 1972
Mr. Al Purdy
R.R. 1
Ameliasburgh, Ontario

Dear Al:
There are some letters to which there can be no adequate reply.
Yours for me is such a letter.

You suggest that I should arbitrate with Town on your behalf.
Arbitration implies power or the ability to influence. I have
already pointed out that in this case I have neither. Town's
position is inflexible. He is clear, totally clear, on this point. In
fact he feels the proposed split is more than generous.

You feel aggrieved because you assumed in good faith a
fifty/fifty split. Town feels equally aggrieved in that he assumed
in good faith that you would accept that his contribution in
terms of time and nature was substantially greater than yours.
Were your contribution previously unpublished Purdy poems, I
believe he would have made no such assumption. As I have said,
arbitration is of no avail. One party is inflexible and adamant.
Now it seems so is the other: both in good faith.

Because your goodwill is important to me, I suppose one
course would be to argue on your behalf with Town, or even to
suggest that I have done so. Truthfully I haven't. And for two
very good reasons. The first, to repeat again, is that Town has
made it clear that nothing will change his position. The second,
unhappily for me in terms of my relationship with you, is that in
all good faith I agree with his view.

You attribute it to his ego. I don't. I attribute it to a straight
calculation of the amount of work and creative effort in the
contribution of both parties and the fact that he originated the
idea. Let me try to take an unbiased look at the relative
contributions and suggest that you check my summation with
some other people.

The first contribution of both—and not the least—is your names. Here it is even. You are one of Canada's leading poets. Town is one of Canada's leading artists. As I have suggested earlier, if you were contributing new Purdy poems to go with new Town drawings, then a fifty/fifty split would be mandatory. No argument.

Next let's look at Town's additional contribution to this book. He was asked to do twenty original portraits. What does that involve? As I understand it, it involves a minimum of two, and sometimes many more, concentrated sessions with each subject—some lasting six hours or more. Then many hours of additional refinement, trial and error, all at a concentrated pitch of creative involvement. Plus the use of costly materials. Then the finished work emerges. Sometimes it is easier than that, of course, and sometimes it isn't. It is because of this that a commissioned Town portrait starts at about $2,500. It is because fees of that sort are charged that very few portraits are commissioned from artists of his standing. I know you are aware why artists like Town can't charge less without destroying their reputation in the art market.

So, in fact, Town is contributing about $50,000 of work to the book, less agent's commission, so let's say about $30,000. Okay, you can argue, if he is going to get $30,000 out of these portraits, what the hell is he worrying about? Sadly, Al, the fact is that he isn't. Who is going to pay $2,500 for a portrait of Earle Birney, Leonard Cohen or Al Purdy? I'm damned if I know. I sure as hell am not. Town can give them away, but he can't sell them at bargain rates, not only because it hurts his established market but because his dealer bloody well won't permit it.

An artist, like a poet, has only so much creative energy and can only do so much first-class work. It is much more than a question of time. Why, then, is he doing this? He is doing it because he believes in Canada and is interested in Canadian poets and because he thinks it is worth doing. The sacrifice is considerable. The contribution is considerable. The amount of return he will get from the royalties on this book, no matter how many copies it sells (and it won't be all that many, in any case), ain't going to be much of a return on this investment. If the book sells, it is surely going to sell largely because of the portraits, which is another aspect of the contribution that must be considered. I don't here denigrate the Purdy name but there are already Purdy anthologies on the market, and there will be others, and in addition to that there are countless fat anthologies on the market that are better bargains, so why is this book going to sell? This book will sink or swim largely on the quality of the portraits. It will be an expensive book.

So then we come to your contribution. The first chore was to select the poets. Were you a neophyte coming new to the chore, were we asking you to evaluate Italian poets, Russian poets, Chinese poets, then that's one thing. For you to make up this list (or for somebody equally familiar with Canadian poets), it's only a few hours' work. In any case it didn't take you very long to prepare the list of poets. You were asked to do the book because of your existing knowledge. So the big contribution in compiling the list was really your expertise or, to put it differently, the contribution already enumerated—your name.

We come to the real contribution (other than your name and reputation), the selection of the poems themselves. You did it honestly and conscientiously. You reread and studied all the poems of all the poets involved. You did an honest and conscientious job but you were hired because of expertise and knowledge. The hours that you expended on this were really of your own choosing. The time was not wasted. It adds up to cumulative knowledge that will be valuable to you in many ways in the future.

Well, that is enough summation. There is nothing further that I can do. I think you should consider this evaluation. I think you should discuss it objectively with others. If you still reach the same conclusion, then that's the way it will have to be. I can't change Town. If I can't convince you, then all I can do is offer you a fair financial settlement for time and effort and cancel the arrangement for this book. There is no other way. I am fresh out of miracles. I sincerely believe that nothing can or will change Town's position, but anyone is welcome to try. Sorry about all this.

Sincerely,

J. G. McClelland

TO AL PURDY

Purdy's response to J.M.'s letter of June 16 repeated that he was unwilling to accept any terms other than an equal division of royalties. With neither Purdy nor Town willing to accept the other's stance, the book of poems and portraits was dropped, and J.M. was left with the job of cleaning up. Despite the serious disagreement, Purdy continued to publish with M&S until 1990, when a dispute over *Reaching for the Beaufort Sea*, his autobiography, resulted in his transfer to Harbour Publishing.

June 22, 1972
Mr. Al Purdy
R.R. 1
Ameliasburgh, Ontario

Dear Al:
The real problem is that no matter what I say or do, it is a fact that the Purdy-Town book is right down the drain. The latter won't change his position, and I judge from your letter that you won't change yours. Even if one of you capitulated at this stage (and that isn't in the cards), I'm not sure it would be advisable to proceed.

So the first problem is the question of a public (or at least semi-public) announcement. By that I mean that the poets who are involved must be informed, and I think they should be informed by us. My own opinion is that the announcement should be simple, direct and non-controversial.

The next step—or maybe it should be the prior step—is to make whatever peace I can with you and with Town. I think the first step here is to compensate you in some reasonable way for time spent. It is difficult to find a yardstick. Certainly we don't want to pay too little, and obviously there is no way we can afford to compensate properly for the time spent. I am going to suggest $500. How do I arrive at that? Well, it is my guess that that is what we would have advanced to you had a contract been signed on a fifty-fifty basis. If you think the amount is totally unreasonable, by all means say so.

As to settlement with Harold, I don't, at the moment, know the answer. Certainly the Poet Portrait Series won't be abandoned and shouldn't be. My recommendation will be that it be completed and published as a portfolio of portraits or perhaps as a portfolio of posters. It's his property, of course, and the decision will be his.

There is only one thing I can add at this stage. I am sure that this matter has not endeared Jack McClelland or McClelland and Stewart to Al Purdy. I accept the full responsibility for what has happened and I dealt with the matter as fairly and as honestly as I could. Unfortunately, I have not had the power to change things or undo whatever harm has been done. You will have to decide whether or not you want to continue publishing with M&S. I don't have to tell you that I hope you will stay. I think you know that we do. I would not want to attempt to keep you against your will, and if there are any contracts or options (and I really don't know whether there are), they can be forgotten. The first principle of our publishing philosophy at M&S is that it is our function to satisfy our authors and do the best job we can for them. Clearly we have done a lousy job in this instance, and I am sorry about that. If you decide to stay, and I hope you will, I can promise that M&S as a whole and J.G.M. personally will do their very best to look after your interests.

Sincerely,

J. G. McClelland

TO MARGARET ATWOOD

July 21, 1972
Miss Margaret Atwood
House of Anansi Press Limited
471 Jarvis Street
Toronto, Ontario

Dear Peggy:
Just a note to congratulate you on the Book-of-the-Month Club. That's really great news. It means *Surfacing* will be off to a flying start. It is our hope that it is going to make it a Selection rather than an Alternate for Canada but we have no final word on that yet. So when do we go on our canoe trip?

Cheers!

J. G. McClelland

P.S. Would you rather come with Leonard Cohen and me? We are hoping to do the grand tour of Western Canada by private railway coach around the middle of October to promote books, Canadian unity, sex, etc. Much more civilized than a canoe, but much less inspirational. You have your choice. Or you could go with Farley. He's going to be alone except for the ninety-four-foot fiberglass walk-through whale. Do let me know.

FROM IRVING LAYTON

Molibos, Lesbos
Greece
July 21, 1972

Dear Jack:
Before the end of this month I'll be sending you the MS for my next book, *Lovers and Lesser Men*. It will contain seventy-five

poems, powerful sockdolagers almost every one of them. I think
L & LM is my most substantial book since God knows when, full
of Greek sunlight and vitality. It's certainly a more gripping book
than *Nail Polish*, and it won't surprise me if it makes the best-
seller list. It's that kind of book. Zany, very, very funny in places,
and in others the magic of poetry coming down plop plop. It's
the sort of book I hoped I'd write one day, and by gum and by
golly I think I've done it. There are more than a dozen really
great poems, the kind anthologists go weak in the knees when
they see.

So, okay, sometime next week I'll have a "sealing party" to
which I'll invite some of the island characters. I'll read from the
MS, get everyone to say some inspired words and then with
benedictions and good wishes raining down on its head and
mine, I'll seal the bloody thing and mail it off to you the
following morning. Then I'll be able to start my vacation, since
I've been working like a bloody fool and slave since I got here.
Will somebody tell me why in the name of Jesus I do it? All
these lovely girls parading in nothing but their pubic hairs, and
here I am scribbling like a fucking medieval monk into my
notebook. I told Anna [Porter] to tell you that I'd like a $1000
advance on this one. I've bought a house in Toronto, and I need
all the bread I can put my hands on. *L & LM* will get it all back
for you in no time. By the way, the photo of me holding up the
column at Sunium is just perfect for the book. It's as zany and
poetic as the poems in the books are.

But one thing I beg of you. Puleese send me a wire saying you
received the MS. Just one word, "yes" or "received" or
"cuntjuice." Anything that will take the worry off my mind.
Afterwards I'd appreciate getting a Xeroxed copy of the book
mailed to me. I shall be here until about the 25th of August.

I hope you will be able to have *L & LM* out by January so as to
hit the campuses with the book. Jack, with some imaginative
publicity behind it or with it, the book ought to grab everybody
by his throat or his genitals. No one, but no one, not even I, have
ever written a book that's as beautiful and gutsy as this one.

Believe me, Jacob.

I've dedicated one of the poems—one of the best, titled "Poetry as the Art of Pugilism," to you.

Aviva sends her warmest love. I hope you're having a wonderful summer. Write when you can.

Yours,

Irving

TO IRVING LAYTON

August 9, 1972
Dr. Irving Layton
Molibos, Lesbos
Greece

Dear Irving:

That's a great letter, for which I thank you. A dozen really great poems out of seventy-five should do it. The sales pitch is redundant but I like it. The last time I heard "by gum and by golly" it was used by a small-town carnival barker at a fall fair somewhere in Western Ontario. He was trying to induce me (and he succeeded) and several dozen other people to go into his tent to see a genuine Aphrodite. We all paid our money and we all went in and we all saw a genuine Aphrodite. A few of us, I guess, were a little bit miffed because it turned out to be some microscopic creature rather than a human, but nobody said very much. It's a great expression. Whatever the hell made you think of it in Greece?

Delighted to hear about the dedication. I look forward to reading it. My best to Aviva.

Cheers!

J. G. McClelland

TO FARLEY MOWAT

August 10, 1972
Mr. Farley Mowat
Grande Entrée
Magdalen Isles, Quebec

Dear Farley:
This letter is in reply to your medical report. One thing should
be understood at the start and that is that it is all clearly
psychosomatic bullshit. You know very well that I'm the sick
one, even allowing for the hypochondria. Christ! You go down
there to the Magdalens, lounge around with nothing to do but
enjoy yourself and think, and this summer, if I recall, a repeat of
last summer, you develop all sorts of dire symptoms. These are
not only psychosomatically induced, they are sympathetic
ailments. You know very well that I am up here working my ass
off, driving myself into an early grave. You develop guilt
symptoms. The fact is that down there you are too relaxed, too
healthy, you have too much time to think. You are probably so
bloody well that even a mosquito bite becomes a major ailment.
Let me assure you that I have a conglomeration of active
symptoms that at almost any given point in the day or night
would make any of your individual symptoms about as serious
as a dose of clap. Actually, when I think of it, that's probably
what you have.
                          Cheers!

                  J. G. McClelland

TO MORDECAI RICHLER

Excerpts from Richler's Plaunt Lectures at Carleton University
appeared in the *Toronto Star* on March 26, 1973, under the headline
"An author warns art isn't good just because it's Canadian." His

lectures expressed reservations about an uncritical nationalistic attitude to Canadian literature, which was leading to the overpraising of Canadian writing.

March 28, 1973
Mr. Mordecai Richler
218 Edgehill Road
Westmount, Quebec

Dear Mordecai:
How about sending me copies of the two speeches? I liked what I read in the *Star* on Monday night. As a matter of fact, I am sending it to you in case no one has done so.

I agree totally with what you are saying. My only problem is that I suspect the casual reader thinks you are attacking the whole nationalism issue. The press usually reports fairly when you are talking about cultural nationalism, but I wish I could believe that the average reader got that. Thus, while I agree with what you are saying—I think you must go on saying it—I can't help feeling that you may be in net result inadvertently doing the country more harm than good at this point in time. The economic issue, as you know, is a very serious one, and it's very crucial at the moment. There are enough U.S. lovers in Canada without you appearing to support them. Oh well, to hell with it, I guess I am past caring.

All the best.

Cheers!

J. G. McClelland

TO MORDECAI RICHLER

April 16, 1973
Mr. Mordecai Richler
218 Edgehill Road
Westmount, Quebec

Dear Mordecai:
I have now had a chance to read the two Plaunt lectures. They are both excellent, but I'm inclined to agree with you that I don't think they should be published in book form by themselves. The material will fit well into your Canada book. As it stands now, though, I think you would be subjected to criticism by allowing this material to be published by itself.

They are really two outstanding lectures. I wish to God that I had heard you deliver them rather than having to read them. What you need is a new typewriter. Failing that, can't you get somebody to repair the letter i. It's enough to drive a person around the bend. Incidentally, although I agree in substance and in principle with what you are saying, I think there are a lot of individual points to which you have not given sufficient consideration. For example, I agree totally with your objection to the publishing policy of the Committee for an Independent Canada.¹ As you know I resigned from the committee because of that policy. However, I don't think the point you make about the Canada Council support of Canadian publishing is valid. By that I mean your reference to the fact that a Macmillan author would be excluded from the Canada Council support under this program, had Macmillan's not been purchased by Maclean-Hunter.

I think we could start by agreeing that in Canada support for the author (particularly those who write on parochial matters) is the prime consideration and that support for publishers is secondary. In fact, I think it is fair to say that the only real justification for supporting Canadian-owned publishing houses is as a support base for authors. The theory behind support of

Canadian-owned publishing houses is that they will publish books that won't be published by foreign subsidiaries. No argument thus far, I assume. The point you missed, though, is that this particular Canada Council program is designed to support Canadian houses competitively (because the foreign houses have a built-in advantage) and is not designed per se to support authors except very indirectly. Doubleday, for example, does not need the support of a federal government book purchase or book export plan. Canadian houses do need those supports to compete with Doubleday, but these are publisher-oriented programs designed to keep some Canadian houses active and thereby of course to help authors.

It seems to me, therefore, that it would be a typically stupid Canadian giveaway program and a typically stupid piece of Canadian nonsense for our federal government to be subsidizing Oxford, Longman's, Doubleday, etc. I do agree that there is a certain discrimination against the authors who choose to publish with those firms, but why are they publishing with those firms? The reason simply is that they are getting a wider distribution internationally. Fair enough. Thus, although it is not a huge issue, I do think you are doing the Canada Council a disservice and Canadian publishers a disservice and just maybe Canadian authors a disservice by confusing the objectives of some of these programs.

Cheers!

J. G. McClelland

1. The Committee for an Independent Canada was founded in 1971 by, among others, Abraham Rotstein, Mel Hurtig, Peter Newman and Walter Gordon to focus attention on the increasing foreign domination of Canada, especially in the economic and cultural spheres, and to propose policies to counter it. Among the committee's publications was *Getting It Back* (edited by Abraham Rotstein and Gary Lax), which summarized its position on various national questions. The extreme nationalism of their policy on publishing was rejected by J.M.

TO THOMAS H. RADDALL

Thomas H. Raddall (1903–1994): short-story writer and novelist, best known for historical novels like *The Nymph and the Lamp* (1950), *The Governor's Lady* (1960) and his autobiography *In My Time* (1976), an early version of which is discussed in this letter.

May 31, 1973
Mr. Thomas H. Raddall
Liverpool, N.S.

Dear Tom:
I would like to start by apologizing once again for the long delay in sending you word about the memoirs *In My Time*. As I told you on the phone, although I was able to read some of it on the plane flying back to Toronto, I found myself involved in some sort of minor collapse from overwork. The doctor described it as fatigue or nervous exhaustion. Nothing too serious if treated quickly and that, in fact, is what I did. The prescription was a complete rest for at least several weeks, and so I am still down in Bermuda and am beginning to feel very well once again.

I would like to start by thanking you for letting me read the memoirs or diary excerpts. I am very conscious of the fact that you have not yet made up your mind about the possibility of publication. It is my hope that I shall be able to persuade you that publication is desirable, but for the moment, at least, it is understood that it is entirely an open matter and you are under no obligation whatsoever simply because you have allowed me to read it.

It is a fine manuscript and a fine record. I am confident that it would be read with pleasure and benefit by a great many readers. I feel strongly on this point and would like to list some of the reasons why I think it should be published:

1. There is a serious lack in Canadian literature of published autobiographies, diaries or memoirs. There are, of course, many

from the earlier years, but by and large this is one area that has
been ignored by Canadians. Possibly it is the result of the nature
of Canadians. I don't know, but I think that it is a fact that
present and future generations are and will be deprived because
of this lack in our recorded writing. Of the few books that do
exist, few are of consequence, and I think that your published
memoirs would do much to offset the lack and possibly
establish a new pattern.

2. It is a particularly fine record of the struggles of a professional
writer in Canada. There are so many insights and comments of
value for other authors, for editors, for publishers, for all
people concerned with the book and magazine industry that for
this reason alone it would be very useful for others to read of
your continuing financial concerns, the struggles that you had
and simply the life of a professional writer with the many
intrusions and influences that make it so difficult to write.

3. I think it is extremely valuable in terms of the picture it gives
of life in Nova Scotia in this century. There are so many rich
and valuable sections—the explosion, the war, home guard,
politics and the many fascinating characters.

4. There is a great deal of material in the manuscript that would
be of particular interest to those involved in Canadian
literature, academic life, historical institutions and associations.
Your impressions are invariably sharp, tremendously revealing
and right to the point.

5. Apart from that, I think the work is extremely valuable as the
study of a man, his interests, his ambitions and his growth and
development. It is unique in Canadian terms in revealing the
two aspects of a very human person. The calm, controlled,
unruffled, charming exterior as contrasted with the struggle
and the inner concern. I would suspect that many people, in
fact most people, who have known you only casually will be

astounded to find that you share the same sort of problems that they face themselves.

All the foregoing is positive. I do have some minor reservations. For a start, I am not able to evaluate the degree to which my special interest contributed to my enjoyment of the script. I suspect that this is not an important point, but it is one that certainly should be checked out. I can't be certain of the size of the market. I am sure that there would be a good market for this manuscript in book form, and I suspect it would be of value to students of Canadian literature for a good many years to come.

One of the particular values of this script, as I see it, in this period of tremendous interest in Canadian literature and Canadian writing, is that it does place Thomas H. Raddall in a more appropriate perspective. I think that it is partly M&S's fault, partly Doubleday's fault and partly your own fault that you do not hold, at the moment, the place in Canadian letters that you have rightfully earned, or even the place that you held ten years ago. Except perhaps in the Maritimes, your novels and your short stories are not being as widely used in schools and in Canadian literature courses as they should be. I think the book would do much to rectify that.

I have to admit to being surprised to learn how tough the financial struggle really was. It shocks me to think how little you earned from book club distribution for example, and from paperback rights. As a North American book publisher, I have always felt that the income from British contracts was pretty depressing, but it shocks me to find how very little money you have actually earned. I certainly came away with the impression that publishing is a racket operated for everybody's benefit but the author's.

I was interested in your reaction to M&S promotion. I think your point of view is undoubtedly valid, as the author sees it. For our part, we feel have been the most promotion-minded firm in Canada. The sad truth though is that today the only type

of promotion that works as far as bookstores are concerned is
direct author promotion and author tours of the sort that you
described so well in the earlier part of the manuscript. It's
becoming virtually impossible to sell a book well today without
turning the author into almost a full-time huckster.

Let me say once again how much I enjoyed my visit with you
and Edith after so many years. I'm only sorry that the time was
so short, but I hope we will have much more time on the next
trip.

With all good wishes.

Sincerely,

J. G. McClelland

1. The book was published in 1976.

TO MARGARET LAURENCE

June 12, 1973
Mrs. Margaret Laurence
Elm Cottage, Beacon Hill
Penn, Bucks., England

Dear Margaret:
Let me start by saying that the manuscript [of *The Diviners*]
contains some of the greatest writing that you have ever done. I
have told you before that you are the only author who has
improved every time out, and I think you have kept your record
intact. I read the manuscript in one sitting from about nine
o'clock at night until four in the morning. It's a very moving
experience. I ended up in tears during the last half hour. I don't
think a man likes to admit it that he sat there like a bloody fool
with tears streaming down his face, but I did and I couldn't do
anything about it. You are a great writer and you have proved it
once again.

This is not to say that I think everything is right about the novel. I don't. I have your letter. I am totally in accord with its contents and most particularly the plan to work directly and solely with Judith Jones [at Knopf] in bringing the script to its final form. One of my great regrets in publishing is that I have never managed to get to know Judith Jones more than casually, but even on the basis of the limited contact I've had with her, I am satisfied that she is one of the better book editors in the world, and I'm more than happy to go along with the decision to work with her. In the best sense it is a very Canadian novel, and there could be the odd point of idiom or spelling where we might have a minor disagreement, but where we would have one, I am sure you would have one too, so there is no problem. Since I am going to be sending a copy of this letter to Judith, I will note here that we will ultimately make a deal with Knopf for repro proofs and a sharing of plant cost, at which point we'll be more than happy to absorb our share of her time and costs.

You have said in your letter that Judith has referred to it as an ambitious novel and that you agree. It sure as hell is. All your novels, of course, have been ambitious. This is more ambitious than its predecessors, I think, only in the sense that you have confronted yourself with the formidable problem of relating the two streams or heritages. You achieve it and it is totally credible—hence the tears, I think—but it is in this area where the fundamental problem exists, as I see it.

In principle—and ultimately I am certain in totality of detail (detail not being my bag)—I'm in agreement with your own functional criticism and that of Knopf and Macmillan. As I see it, the problem with the novel is essentially that you have not been confident enough in your own achievement and as a result have larded the script with material that impedes the flow and that really is unnecessary in terms of what you are trying to do. I read every page, but I can be honest and tell you that it bugged me as a reader to have to do so because too often I was taken away from the narrative, from your own beautiful writing and characterization, and forced to read background material that I really didn't want or need.

I don't think we have any concern about the length of a

Margaret Laurence novel in real terms any more than Macmillan or Knopf would have, but this one needs artistic paring, and once you have done that, we'll have a great book.

Having said that, I should probably stop. I didn't make notes while I was reading, and in any case very detailed comments from me would be gratuitous. You have your own judgement and a damn good editor. For what it is worth, though, without any attempt at being comprehensive, let me jot down a few random thoughts not in chronological order or in order of importance:

– Morag, Jules, Pique, Christie, Prim are superb—I am old-fashioned enough to believe that you should grab the reader at the outset. You don't really grab this reader until page 14.

–one character that didn't come alive for me, really, was A-Okay. It may be that I simply didn't identify with his name or him, but I think he may need some thought

–I liked the Catherine Parr Traill material but wondered if there might be a bit much of it for a non-Canadian reader

–the insert plots bothered me for the most part, except in the early stages of the book

–I thought there might be some paring at the university stage of musings re John Donne, etc. It may be necessary. I'm just not sure

–I wondered a bit about the fictional credibility of the visit of Brooke and his new wife in Vancouver

–I wondered, too, about the meeting with the young undertaker. You have done this area so well before that I just raise a question here

–I could see minor cutting of the Piper Gunn and Ryder Tonnerre episodes

–Milward Crispin and the communications with him may be a bit "in" and not the best thing you have ever done

–for some reason the expression "go like 60" stands out in my mind. It appears several times, and I wondered if it was anachronistic. I have no idea where the expression comes from

–I had made a note about being less than enthusiastic about some of the English material, but you have covered that in your letter and I can only say that I agree, both that some of it should go but that some should be retained

–the only other note—mental note—that I made was that I was not totally sold on the heading technique. I'm not referring here to "rites of passage" which I am inclined to think is an obvious horror, but rather that I am not sure about using terms like "memory bank movie" or "inner film." This is probably personal prejudice because I have never really liked this type of thing; so making allowances for that personal prejudice I would say that I am unsure about it and maybe a typographic distinction is a workable alternative.

In putting together a list of comments like that, any good or competent editor would have been certain to achieve some appropriate balance between positive and negative comment. I haven't bothered to do that. I've stuck with the negative because I don't want to waste your time. If any of the negative comments are useful, fine. But whatever you do, don't take the time to reply to the comments. Where you and Judith agree with what I have said, you'll have a further reassurance; where you don't, I wouldn't lose too much sleep.

Re Jack McClelland personally, I can report that I had a great three-week holiday. I've returned to the job not only somewhat renewed physically but almost totally renewed mentally and philosophically. I now know what I am going to do in the future and what I am not going to do, and there is no way that I am ever going to get back on the treadmill that I operated for so many years. I even go to bed early most nights (for some reason this doesn't incline me to get up any earlier, which is a phenomenon that I haven't been able to understand) except when I stay up most of the night reading a new manuscript by Margaret Laurence. That, I need not tell you, comes under the heading of pleasure, not business, and it is one of the pleasures that I hope to be indulging in from time to time for many years to come.

So there it is, Margaret. I hope this letter is helpful. Again, my congratulations.

Sincerely,

J. G. McClelland

TO LEONARD COHEN

July 12, 1973
Mr. Leonard Cohen
8303 St. Dominique
Montreal, Quebec

Dear Leonard:
It was good to see you in Niagara-on-the-Lake [at the Shaw Festival]. I don't really know what to feel about *Sisters of Mercy* itself. I said to you at the time, it is clear that there are some very good lines in the play—as a matter of fact, I think the script is damn well put together—but I have some serious doubts about the cast, particularly the main lead. I guess the real problem with the play—if there is one—is that it is really "An Evening with Leonard Cohen" and there is no way that it can ever be as successful as the real thing. It seems to me that this is a built-in limitation that it can't overcome. This doesn't mean that it won't

be successful. It may well be very successful, but it is still always going to be compared with an evening listening to you read your poems and sing, and ultimately it has no hope of standing up to that comparison.

I still would like to do a book using the script from the play and some pictures, if you continue to think it is a good idea. I am convinced that it is worth doing, even if the play itself should turn out not to be as successful as one might hope.

Cheers!

J. G. McClelland

FROM AL PURDY

English Department
Loyola of Montreal
November 14, 1973

Dear Jack:

The party was great. I was a little surprised that it was. On the face of it, if you bring authors and booksellers together it doesn't guarantee a free and easy and enjoyable party. But I thought it was just that. Odd to be asked for so many autographs. I must've signed the McStew catalogue at least six or eight times, as well as many books. I had been drinking rum most of the afternoon, then tapered off with beer at the party— maybe that was why it was enjoyable—

I'm pleased, naturally, that the *Selected* sold so well, or at least 3,100 and some copies till June seems not bad to me. Titles seem to make a helluva difference. *Wild Grape Wine* is not selling well at all, but I will lay a bet *Sex and Death* will.

I'm sorry Farley Mowat wasn't there. I killed Angus Mowat's dog accidentally a while back. Turned into Angus's drive at about ten mph and the dog ran right under the wheel. Bit Eurithe and Angus, the latter badly. We drove thirty miles to

Napanee to the vet and then hospital for tetanus shots. Too late
for the dog. I dug his grave under an apple tree, Angus being too
old for that. Very odd feeling, in my shirtsleeves, wind off the
Bay of Quinte, digging a grave. And even if it wasn't my fault, I
was still the one who shoved grief into another person's life—
and I like Angus much, as well as the dog.

This letter is not apropos of anything in particular—except
to say I enjoyed the party and thank you for it.

Best,

Al Purdy

TO MALCOLM ROSS

August 27, 1974
Dr. Malcolm Ross
Dalhousie University
Halifax, N.S.

Dear Malcolm:
Through a close friend of Gabrielle Roy's I have learned that she
is privately very upset about the introduction to *The Hidden
Mountain*. I just read it and I don't blame her. Most authors of my
acquaintance would have stormed with outrage. Gabrielle Roy,
as you know, is a quiet, modest reserved person and has chosen
not to make an issue of it, but it is clear from her friend that she
is upset and somewhat confused why a publishing house would
put a book in the New Canadian Library and then proceed to
destroy it.

I have read the introduction carefully, and in actual fact
slightly over a third of the introduction is devoted to criticism
of the translation and criticism of the work itself. The criticism
is always somewhat qualified with praise but it's nonetheless

bloody direct in terms of its references to other reviews and in my opinion at least highly subjective and highly questionable. I don't know the author but I would be of the opinion that the rest of the introduction itself is at the level of a good undergraduate essay. Listing the number of references to animals and trees etc. may be worth points in academic circles, but in terms of space consumed in relation to the total length of the introduction it seems to me that this particular intro should have been judged not only unsuitable but also inadequate.

I have always considered the introductions to the New Canadian Libraries as strictly your business. To the best of my recollection, it is the first time I have encountered and stated any objection, but then I think that you have always followed the principle that the introduction be written by somebody who is favourably disposed towards a book because the concept of the New Canadian Library implies a long term, and it clearly doesn't make sense to saddle a work with a negative introduction in perpetuity. It is possible that you did not read this particular introduction before it was published. In that event, I would have expected a house editor to draw it to my attention (or to Anna Porter's), but that was not done. It is a judgement issue. We have never given specific instructions to house editors re policy on such matters and don't intend to start because it shouldn't be necessary.

I hope you will agree that we are going to have to do something about this one. I suggest this not because Gabrielle is an old and dear friend but because the principle is wrong. I am unalterably opposed to interference with free critical opinion of our books. I am also opposed as a publisher to limiting the potential of a major work with a substantially unfavourable critical introduction. It makes no publishing sense. It seems to me that there are two choices: ask the author to rewrite her introduction, or tell her that her introduction will be dropped from the next edition because we don't think it's appropriate. I don't think there is any other alternative. It requires fairly immediate action because the book is scheduled for a new printing early in the new year. [1]

I feel very strongly about this point, Malcolm, and I hope you will not find my position unreasonable.

Best regards,

Sincerely,

J. G. McClelland

1. The novel was published in 1974 with an introduction by Mary Jane Edwards, and in 1975 with one by Ross.

TO CLAIRE MOWAT

Claire Mowat (b. 1933): wife of Farley Mowat and author of *The Outport People* (1983), *Pomp and Circumstance* (1989), and *The Girl from Away* (1992).

November 18, 1974
Mrs. Claire Mowat
25 John Street
Port Hope, Ontario

Dear Claire:

I've been brooding about the fact that I seemed to have caused a stoppage of progress on your manuscript. That wasn't my intention. I wish we had taken the opportunity to discuss the whole thing at greater length the other night.

I think that my statement in the Magdalen Islands should be remembered only in context. That specific context was that you were looking for something to do—a career—to offset the partial isolation caused by Farley's work. My comment was that of all the careers that you could have selected, it seemed to me that writing would perhaps be the least suitable in terms of *that* objective. I gave my reasons. I still feel that way about it, in that particular context. But, for God's sake, this does not mean that you should, having started a book, be discouraged from finishing it.

I came to understand that evening that the writing of this particular book was not really the start of a separate career for you—as I had first understood it—but rather something that you wanted to do to occupy your time and to tell a story that you wanted to tell. That's fair enough. It really has nothing to do with what I was talking about. My concern related to the long-term prospect of a wife developing a career that parallels her husband's. There have been many occasions, of course, when this has been done but usually before the fact, not after. I merely expressed an opinion that I didn't think that this was the wisest solution to the particular problem that had been described to me.

I would urge you to go on with the manuscript. Farley doesn't know that I am writing this letter, but I am concerned that when you have gone this far with the book, you could become discouraged by my remarks that related to a separate problem. It is still my personal view that a professional writing career is not what you should choose as a solution to the problem. Become a painter (you are one), a photographer, a collector, a musician—even a hooker (these are my views, not F.M.'s) if you must, but one writing ego per family is enough. *However*, do finish this book. It would be crazy not to. After it is published, you can then decide whether I am right or not in terms of a continuing career. It's a matter of record that I have been wrong once or twice in my life.

> Love,
>
> *Jack*

TO MORDECAI RICHLER

September 13, 1974
Mr. Mordecai Richler
218 Edgehill Road
Westmount, Quebec

Dear Mordecai:
As requested, I will try in this letter to give you a few of my views on the American publishing presence in Canada for your speech. If you are going to quote me directly, please bear in mind that I am dictating this off the top of my head without too much thought or planning, and it won't be as polished as one might wish.

There is no doubt in my mind that U.S. publishers (and for that you could read British publishers and any foreign publishers because it has nothing to do with the U.S.A. per se) are a real problem in Canada. I don't think it is an immediate problem, nor do I think it is one of such major proportions that anyone should stay awake at night worrying about it. Nonetheless, it is real. Canada has become increasingly nationalistic in the last decade. It is my opinion that this is a trend that is irreversible and a trend that will grow in the years ahead. It is not anti-Americanism, it is a simple and logical desire (and a common one in the U.S.A.) to resent foreign intrusion and takeover.

As you know, I could go on at great length on the general issue. I won't do so. I think it is important for U.S. publishers to realize that it is a general issue and a logical one, not a publishing issue. But because book publishing has to do with education and book publishing has to do with the basic culture of a nation, this industry is caught in the most sensitive core of the problem.

The basic problem with our federal and provincial governments is to find a way of ensuring that a substantial percentage of the book publishing apparatus in Canada be owned in Canada and controlled by Canadians. You will be speaking to a group of book publishers, and it is my expectation that book publishers will understand that point readily enough. The serious book publisher is involved in the mainstream culture of his country, and where the objectives are commercial and solely commercial, we believe that there must be an element of this identification, even if only for purposes of self-interest. However, a publisher operating a subsidiary in another country does not identify with the culture of that country. It is totally meaningless to him. His purpose in having a subsidiary can only be twofold. First, he is interested in moving his publishing product, and second, he is interested in making money. Those are his sole objectives. They would be my sole objectives if I operated subsidiary companies in countries outside Canada. This does not mean to say that the publisher, through the subsidiary—again, generally for purposes of self-interest—does not involve himself in some token publishing. If he is sensible, he will and should, but that's not why he is there. He will do so and continue to do so only as long as it supports his main objectives.

Nobody can object to those objectives. The problem in Canada, however, is the almost total takeover of the industry by foreign interests; this means that many vital forces in the cultural growth of the country can be lost because of inability to compete with massive foreign presence.

The result, specifically at the moment, is that there is an urgent need for more Canadian participation in the publishing industry and certainly much more Canadian ownership than exists at the present time. What does this mean in terms of a trend? It is my guess that in the area of general publishing, there will be a trend towards a steadily increasing Canadian content. Does this mean that American books will be pushed out of the market? I don't think so. Because the market is growing steadily, there may be a growing market for American books in Canada in absolute terms, but certainly not a growing market in terms of percentage of the whole market. Trade publishing will become much more competitive; there will be much more Canadian product available; the sale of secondary foreign titles will gradually dry up.

In the educational field, I see a rather different form developing. Foreign presence is very large in educational publishing in Canada. There are few Canadian-owned firms of consequence competing, and even those that do, do not have access to sufficient capital. My guess is that the solution to this problem will ultimately be a return to direct government involvement in book publishing. It is my guess that the provincial governments will set up their own publishing houses to supply a substantial portion of the educational markets. The alternative to this is for the governments to supply vast sums of money to Canadian-owned firms. They will do this initially. In the long run, it is my guess that there will be substantial direct government involvement in educational book publishing in Canada.

My advice to U.S. publishing firms that have Canadian subsidiaries would be that they should anticipate over the next decade a decline in the market for American product in Canada, although not necessarily a decline in absolute terms. If they have subsidiaries, I think they should plan to publish more Canadian books and accept the reality of Canadian determination to have a substantial measure of independence.

I don't, by the way, suggest that U.S. or British firms have a bad record in Canada. Some of these firms have played a major role in Canadian publishing and continue to do so. On the whole, I think the record has been superb. However, being a good corporate citizen in Canada may not be enough in the years ahead, as far as book publishing is concerned.

Two large American houses have recently opened educational subsidiaries in Canada. These are Houghton, Mifflin and Allyn (Mordecai, pronounced Alline) and Bacon, despite official and unofficial warnings that have been issued against such developments. I think it is entirely possible that the whole industry may suffer because these two firms have chosen

to ignore Canadian attitudes in this area. I am not predicting
what might happen because I simply don't know. I do have some
feeling, however, that incorporation of these two firms in
Canada may lead to more rigid controls over foreign-owned
publishing in Canada than might otherwise have been .
developed. We will have to wait and see.

In summary, then, I don't think it is a bad scene for U.S.
publishers, but I do think that sensitivity to the Canadian fact
would pay dividends in the long run.

Cheers!

Jack McClelland

TO MARGARET ATWOOD

November 12, 1974
Miss Margaret Atwood
Box 1401
Alliston, Ontario

Dear Peggy:
Thanks for sending along the copy of the U.S. edition of
Surfacing. It is horrid, of course, but I must say I like their claims
and their cover copy. American paperback publishers may not
care much about the sensibilities of the author or of the
public—but they sure as hell know how to sell books. It will
probably work very well.

How's the new novel [*Lady Oracle*] coming, by the way? I keep
hoping you are making great progress and that maybe it will be
ready for next year. I really can't believe the change that has
taken place in the fiction market in the last several years in
Canada. Where it seemed to have been almost impossible to sell
in any quantity for quite a long period, the market has really
turned around—for both serious and not-so-serious fiction—to
a degree that I wouldn't have believed possible. I don't mean that

the book market has improved all that much—it sure as hell hasn't—but suddenly fiction is very strong again. This may have started with *St. Urbain's Horseman* or maybe it was *Surfacing*, but whatever has occurred, I now think we may be coming into a period where fiction will actually outsell non-fiction for a while.

Can you tell what is going to happen at Anansi? Press reports continue to conflict with private reports, and I no longer know what to believe. Does it really have to be sold? Is there a time limit? Are there any prospective buyers? Should we be trying to make a deal? If you have any advice on this subject, I would be glad to have it. I don't really think it would be to anybody's advantage to have Anansi taken over by McClelland and Stewart or any other of the larger houses. It can and should continue to do things that we just can't do, or at least that we shouldn't be doing. The solution might be the sort of deal that we proposed to Dennis Lee a few years back. I am sure it was reviewed with you at the time. In any case, Peggy, if you have any thoughts on the matter or any ideas what I should or should not be doing, I wish you would give me a call.

All the best.

Sincerely,

Jack McClelland

TO GABRIELLE ROY

Gabrielle Roy (1909–1983): one of the major Canadian writers and one of the few popular both in French and English. Among her books are *Bonheur d'occasion* (1945 [*The Tin Flute*]), *Alexandre Chenevert* (1955 [*The Cashier*]), *Cet Eté qui chantait* (1972 [*Enchanted Summer*]) and *Ces Enfants de ma vie* (1977 [*Children of My Heart*]). J.M. always considered *Bonheur d'occasion* one of the great Canadian novels, and reissued it in 1980 in a deluxe boxed edition in a new translation illustrated by Harold Town.

December 24, 1974
Mrs. M. Carbotte
Apt. 302
135 Grande-Allée West
Quebec, Quebec

Dear Gabrielle:
Have I ever told you that you write the most beautiful letters
that I ever receive? I am often tempted to bother you with a
continuing stream of letters just so that I can have the reply.
Why should I be surprised, though? As I have told you so many
times, you are the greatest writer in the country, and it is not
surprising that you should write such lovely letters.

Let me speak for a moment about the New Canadian Library.
It has become a real problem to us. I am being very candid
about it. We don't have a committee. Malcolm Ross is totally in
charge. We can, if we wish, direct the selection of titles, and I
guess we do to a degree. He selects the books and he selects the
people to do the introductions. Malcolm Ross is one of the great
figures in Canadian literature. In my view, he has had a far
greater understanding of it than almost anybody else that I have
ever known. His problem, however, is that he has lost touch
with the people who know how to write an appropriate
introduction. He has lost touch really, as I have lost touch. The
Canadian literary community has changed more in the last ten
years than it has changed in the fifty years that preceded. It is
really a terrible problem. We have been going through a period
of incredible change. There was a time when, if it were needed, I
could have assisted Malcolm. Today I can't. Quite literally, I don't
know how to advise him.

I've learned more from Joyce Marshall than I could ever
learn from you about your recent illness. I gather you have had a
really difficult time. We talked once about asthma, but only
very briefly. My own guess is that it is the most terrifying of all
ailments. I contain my own through constant use of inhalators
to a degree that would shock my doctor if he knew about it, but

I have always believed in the principle that immediate survival is more important than long-term survival. We will deal with that subject one day.

The nicest thing about your letter was the very tentative suggestion that you might, after all, sometime, come up to Muskoka. Gabrielle, that is going to be next summer, and I am going to insist on it. That's a promise on my part, and I am going to accept it as a commitment on your part. If I told you that that would be the nicest thing that could happen to me in 1975, you wouldn't believe it. It is true, though, and I hope you will accept it, because I mean it with great sincerity. For the moment, though, let's leave it at that. I am going to come down to Quebec City sometime between now and next summer and get you to commit yourself to specific dates.

So have a great Christmas and New Year. This letter may reach you too late. The new edition of *The Hidden Mountain* will be out about January 6, and copies will be en route to you. Incidentally, I hope we are going to be able to do new covers for all the New Canadian Library books in the very near future. I'll tell you about the program when next I see you. I hope we can do much better with the covers in the future than we have done in the past.

Love,

Jack McClelland

1. Joyce Marshall (b. 1913): Montreal-born short-story writer (*A Private Place*, 1975) and translator. She worked closely with Gabrielle Roy on *The Road Past Altamont* (1966), *Windflower* (1970) and *Enchanted Summer* (1976). She was awarded the Canada Council Translation Prize for the second. Her collection of stories, *Any Time at All*, was published in the New Canadian Library in 1993.

TO HUGH FAULKNER AND
ANDRÉ OUELLET

Like other Canadian publishers and most writers, J.M. was angry
that American publishers could sell remaindered American
editions of books by Canadian writers in Canadian bookstores
even if the Canadian editions of the same books were still on
sale at full price. The following letter is one of dozens written
about the issue during this period.

February 4, 1975
The Hon. Hugh Faulkner
Secretary of State
House of Commons
Ottawa, Ontario

The Hon. André Ouellet
Consumer and Corporate Affairs
House of Commons
Ottawa, Ontario

Gentlemen:
Sometime within the next few weeks, full-page ads will appear
in the *Ottawa Journal*, the *Ottawa Citizen* and, if it can be afforded,
the Toronto *Globe and Mail*. They will be signed and paid for
cooperatively by almost every major author, French and English,
in this country.

The sole purpose will be to attack your administration for
equivocation and lack of action on this copyright issue. This is
an incredible waste of their money! They shouldn't have to do it,
but they intend to. They won't soon forget why they had to
spend that money.

I am not a politician, but if I were I am certain that I would
not want to antagonize the single most articulate group of
people in this country. But that is exactly what you are now
doing.

Let me quote from a letter that appeared in the *Globe and Mail* recently, written by one of the top copyright experts in the country. "If the government feels that there is legal protection under the Copyright Act, as there appears to be, it surely should act to see that there is immediate enforcement. If the government does not accept this interpretation, then it should introduce an amendment to the Act. It was not hesitant in amending Section 4 of the Copyright Act in 1972 in respect of royalties payable to record companies." On Friday, December 13, Inspector Howe of the RCMP informed me that he had been empowered to begin an investigation of Coles Bookstores. It took almost two years to bring the RCMP to that position because they were acting under instructions from Ottawa, presumably from the minister of Justice. That makes a beautiful story in itself. If somebody is breaking the law, the RCMP usually doesn't have to wait for permission from Ottawa. However, that investigation has been stalled again as the result of the dismissal of our injunction applications.

I don't like writing this sort of letter. I think you must concede that I approached this subject initially in a reasonable and friendly way. I took no public action for at least six weeks. I am aware that neither of you is in any way responsible for the fact that this particular situation exists. Fair enough, but if you don't act very quickly, I believe your respective positions will become untenable.

Now this is a very bad scene. If I were a cabinet minister and I got a letter like this from somebody called Jack McClelland, I would say, "Who the hell does he think he is? Does he really think he can intimidate us?" Frankly, gentlemen, I don't think I can, but I think a force is developing that will. Let me name a few of the authors who will pay for the advertisement and who will perhaps then go to Ottawa to confront you. Let me start with Farley Mowat, Pierre Berton, Peter Newman, Robertson Davies, Margaret Atwood, Margaret Laurence, Mordecai Richler, Irving Layton, Leonard Cohen, Hugh MacLennan, Morley Callaghan, to name a few.

For you, Mr. Ouellet, I have a special message. I mentioned no French-Canadian authors. It may or may not surprise you to know that many of the leading French-Canadian authors are friends of mine. It may also surprise you to know that they are even more directly and definitely affected by this apparent loophole in our copyright act than English-Canadian authors. It hasn't yet been made an issue in Quebec, but believe me, it will be. As far as Quebec is concerned, there can be no question about it. The Canadian author has no protection from France. It is a Berne Convention country. But France protects its citizens.

I know very little about politics. That is your business. You may think that copyright is a dull, uninteresting topic without political appeal. I agree with you. However, there is one thing I do know about. I know more about Canadian authors than almost anybody else in this country. They can and do get the attention of the media—hell, they are the media. Unless you want them all at your throats—and you can calculate the political effect of that—you should make some sort of sensible pronouncement on this issue in the House of Commons. I hope you can do something. I know that you are busy people. I know that you are under constant pressure. So am I. We all need this problem like a hole in the head. You are the only ones who can deal with it before it develops into unmanageable proportions. As a matter of fact, you could still get a substantial political advantage by moving quickly. If you don't, I wish you good luck.

Yours sincerely,

Jack McClelland

TO HARRY BRUCE

Harry Bruce (b. 1934): essayist (*The Short, Happy Walks of Max Macpherson,* 1968) and biographer (*The Life of Lucy Maud Montgomery,* 1992).

March 13, 1975
Mr. Harry Bruce
6341 York Street
Halifax, N.S.

Dear Harry:
Our two letters crossed in the mail. Mine may or may not have been adequate as an answer. Let me have another go at it.

My point—and the one that I did not express all that clearly, apparently—is that if there is a foreign-ownership problem in Canada (and I believe that there is), then the person most affected by it in the publishing field is the author, not the reader. The reader is affected in the sense that the heritage of Canada is substantially affected, but the more direct effect is on the author.

I mentioned to you, I believe, my theory and my belief that there should be no limit on the existence or growth of U.S., British or other foreign publishing houses in Canada. At the same time, I recognize that unless Canadian-owned houses are given artificial support, they simply will not continue to exist in that competition because it is an unequal competition. It is demonstrably unequal—as few people know as well as I do—because I have managed and continue to manage several American subsidiaries in Canada while managing M&S. The artificial support—government-guaranteed loans, subsidies and whatever actions the government takes—may keep a reasonable proportion of the Canadian-owned segment of the industry alive. I don't know the answer to that.

The point I was making to you was that from the standpoint of the writers of this country, it is important to keep those options open. I have argued many times publicly against restrictions on foreign publishing companies in Canada because I think the author needs all the options here he can get. There are a lot of books that can't and shouldn't originate in this country. There are other books that could originate here, but that can be done more successfully if they originate elsewhere.

But what about the Canadian author's option? Foreign houses operate in Canada for only two reasons. The first is to push their product. That is to say, their American, British or whatever product. The second is to make a profit. There is no other reason. I suggest to you that Canadian-owned houses— and the same holds true for serious native houses in any country—have a sense of purpose and identification with the culture far beyond that. There are a growing number of good Canadian houses that have that sense of purpose and that identification.

If that Canadian competition ceases to exist—and it may well; I don't know the answer to that—then I suggest to you that much of the tokenism that now exists as far as foreign-owned firms are concerned will disappear and the total market will be rationalized. Why not—it is entirely logical. Selling will become totally American. Canadian allusions that are not understandable in the United States will be eliminated. Where the market can be improved, locale [in a book] will be switched across the border. This may sound far-fetched to you, but it is not to me because I have been through it.

End of message. When things are equal, then I think the serious writer will publish with Canadian-owned firms. When they are not equal, then that's an entirely different matter.

Cheers!

Jack McClelland

TO ANNA PORTER

Anna Porter (b. 1947): an editor at M&S during the second half of the Jack McClelland era. More recently, publisher of Key Porter Books (1982 to the present). She is also the author of three mystery novels. The object of J.M.'s wrath in this memo is Edmund Wilson's *O Canada: An American's Thoughts on Canadian Culture* (1965).

August, 19, 1975
MEMO TO: Anna Porter
FROM: Jack McClelland
RE: MALCOLM ROSS

Re the Edmund Wilson¹ book, tell Malcolm, no, no, no. I don't remember Malcolm's earlier letter on the subject, but I do know what I think. Let me give you a quote for your next letter to Malcolm.

"Re Edmund Wilson, pass on to Malcolm my extremely vehement veto. There is no way during my lifetime that that book by Edmund Wilson will ever be included in the New Canadian Library or issued under a McClelland and Stewart imprint. Wilson acquired a staggering (and well-deserved) reputation as both a writer and as a critic in his earlier years. He became senile. Some ill-advised people encouraged him to come to Canada and take a fast look at Canadian literature. Christ! He did almost none of his own research. His judgements couldn't stand the test of time. In fact, they didn't even stand the test of exposure when they were published. I spent a drunken evening with him while he was in Canada doing his two-week survey, and after listening to him politely for a couple of hours, I told him he was an ill-informed, egotistical old bastard. And he didn't know what the hell he was talking about. The fact is, he didn't. He still writes superbly well [though] his mind has gone. Migod and Malcolm wants to publish him? In about two weeks he undid most of the good work that Malcolm himself had been doing for the previous fifteen years. The answer is a categorical no!"

1. Edmund Wilson (1895–1972): influential American literary and social critic whose books include *Axel's Castle* (1931), *The Triple Thinkers* (1938) and *To the Finland Station* (1940). He had a long association with the *New Yorker*. In his last years, he prepared his voluminous journals for posthumous publication and studied Hungarian.

TO KENNETH GLAZIER

January 6, 1976
Mr. Kenneth Glazier
Chief Librarian
University of Calgary
2920 – 24 Avenue N.W.
Calgary, Alberta

Dear Ken:
I have finally had a chance to talk to Gabrielle Roy about the University of Calgary. She is mildly interested. I say mildly deliberately because she has some concern as a French-Canadian that her papers should remain in Quebec or at the least in Ottawa. The good news, however, is that her papers are still intact. She has not yet made a decision, although she has been approached by the National Archives, the National Library, one Quebec university and, strangely enough, the University of Massachusetts.

I have given her a reasonable sales pitch on your serious intent, the fact that you have Richler, Moore, some MacLennan, etc. and are determined to build up the top archives in Canada. She is impressed by this. I've also told her that you are quite likely to make a proposal that would be more financially rewarding than she would receive from any of the other interested libraries. This could be important to her because she's not in the best of health and I think would be impressed by the possibility of having a small nest egg set aside for the future.

I think, then, that the picture looks promising. She has received your letter and will be writing you and inviting you to come to see her. I urge you to do this. She is one of the most enchanting and intelligent women I have ever known, and you will enjoy meeting her. In addition, you will have a chance to assess what she has. Some of her papers are stored with a neighbour and she has some of the others in her apartment. She tells me that she has made only very preliminary attempts at sorting things out, and she would probably welcome some help in that area. She has some unpublished manuscripts—some that might be published after her death—but I think she would certainly want to place restrictions on the unpublished manuscripts. I would certainly guess that some of them should never be published but might be of great interest to you. She talks in terms of setting up a small committee that might, after her death, decide what might or might not be published.

Her meeting with you, Kenneth, would be only dealing with the matter in principle. I am sure you could charm her and convince her that Calgary is the right place for her papers. She is very much aware, having just returned from a visit to her relatives in St. Boniface, that the attitude towards Quebec becomes increasingly unfriendly west of the Ontario border. In short, you will have to do some selling, but as I have told you, it is an absolute certainty that her papers are worth going after because she is clearly the only Canadian writer who has achieved pre-eminent success in both languages. Not only is this true but it's my estimate that the majority of critics in both Quebec and in English Canada would rank *The Tin Flute* (*Bonheur d'occasion*) as probably the top Canadian novel in either language.

All that is good news, but what will make things tough for you is her decision to appoint me as her unpaid financial adviser. In other words, I'll negotiate with you on the terms of the deal after she has made a decision whether she is prepared to have the papers go to Calgary. Obviously I value her work very highly—although I'm not an unreasonable person and we should be able to reach a sensible sort of deal. I must warn you, however, that I tend to negotiate much more successfully when

I have no direct financial involvement myself.
  Best personal regards.
                              Sincerely,

                          Jack McClelland

TO DONALD CREIGHTON

Donald Creighton (1902–1979): the pre-eminent Canadian historian of
his era. Creighton wrote more than a dozen books, including the influential
The Commercial Empire of the St. Lawrence: 1760–1850 (1937), *Dominion of
the North* (1944) and the two-volume biography of Sir John A. Macdonald
(*The Young Politician*, 1952, and *The Old Chieftain*, 1955). He was advisory
editor of M&S's eighteen-volume Canadian Centenary Series, edited by W. L.
Morton.

February 16, 1976
Dr. Donald Creighton
Box 225
Brooklin, Ontario

Dear Donald:
Those are two really great chapters [of *The Forked Road*]. I took
them out West with me last week—I was away on a promotion
tour—and started reading them very late one night (actually
early one morning), and even though I was dead tired, I became
so absorbed that I read the two chapters at one sitting and
would have read the rest of the manuscript had it been
available.
  I was fascinated by your treatment of Mackenzie King. I
obviously had never thought about him very much and had
tended to accept him at face value. The picture that was so often
presented was a dull, colourless, plodding, unimaginative and
indecisive prime minister. I have always thought what a typically

Canadian thing it was to have allowed him to remain in office so long. Instead I see him emerging from your pages as a cunning political strategist—he really had to be to stay in office all that time—always several steps ahead of his associates, his opposition and the public in his planning.

As I say, it is really great stuff, Donald. The perspective is sharp and clear on so many things—Canada-U.S., Canada-U.K., U.K.-Newfoundland, etc. Incidently I see no problems of libel, but we will have it looked at from that point of view when the script is complete. It is going to be a very fine book indeed. All the best.

Sincerely,

Jack McClelland

TO AL PURDY

February 16, 1976
Mr. Al Purdy
Department of English
Fletcher Argue Building
The University of Manitoba
Winnipeg, Manitoba

Dear Al:
I am not surprised about your report on Winnipeg. When you think about Winnipeg, you find it is noteworthy for the people that have left there, not the people who have moved there. Well, winter will soon be over and things will look up. Remember, too, that it is a very good book town. Our statistics indicate that. Always remember that things could be worse. I am dictating this letter on the eve of my departure for Saskatoon. Fortunately I am not going to have to live there.

Cheers!

Jack McClelland

TO SYLVIA FRASER

Sylvia Fraser (b. 1935): Toronto-based novelist, author of *Pandora* (1972), *The Candy Factory* (1975), *The Emperor's Virgin* (1980) and *The Ancestral Suitcase* (1996). To publicize *The Emperor's* Virgin, J.M. and Sylvia Fraser rode up Yonge Street in a chariot during an unexpected spring snowstorm.

February 16, 1976
Mrs. Sylvia Fraser
382 Brunswick Avenue
Toronto, Ontario

Dear Sylvia:
I have heard from a reasonably reliable grapevine that you weren't overly enchanted by the piece in *Weekend Magazine*.¹ I don't really understand why you feel that way. I am not thinking only of the prevailing wisdom that since they spelled your name properly it's okay, when in actual fact the article presented you as an interesting, opinionated and somewhat mysterious lady. What more can you ask? The painting presented you in exactly the same way. All the article will do is increase the market for your books. That's the only function served by such articles, in any case.

As confirmation of that, the stewardess on a flight west that I took last week recognized me from TV and started to talk to me about Canadian writers. She mentioned you and I asked if she had read the article and what she thought of it. She had read it and she thought you were a really interesting person and it made her want to read your books. It is as simple as that.

As a matter of fact, I now begin to wonder why I am writing this letter. I have been told that you were upset by the article, and after thinking about it, I realize that that is unlikely, and even if you were, it is unlikely that you would admit it. But if you were upset, remember that the only people who ever read this sort of thing with any care—and journalists should remember this—are friends of the subject, and they know what is true and what is not true. So what difference does it make?

The only difference it makes is that such articles should help
the subjects in whatever field they may be involved in. This one
sure as hell helps you in yours and you should be pleased.
Cheers!

Jack McClelland

1. J.M. refers in this letter to Margaret Drury Cane's article about Sylvia Fraser, "In
the Palace of the Snow Queen" (*Weekend Magazine*, February 7, 1976, pp. 8–11).

FROM HUGH MacLENNAN

Hugh MacLennan (1907–1990): one of the major figures of Canadian
literature, MacLennan is the author of realistic novels like *Barometer Rising*
(1941), *Two Solitudes* (1945) and *The Watch That Ends the Night* (1959), as well
as popular collections of essays that have lasted better than the fiction, now
read primarily by university students. He received five Governor General's
Awards. None of his novels was originally published by M&S.

McGill University
March 26, 1976

My dear Jack:
With Alistair MacLeod's *Lost Salt Gift of Blood*, you may well have
published the finest book ever written in this country. He's a
marvellous writer, and profoundly modest. I wrote to him and
suggested that he send the letter on to you, but it's quite possible
he didn't.

This book reminded me of what Luther said of St. Paul: "His
sentences are limbs. They bleed." To use my own metaphor,
there's an iceberg depth of feeling and ultimate human
knowledge under the visible surface.

From the standpoint of sales, the title is probably unfortunate.
But once you've absorbed the book, it's just right. This is a book

which will grow with the years, perhaps as Joyce's *Portrait of the Artist*, but it's more fundamental than that. I'd guess it owes something to Joyce. We all owe something to Joyce. Yet the craftsmanship here, which I think is marvellously subtle, is Alistair's own. I do hope it sells well now and I'm sure that if it goes into paperback it will be taken up by every university in the land.

Best wishes,

Hugh MacLennan

TO HUGH MacLENNAN

March 31, 1976
Mr. Hugh MacLennan
McGill University
P.O. Box 6070, Station A
Montreal, Quebec

Dear Hugh:
Migod, that's a great letter re Alistair MacLeod and I am grateful to you for it. I agree with your evaluation totally. The publication came about as the result of my reading one of the stories in *Tamarack*. I was totally turned on by it and I got in touch with MacLeod, who, as you say, is a very modest man but he certainly is a major talent. In retrospect, I agree with what you say about the title, but the book in the long run is probably good enough to rise above it.

Hugh, I want to impose on your interest and good nature again by asking you to read a novel that we are publishing this fall. It has been a long time since I have been so truly excited about anything. Let me tell you a little bit about it because I realize that you may, in fact, have already read it. It's André Langevin's *Une Chaîne dans le parc.*[1] It has just been translated by Alan Brown and we are bringing it out in the fall under the title

(I hope) *Orphan Street.* Langevin hasn't accepted that title yet, but I am praying that he will. It's Alan Brown's inspiration.

Even if you did read it in the French, you may be interested in reading it in the English because it is a superb translation. We published Langevin's first novel, *Dust Over the City,* quite a long time ago—maybe fifteen years ago. It had some very good writing, showed a lot of promise, but was a pretty slight book. Several of my Quebec publishing friends have told me recently that Langevin has become a very major figure in Quebec and that his books are used widely now in colleges and high schools. I really wasn't aware of this until they said that his books were almost as widely read as Gabrielle Roy's. We accepted *Une Chaîne dans le parc* without my reading it in French. I didn't read it mainly because my French is so uncertain that I never know whether a book is good or not. About all I get out of it is the plot, so I have just finished reading the translation and I am totally turned on by it.

It is my personal guess that it may be the first major universal novel out of French Canada since *Bonheur d'occasion.* Obviously there have been some very good books in the meantime, but I don't think there has been a major work in the full sense of the word that combines literary appeal with some commercial appeal.

I am tempted to get really carried away on this one and really try to force-feed the market. We don't do that too often, but there is some justification for it because, as I am sure you know, French-Canadian novels in translation almost inevitably bomb in English. We never seem to sell more than a couple of thousand copies of books by major writers like Aquin, Ferron and others. As a matter of fact, allowing for the moderate successes like Lemelin, perhaps Carrier and the success of Anne Hébert's *Kamouraska*—which was largely inspired by the film, but which was still limited—English Canadians and English-speaking people anywhere simply don't pay much attention to French-Canadian literature.[2]

I have a hunch that this may be a very important book, and if you have time to look at it, I would really appreciate your reaction. I am having it sent to you separately.

Getting back to Alistair MacLeod for a moment, obviously our people are going to want to quote your letter. Can we do that? It would certainly help Mr. MacLeod, to say nothing of us.

Best personal regards.

Sincerely,

Jack McClelland

1. André Langevin (b. 1927): best known for *Poussière sur la ville* (1953 [*Dust Over the City*]). Langevin was one of Quebec's most celebrated novelists in the fifties and early sixties. His later works, including *Une Chaîne dans le parc*, were never quite as well received. Nevertheless, J.M. continued to promote his work throughout his tenure at M&S.

2. Hubert Aquin (1929–1977): major French-Canadian novelist (*Prochain episode*, 1965) who was also a producer at Radio-Canada (1955–59) and a scriptwriter and film director for the National Film Board (1959–63). Aquin was a political activist and a member of the Rassemblement pour l'indépendance nationale. He was the first Quebec writer to refuse the Governor General's Award on political grounds. Jacques Ferron (1921–1985): doctor, political activist and prolific writer of short stories, or *contes*. He received a Governor General's Award for *Contes du pays incertain* (1962). Roger Lemelin (1919–1992): publisher (*La Presse*) and novelist, best known for *Les Plouffe* (1948), a family saga that was continued in *Le Crime d'Ovide Plouffe* (1984) and made into a very successful television series and a film. Together with Ringuet and Gabrielle Roy, Lemelin was a key figure in introducing social realism into French-Canadian fiction. Roch Carrier (b. 1937): novelist, short-story writer and recent head of the Canada Council. Among his many books of fiction are *La Guerre, Yes Sir!* (1968), *Le Jardin des délices* (1975) and *Il n'y a pas de pays sans grand-père* (1979). Anne Hébert (b. 1916): major figure in French-Canadian literature both as poet and writer of fiction. Some of her poems, like "Le Tombeau des rois," are classics of modern Québécois literature.

FROM ERNEST BUCKLER

Ernest Buckler (1908–1984): short-story writer and novelist, much of whose work is set in the Annapolis Valley. *The Mountain and the Valley* (1952) is a Canadian classic.

Bridgetown, N.S.
September 1, 1976

Dear Jack:
Did you survive the Queen? I rather liked her, even in her dowdy Golda Meir street clothing. And she was certainly less wearing than those endless Olympics. Beset as I was by corrosive health and family upheavals, I simply didn't *care* that Uruguay could jump a millimetre higher than Paraguay.

I write now, because I still keep wondering about *Hamlet* [*Whirligig*]. For God's sake, Jack, why don't you publish the damn thing to keep me quiet? Maybe under another title, for those readers who may not be familiar with Kopit's *Oh, Dad*.¹ How, for instance, would something like *Inklings* (if the double pun is not too hidden) or *Never Laugh at a Giraffe* grab you? In any case, please believe that I don't mean to be unreasonable. I know full well that authors can be as irritating as wood ticks. Incidentally, we've had a pestilence of those creatures this season, and not even one's "sine qua non" is exempt from their burrowings.

To interject a personal note, I've fallen in love. With a four-year-old moppet of my acquaintance. The other night she called out to her mother: "Mummy, can we have some Kenfucky Tried Chicken for supper?" With that, she earned my imperishable devotion and I can't resist passing her splendid utterance on.

With all warmest regards,
Sincerely,

Ernest Buckler

---

1. Arthur Kopit (b. 1937): American dramatist, best known for *Oh, Dad, Poor Dad, Mama's Hung You in the Closet and I'm Feelin' So Sad* (1960) and *Indians* (1969).

TO ERNEST BUCKLER

September 14, 1976
Mr. Ernest Buckler
Bridgetown, N.S.

Dear Ernie:
Migod, I barely survived the Queen. Would you believe that I was invited to have dinner with her and declined because it required me to travel all the way to Montreal. I am disappointed that you didn't enjoy the Olympics. I enjoyed them immensely, but would have felt happier about the whole thing had the Queen participated as a volleyball player or something of that sort.

I am delighted that you have fallen in love. She sounds a bit young, but I like her style.

Can I tell you the truth about *Hamlet?* I really don't think, Ernie, that there is enough yet to make a book that we can sell well enough. We will do it if you insist, but migod, what are you up to? What are you writing? Can you give us some additional material? I honestly feel that it needs strengthening. The real problem is that you have this monumental reputation and we don't want to bring out a book that will do anything less than add to it. *Hamlet* won't add to it. What are you up to? I am prepared to come down to Bridgetown to find out—and that's a promise rather than a threat, although you may regard it as the latter—but do bring me up to date on what you are writing and how things are progressing. And I really am sorry about the delay on *Hamlet.* We are just not entirely happy with it yet. So do write at length. I look forward to hearing from you!

All the best.

Sincerely,

Jack McClelland

TO GABRIELLE ROY

The autobiographical article by Gabrielle Roy mentioned in the next two letters appeared in the *Globe and Mail* on December 18, 1976, with the title "The disparate treasures of a young girl who came from Deschambault Street." It dealt with her schooldays in St. Boniface, Manitoba, and described occasions when she found herself caught between the French and English languages.

December 20, 1976
Mrs. Marcel Carbotte
Apt. 302
135 Grande-Allée West
Quebec, Quebec

Dear Gabrielle:

That was a very nice piece in this morning's *Globe*. Sometime when the spirit moves I'd be interested in knowing how it came about. Did you write it at their request? Is it part of something else?

My real reason in writing, however, is to ask whether or not you have had a meeting yet with Alan Brown. I spoke to him several weeks ago about our continuing interest in a new translation of *Bonheur d'occasion* [*The Tin Flute*]. He would be willing to undertake this, but he wanted to be sure first—as of course I do—that you like the work that he has done and that you are satisfied with him as a translator. We think he is one of the finest in the country. He has great admiration for you and your work and I think he would be an ideal person to do *Bonheur d'occasion* if you are willing. I would like to get that translation started early next year with a view to publication in the spring of 1978.

One of the reasons that I would like to do that, Gabrielle, is that I think its publication might be effective in terms of the problem of Canadian unity. Don't misunderstand me on this. I don't for a minute believe that one book or a dozen books can have much effect on what I believe to be a terribly serious problem that is facing Canada. I am not altogether gloomy about the prospects because I do think some changes are needed in our structure, but I am concerned about the real possibility that many of those changes will be of the negative sort. I mention *The Tin Flute* specifically because it remains the fact that you are unique in being the only Canadian writer who has totally bridged the gap between the two cultures. You are the only writer who is critically accepted and widely read in both our two languages. There simply is no one else. This is a unique situation. We will be starting early in the new year to distribute books directly in mass-market paperback. I believe that 250,000 copies of the new translation of *Bonheur d'occasion* could be sold in English-speaking Canada in a very short period of time, and I feel sincerely that this could have a useful effect on understanding in our country.

 With all good wishes to you and Marcel for Christmas and the New Year.

Sincerely,

Jack McClelland

FROM GABRIELLE ROY

Quebec
December 30, 1976

Dear Jack:
Thank you so much for your good and most interesting letter. The *Globe and Mail* invited me to their "Mermaid Inn" for a column. At first I was a little reluctant, finally gave in as the memory awoke in me of my school days in St. Boniface, which for the first time in my life, as I looked at them from a great distance and in a strange, new light, appeared to me as they are indeed, rather unique, perplexing and in a sense rich, sad and

humorous. Hence, the article, and I am pleased that you enjoyed it. It has dawned on me lately that my own life, could I relate it simply as it unfolded and went on its bizarre way, would be my best novel. The drive to do so somewhat left me since November 15. It may come back. Like you, I am far from feeling beaten, but I am worried. What you write about my unique position as a Canadian writer is heartwarming. It is also a little heavy to bear, for much as I would love to be of real use to my country—on both sides—at the moment I can't see my way clearly, it is so confused. I have a feeling that a period of silence is almost necessary before tackling the job. All of us, especially on the French side, have given way to too much talk. It is very wrong to think that talking will resolve problems. Most of the time it only makes them worse.

Now about Alan Brown. That—meeting him—has been the most enjoyable experience of these last few months. I think he is the best possible translator I could hope for, and it is a pleasure to work with him. He came over for a weekend, and in two days of arduous, but oh so pleasant and enriching work, we went through the manuscript. Both of us, so far, have in mind for the title *A Garden in the Wind*. Alan Brown should send you the manuscript very soon—after a few little corrections of his own—and you will be able to judge.

Now about *Bonheur d'occasion*. We did talk about a new translation, Alan and I. That is, he told me of your continuing interest in a new translation and let on that he would be willing to tackle this enormous job, if a certain project for going to Europe for a few years doesn't materialize and if myself were consentaneous. I certainly would give him the job, for I have no doubt now that he is the man for the job. I myself hesitate a great deal, though, for naturally I would love to work with Alan at some time or another—a good translation, a really good one, can only be achieved at that cost, I think—I dread plunging myself in that big book of which I am truly weary. Jack, honestly, dear friend, the mere thought of going back to it gives me goose-flesh. Either I would want to write it all over again, which is impossible, or throw it in the furnace. I wonder if you are not under an illusion when you expect another boom of this book. It is a mystery to me that it has continued this long, and I feel, somehow, that it is about to peter out slowly, not flame again, God forbid. And I can't see that it could do much to draw us together, all the fools in Canada who have not been able yet to realize that we are blessed with a wonderful country, despite a few clashes, and which could easily be improved to satisfy the essential needs of East and West. We are, almost all of us, too small yet to see its greatness—in the seed, so to speak.

Gabrielle

TO ANDRÉ LANGEVIN

February 9, 1977
Mr. André Langevin
Frelighsburg, Quebec

Dear André:
I was glad to have your letter. I really feel sad that we were not able to do more with *Orphan Street*. The initial response in English Canada was certainly disappointing. Don't despair just yet, however. We are still working on it. There are a lot of people around the country now who have read it, are talking about it and who are recommending it, and it would not entirely surprise me if it turned out to be a slow starter that will eventually gain momentum and do extremely well.

Unquestionably one of the difficulties with the book in English is that it starts more slowly than the English-reading public have come to expect. They found the opening chapter slow, somewhat baffling, and the truth of the matter is that from a large file of reports I have, a lot of readers just didn't really get into the book.

This is not your fault, nor is it the fault of the translation. It is a matter of fact that taste and reading habits vary between two cultures. The real solution is for more liberties to be taken in the translation than is normally the case, but translators are often nervous about this, and usually the original author objects to any cutting or deletion or change that would in any way alter the impact of the original.

I am still convinced, as I have said publicly on many occasions, that it is one of the finest novels that we have ever published and that it will ultimately stand as one of the great works of Canadian literature.

I haven't yet seen the translation of *L'Élan d'Amérique*. It is in the house and is being considered by our editors at the present time. I will read it within the next few days and then get back to you with whatever suggestions I can make on the question of timing and related matters. Certainly it is not our wish to interrupt you during the writing of the new novel. We also want to give *L'Élan* the very best possible opportunity in English both for Canada and the United States. Leave it with me until I have had a chance to read the translation, and I shall get back to you very soon.

With all good wishes.

Sincerely,

Jack McClelland

TO AL PURDY

February 11, 1977
Mr. Al Purdy
R.R. 1
Ameliasburgh, Ontario

Dear Al:
I have just had a look at *Al Purdy's Canada [No Other Country]*—minus three or four pieces that weren't with the script—and it

was really an outstanding reading experience. It is clear that you have put a helluva lot of time and effort into it now, and it shows. The manuscript really zings along. It has got a lot of colour, a lot of variety, a lot of guts. It is vintage Purdy. It is a very special view of Canada. It is a view that a lot of people are going to enjoy, and funnily enough, I think it is a book that can do a helluva lot of good in terms of our unity problem.

One of the things that was new to me was your piece on Rod Haig-Brown.[1] I don't know whether or not it was previously published and adapted for the book. If it was, I missed it. It's a helluva good piece. Although we only ever published one of his books, he became a very good friend through the years, and there are few people that I have admired more. As you probably know, he died several months ago, very suddenly and very unexpectedly. We hope to be publishing two or three books from material that he left behind over the next few years. He was really a fantastic guy.

But the whole book is good, Al. It is really solid stuff. Interesting people. Fascinating experiences, and it shows a really moving and important part of Canadian life. Even Leonard Cohen may forgive you.

One of the pieces that was missing was the one on René Lévesque.[2] Not having read it, I can only guess that you like him and admire him. As I say, that's only a guess because I feel that way about him myself. He has a lot of guts. He has the courage of his convictions. He has stood by those convictions a long time. What I wonder about, however, is your dedication. If it is not a cynical dedication, do you really think you should be dedicating *Al Purdy's Canada* to a man who, despite any respect we may hold for him, is determined to destroy the very country you have written about? That is what he is trying to do. That is what he is intending to do. It is perfectly clear. Now, he may have ample justification for that—in fact I suspect he has—but that doesn't mean I have to like what he is doing to us. I don't like what he is doing to us, and frankly, I don't think he will succeed, but he is going to try. So I for one say fuck him. I am not about to thank anybody who tries to burn down my house, even though I might end up liking better the new one that the insurance company pays for.

So, hell, Al, when you have time, do satisfy my curiosity. The dedication of the book is strictly the author's business. Dedicate the book to Adolf Hitler, if you wish, but do tell me why a man who loves Canada as you do—and I can't think of anyone who loves Canada more—wants to thank a man for kicking him in the teeth.

Cheers!

Jack McClelland

1. Roderick Haig-Brown (1908–1976): naturalist and well-known nature writer whose books include *Silver: The Life Story of an Atlantic Salmon* (1931), *The Western Angler* (1939), *Fisherman's Winter* (1954) and several books for children. He also served as a provincial court judge for thirty-three years and was director of the National and Provincial Parks Association. M&S had published his *Return to the River: A Story of the Chinook Run* in 1946.

2. René Lévesque (1922–1987): premier of Quebec from 1976 to 1985. M&S published his *Memoirs* in 1986. Purdy eventually dedicated *No Other Country* to Jacko Onalik and Martin Senegak, two Inuit hunters who disappeared in February 1975. Purdy had participated in the search for them and wrote an article about it, "Argus in Labrador," collected in *Starting from Ameliasburgh: The Collected Prose of Al Purdy*.

TO EARLE BIRNEY

Few of M&S's writers could match Birney's almost Talmudic attention to the details of his contracts and royalty statements. Birney probably thought that he was helping keep M&S on its toes, while ensuring that he received the royalties that were his due. J.M., not surprisingly, found Birney's letters a nuisance, although he was willing to admit to various mistakes made at the office. The following is his side of one of their last skirmishes.

April 26, 1977
Dr. Earle Birney
Apt. 2201
200 Balliol Street
Toronto, Ontario

Dear Earle:
I understand that you have been complaining about the delay in
response to your letter of March 30 to Anna [Porter]. In a sense I
suppose there is some justification for that, but yours was not
exactly a run-of-the-mill letter to which Anna or anybody could
simply sit down and dash off a reply. A girl in our contracts
department passed on your most recent threat and I said, "Tell
Dr. Birney to go fuck himself." She was rather shattered by this
and said, "You don't mean it." I said, "Of course I do mean it, but
perhaps you are right. You better not do it."

When Anna received your letter, she passed it on to me with
a note: "I am just not strong enough for this—are you?" To this I
replied in effect that I have a particular sympathy for you about
our present contract. You are right. There are a lot of silly
clauses in it that are neither suitable nor applicable. It was not a
contract devised for your book. It's a standard contract form
that has been in use around here for many years. It is an
amalgam of the best British and American publishing contracts.
It is constantly being amended, but has never been totally
revised. So I replied that I had great sympathy for you but that I
didn't want to deal with the matter because as is always the case
when I read one of your letters, while I started out with
sympathy, I ended up in a fury because of your continual
incessant petulant sniping and carping about the past.

I don't really understand the point of all this shit, Earle. I
don't know why you persist. You can't undo the past. What you
are complaining about had absolutely nothing to do with
contracts. I personally don't ever remember a dispute about a
contract where we haven't been willing to amend or waive a
clause. If you are doing this for some future historian, it has

been done thirty times over. It is not going to help you or me or anybody else to keep bringing the goddamn thing up.

Let me put it to you this way. If you really want to leave McClelland and Stewart, then I for one am not going to stand in your way. Anna objects to my saying this, but I am going to say it nonetheless. If a publishing relationship has to be this damn unfriendly, then let's put an end to it. I have never held an author to an option agreement. The firm, to my knowledge, has never imposed an unreasonable clause. Some authors are well pleased with our performance in sales and promotion. Others are not. We do what we can do!

It has been suggested on more than one occasion that I have been altruistic in my approach to Canadian publishing. I have denied it because that has never been my motivation. It has always been what I have called "enlightened self-interest" and now call "ill-conceived self-interest." Of one thing I am certain. The problems in this business are enough without adding to it the problems posed by holding an author who is persistently unhappy and dissatisfied. It is simply not worth it.

I would hate to see you leave, of course, and it shouldn't be necessary to say that. Should you decide to stay, I am not going to ask you to stop complaining. I am going to ask you to try to find some new subjects to complain about. The fact that we have not done an effective job of selling some of your books in the past has registered.

Cheers,

Jack

FROM IRVING LAYTON

Department of English
York University
May 11, 1977

Dear Brother Jacob:
Seeing you the other night on the stage chivvying the audience
for not rising to your bid of $2000 for Cohen's MS, I thought of
how much this country owes you. There's no mistaking your
genuine devotion and zeal in the cause of writing in this
country. They have been an inspiration to many Canadians who,
like myself, might have been left to wander in the cultural
wilderness had you not picked up your staff (no pun intended)
and told us to follow you out of it.

May your shadow never grow less, Jacob. I want to thank you,
somewhat belatedly, for the letter you wrote to me after the
testimonial dinner which you emceed so superbly. And thanks
for that too. It was a great evening, and my one regret is that I
didn't mention anything about my great debt to you in the brief
thank-you speech I made. I should have told them all about your
encouragement and support and what they have meant to me
during all these very good years of our association. I think we
faithfully kept the bargain that we made: that I wasn't to tell you
how to run your business, and you were never to censor a poem
of mine. Well, I didn't, and you haven't. You're a beautiful soul,
and one day my affection for you and my great esteem will spill
over into an ode that will astonish the world. Who knows, I
might even include it in my love poems scheduled for M&S
publication some time in 1978.[1]

Until then, always, peace and joy.
                    Best wishes,

                    Irving Layton

1. *The Love Poems of Irving Layton* appeared in 1980.

TO IRVING LAYTON

May 18, 1977
Dr. Irving Layton
Department of English
York University
Downsview, Ontario

Dear Irving:
That's a beautiful letter and I thank you for it.
                              Cheers!

                         Jack McClelland

TO THE *TORONTO STAR*

September 26, 1977
The Editor
The Toronto Star
1 Yonge Street
Toronto, Ontario

Dear Sir:
One of your book reviewers, Robert Fulford, recently revealed
in print that he was a school drop-out at age thirteen. This
confirmed my suspicions of a good many years. There was
another confirmation in his review of Charles Templeton's *Act of
God (Toronto Star*, Saturday, September 24).

Among other things, Fulford describes the novel as "dull."
The novel may have flaws, but being dull is hardly one of them.
I have over a hundred letters from early readers of the book that
say just the opposite. Let me quote one. William Stevenson,[1]
author of *A Man Called Intrepid*, warned us in advance that he was
not a Templeton fan and would probably dislike the book. After
reading it he said, "It is an absolute winner—high controversy in

the best sense—and is the best novel I have read in a long, long time."

Now that Mr. Fulford is regularly employed, it seems to me that he should make up for his lack of formal schooling by investing in one or more of the excellent adult education courses now available. After reading Fulford's review, Templeton himself intends to do that. He, too, is a school drop-out.

Yours very truly,

Jack McClelland

1. William Stevenson (b. 1924): author of *A Man Called Intrepid* (1976) and *The Ghosts of Africa* (1981). For Charles Templeton, see November 17, 1978.

FROM AND TO PIERRE BERTON

This note was returned to Berton with "bullshit" stamped all over it.

121 Sackville Street   *BULLSHIT*
Toronto, Ontario   *BULLSHIT*
January 3, 1978   *BULLSHIT*

Dear Jack: *BULLSHIT*
I find that due to the pressure of other business, I can no longer serve on the Board of Directors for Magook Publishers. Please accept this letter as my official resignation.

Sincerely,

Pierre Berton

Jack McClelland	*BULLSHIT*
President	*BULLSHIT*
Magook Publishers	*BULLSHIT*
254 Bartley Drive	*BULLSHIT*
Toronto, Ontario	*BULLSHIT*
	BULLSHIT
	BULLSHIT

Received Jan. 24 and noted for consideration at next meeting. Pressure of other matters prevents me dealing with it more quickly.

JGM

TO BOB YOUNG, ART DEPARTMENT

February 15, 1978
MEMO TO: Bob Young
FROM: Jack McClelland
cc: Pierre Berton
       Anna Porter
       Linda McKnight

I have read Pierre Berton's memo of February 13 re *The Wild Frontier* with great interest. Please proceed with the preparation of the rough along the lines that Pierre has described. However, as publisher of the book, I would like to have my own input. The jacket that Pierre has described sounds revolting to me. As a matter of fact, the colour combination that he suggests, from my experience, is almost certain to guarantee that the book will end up on the remainder table in very short order. Let him see what it looks like, but please do an alternative with some rich, expensive-looking colours. The key to these Berton jackets is that they must look like gift books. His colour combination will almost certainly produce a gift book that will look as if somebody has just thrown up on it.

TO MORDECAI RICHLER

The following three letters all deal with the ill-fated conference held at the University of Calgary (February 15–18, 1978) to determine the hundred greatest Canadian novels. J.M.'s two letters offer his reasons for wanting such an academic conference to produce such a list; Margaret Laurence's expresses the reservations of many writers, teachers and critics. The list and the proceedings of the conference can be found in Charles Steele's *Taking Stock: The Calgary Conference on the Canadian Novel* (ECW, 1982). Whether one agrees or disagrees with the idea of such a list, it's worth noting that this may have been the only conference on Canadian literature that ever generated any controversy. For that alone we should be grateful to J.M. and the University of Calgary organizers.

February 28, 1978
Mr. Mordecai Richler
218 Edgehill Road
Westmount, Quebec

Dear Mordecai:
I have just finished reading the comments on your Canada article in *The Atlantic.*¹ That is really a fantastic response, and I can imagine that you are feeling quite pleased. If not, you should be. The response indicated clearly that the article did a helluva lot of good and gave a lot of people a clear understanding of what is going on for the first time. If you weren't such an antisemitic bastard, the world would be your oyster. There is a real metaphor.

The real purpose of the letter is to thank you for going to Calgary. I imagine that you found it a horrible experience. I must say I was tremendously impressed and grateful for the fact that you really went out of your way to be cooperative, pleasant and available. I know that they were all pleased, and I think it did a helluva lot to make the conference a success. Obviously there are a lot of people who think that it wasn't and who think the whole conference was wrong. I have been trying to peddle Canadian books for over thirty years, and I am completely convinced that given a few years for the results to show, that conference will have done more to ensure the use of the right Canadian books in the schools and colleges than any other single event that has occurred in the last thirty-odd years.

The thing that a lot of purists fail to recognize is that the teachers in our high schools and the teachers and critics in our universities—what an inept bunch they are—really don't know a goddamn thing about Canadian writing, what is important and what isn't important. Teachers desperately need guidance. This list, imperfect as it is, indicates how desperately it is needed, but it is a start. I know that you are nervous about pushing Canlit too far—and I agree with you within limits—but the truth is that the English is deplorable. We are really suffering from the fact that the British, the Americans, the French, the Italians, etc., etc. have been publishing their own literature for a long, long time and we have a lot of catching up to do before we have even a minor foothold for our own. What I am really talking about is best stated in the letter from Kristin Foss in *The Atlantic.* "Mordecai Richler captured the very essence of our contradictory nationhood; through him I have gained a sense of country...." I know you abhor nationalism and parochialism, but Miss Foss has underlined what the whole cultural independence battle is about.

So, again I thank you for going to Calgary. You may never forgive me, but I think it was worth it.

Cheers!

Jack McClelland

1. Mordecai Richler's "Oh! Canada! Lament for a divided country" appeared in the December 1977 issue of the *Atlantic Monthly* (pp. 41–55).

FROM MARGARET LAURENCE

8 Regent Street
Box 609
Lakefield, Ontario
March 7, 1978

Dear Jack:
I'm glad you felt I did all right at the conference. I enjoyed it, really, and it was marvellous to meet Gabrielle Roy, and also Roger Lemelin, and to see old friends.

However, I have to say that I am uneasy on several counts. What causes me considerable anxiety is your talk of using the list in an ongoing way. You say that if the U. of Calgary doesn't want it, then perhaps some other institution or publishing company, and maybe—wait for it!—McClelland and Stewart would like to use it. Well, surprise, surprise. I have to admit that I have for some time been worried that this is precisely what you were aiming for with that damn list, and now my worst fears are confirmed. Please, Jack, I beg you to rethink this one. Listen, believe me—I am *trying* to be loyal to you and to the old firm. Please don't make it impossibly difficult for me to support you in public utterances I may make. Let me tell you why I am so much against your using this list.

1. The list, as it was visualized by Malcolm [Ross], was, as I said in my letter to the *Globe* (which was printed in tandem with yours), *not* a list of *the hundred best or the hundred greats*. Good God, we don't have a hundred "great" novels. And as for "best," well, that would have been the arbitrary choices of not more than 140 academics, hardly a referendum on a national scale. Malcolm, as he explained, intended the list only as a talking point at the conference, and to show which books were being the most widely used in courses. As several people pointed out, there are far too few translations from French-Canadian writers, and also, only books out in paperback can be used in course work, so there are wide gaps in the list in terms of its being

representative of the whole of Canadian writing. So a use of the
list as "the best" would be a total distortion. I would like to see
the list gracefully forgotten.

2. A use of the list could only damage the reputation of
McClelland and Stewart. There has been a lot of talk, and not
idle talk either, about the nature of the conference. Perhaps no
one tells you these things, Jack. I hope you are not going to be
offended, but someone has got to let you know about this
situation. The fact that *only* M&S writers were there, apart from
Yves Thériault (whom maybe you have also published, for all I
know) did not go unremarked. I did not realize, until I arrived
at the conference and began to look around, that only M&S
writers were there. Of course, it was marvellous to meet
Gabrielle Roy and Roger Lemelin, and to see Rudy Wiebe,
Marian Engel, James Houston, Mordecai Richler, Brian Moore,
etc. But then one began to think—where are the writers
published by other publishers? Where, for that matter, are the
other publishers? I have since learned that Doug Gibson of
Macmillan had to *ask* for an invitation, and the only other
publisher I saw was Francess Halpenny of the U. of T. Press. I
know of at least one other publisher who was sent an invite so
late it was impossible for him to go. I don't blame you for that,
of course—but I can't entirely blame the U. of Calgary, either.
Someone, however, at some early date, should have made sure that
a large number of publishers and writers were invited, not just
M&S writers. It did not take much eyesight to spot the lack of
representation on the part of other publishers and writers. The
press, naturally, noticed this, as why wouldn't they? This has
caused a good deal of hard feeling on behalf of other publishers
and, from my point of view even worse, on the part of writers
published by other publishers. Am I supposed to cheer with
happiness when my colleagues, published by other publishers,
have been totally left out and are understandably annoyed? Am I
supposed to chirp with glee when it appears that I am a party to

this kind of exclusion, when I didn't know a damn thing about it until I got there? Anyway, forget my role in all this. If you use that blasted list for advertising or other purposes, it will confirm what the press has already noted—the conference was predominantly M&S writers, and the list, naturally, has a huge percentage of M&S writers, simply because of the very valuable NCL—and full marks to you and Malcolm for the NCL. But you don't need to advertise the NCL in that way—it cheapens it, and it will do your own reputation no good. Of that I am sure.

3. I have heard (and I do hear a lot, believe me—Lakefield is not far from *anywhere*, and things filter through like prairie smoke signals) that there is a good deal of rather bitter comment, on the part of (a) academics who weren't invited; (b) writers; (c) publishers; (d) media people—to the effect that a very great deal of Canada Council money (i.e., taxpayers' money) was poured into that conference, which, it is being said, was a clever front for M&S (who had conned the U. of Calg) to publicize its own books and writers. Well, obviously, the conference was not that—the papers were serious, and, for the most part, interesting attempts to deal with aspects of our literature; I'm damn sure none of the academics thought they were there to boost M&S (and heaven knows, it would be terrible if they ever came to feel they'd been used). But because M&S had such a high profile at the conference, and the other publishers virtually were not given a chance at all, one can see how such a feeling could arise in various quarters. I for one, although naturally I did not say so at the time, felt highly upset by the absence of writers other than M&S writers, and so did some of the other writers. Any use of the list for any purpose of your own would simply serve to confirm people's suspicions in this direction. It would harm the firm; it would harm your own reputation; it would harm Malcolm; and it would harm all your writers who attended that conference. Jack, I do hope you will take my remarks seriously.

As far as the NCL is concerned, I would be delighted to meet with you at any time to discuss it. I think you are perfectly correct in saying you don't want it to be a house list. I also think you are right in saying that you don't want it to contain novels which might appear more appropriately in some other paperback form. I do feel, however, that it would be a great pity if some of the turn-of-the-century novels were not kept in print, even in small quantities, for the use of scholars. I know you are not in this as a charity operation, but I hope there can be found some way to keep these books available. Also, I would hate to see the NCL simply cut to a hundred titles and the list closed forever. I think all these things should be discussed. I quite agree with your idea of some kind of cut-off point; the Everyman Library is a good example of what *not* to do—it got so many titles that they all began to look the same. Anyway, I would really like to talk about the NCL with you, as I believe it is absolutely crucial to the teaching of Canlit in our schools and universities.

But please, I beg you, let the list go. Just let it go. Enough harm and bad feeling have been caused by its being interpreted as some kind of exclusive club. Please don't add to that. It can only put you in a very bad light, and I would hate to see that happen. Believe me, I am not exaggerating the things I have heard. Nor am I exaggerating my own profound sense of unease at the apparent exclusive nature of the conference. It's over now—let's for heaven's sake let it be.

All the best,

Margaret Laurence

TO MARGARET LAURENCE

April 6, 1978
Mrs. Margaret Laurence
8 Regent Street
P.O. Box 609
Lakefield, Ontario

Dear Margaret:
You seem to think that I can be guilty of the most horrendous
acts. I suspect you are overly impressionable and too easily
influenced by the vast number of young authors, critics, editors,
etc. to whom you have become den mother or whatever. Maybe
it isn't that at all. Maybe you really do detect in me a deep,
sinister streak that unnerves you from time to time.

Let me tell you the absolute truth about the Calgary
conference, for starters:

1. Yes, I did propose it to them in the first place.

2. Yes, my sinister purpose was really to find a way of honouring
Malcolm Ross appropriately and to ease the way for his
retirement. Initially Malcolm was to have been the core of the
conference. This was watered down considerably in order to
ease the fund-raising activities for the University of Calgary.
Dissipation of original purpose was such that I despaired from
time to time whether he would even play a central role in the
closing banquet. Thanks to you, that, at least, was retained. I
think the fine tribute that you paid to him was appreciated by
everyone present and probably by me more than anyone else.

3. From that point on I had surprisingly little to do with the
conference. I attended the initial committee meeting in Calgary,
where I outlined the overall plan. Beyond that I had no
connection with the committee. There were a lot of telephone

calls, a lot of correspondence and we did a lot of work for them, but beyond the overall form of the program—the fact that there was an opening reception and a closing banquet, the fact that Malcolm made his report on the Saturday morning and that there was a film festival and that the whole thing was covered by the National Film Board (which I arranged)—almost every suggestion or proposal that I put forward was ignored.

4. It is a matter of fact that beyond supplying a list of living New Canadian Library authors, and living New Canadian Library introducers, I had nothing to do with the invitation list. To this day I don't know who was invited and who was not invited. It was strictly their conference, but when they asked me to do something, I did it. When they asked me a question, I answered it. I suggested, for example, that they write and send an invitation to the head of every English department at every Canadian university, community college and high school.

5. I suggested that they get in touch with both publishing associations, in fact three including the French, and ask them if they would set up book displays and also ask them for suggestions and also ask them to circulate invitations to their members to attend, etc. I also asked that they approach other publishers re author lists. I then wrote and talked to both associations to take the whole thing seriously, which in the end they did.

I then leaned on a certain number of authors they were particularly anxious to have present. Some McClelland and Stewart authors were in this group, including Margaret Laurence, Gabrielle Roy, Roger Lemelin, Margaret Atwood (who, as you know, was out of the country), Mordecai Richler, James Houston, Sylvia Fraser, to name only a few.

6. Also at their request, I wrote to a number of non-McClelland and Stewart authors and pressed them to attend. That list included Robertson Davies, Northrop Frye, Morley Callaghan,

Hugh MacLennan, Richard Wright, Alice Munro, and that's to name only a few.[1]

7. You already know how the list was prepared. It was entirely open and straightforward. The ballot list was prepared by Malcolm's original group of ten. People were invited to add names. The thing wasn't doctored or edited in any way by us. We did prepare the physical ballots. We did mail them out. The tabulation was done by our people. The results were exactly as compiled by the tabulator.

Now, before I deal with your numbered sequence re the list and use of same, let me say one more thing. I did have a second motive for arranging this conference. Let me say a word about Margaret Atwood. I admire her intelligence and her energy. I think she is a fine poet and a pretty good novelist. I think she is a lousy critic. While *Survival* has in some ways helped Canadian writing and the study of Canadian literature—because it has been widely read—it has also done a great deal of damage. I consider it to be uninformed, half-baked and in some respects extremely damaging to the main body of Canadian literature. One of the high spots of the conference, for me, was when one of the critics on the panel the last day said how appalled he was to find it listed as one of the ten essential books for the study of Canadian literature. He was absolutely right. As a matter of fact, the study of the list of the hundred books indicates the damage that *Survival* has already done.

Why has that book had such an impact? There are a number of reasons. First, Peggy is high profile. Second, the timing was right. Third, there was no other contemporary book available—it filled a much-needed gap. That's fine except that it has become the school teacher's bible and it does a disservice to Canadian literature. It was my hope that something would come out of this conference to serve over a period of years to replace that book. This will happen. I couldn't care less whether such a replacement is published by M&S or not. I have absolutely no financial interest in the matter, but I do care about our literature and I do care that some balanced, reliable guide be available to undo some of the damage that that book has done.

Now let me look at some of your specific points as you list them:

1. I agree that we don't have a hundred great novels and that this list doesn't represent the hundred best. I think it is a starting point in determining what our hundred best are. The very fact that 140 academics (and almost 600 were invited to respond) didn't perform with particular intelligence after they got through the first two dozen books is a fair indication that such a list is needed. Why do you say it is nothing like a national referendum? If you go to almost 600 teachers of Canadian literature across the country and over 20 per cent respond, surely to God that is a pretty good poll. It is a more extensive poll than most of those conducted by Gallup or anybody else.

Next, under item #1 you make two points that simply aren't valid. You say "there are far too few translations from French-Canadian writers." While it is true that a lot of outstanding English-Canadian novels have not been translated into French, the reverse, in terms of my experience, is just not true. I think any intelligent French-Canadian publisher would agree with me. The best of French-Canadian literature has been translated into English. Translation money has been readily available. There are some very recent books that haven't been translated yet. It is doubtful that there are any great ones. It is true there might have been a higher French content at the lower level, so my answer to that one is that although I heard the point being made, I don't think it was made by anybody who knew what they were talking about. I consider it at the same level of statement as the one made by somebody who wanted the conference to make the overall recommendation to the Canada Council that more money should be made available for translations. It's a joke. The Canada Council has, in fact, more money available for translation into French and English than anybody can possibly use.

And then there is this argument about all these great Canadian works that aren't available in paperback. Name one. I challenge you to name one. Conceivably you might come up with a title that could worm its way into the lower quarter of the list, or a book by an author like Willa Cather[2] who refused to allow her books to be done in paper, but I know of no such book. Migod, Margaret, are you not aware that Malcolm and a whole body of people have been looking for such books for twenty years? They do not exist.

2.Well, you softened your position on point #2. The talk about the sinister Jack McClelland at the conference didn't trouble me then, and it doesn't trouble me now. You now know why there were mainly M&S authors present. I worked at it. I even got Richard Wright[1] to agree to attend and then they wouldn't pay for him. As to Doug Gibson's having to ask for an invitation, that's straight bullshit. The Publishers' Association circulated all the details of the conference to their membership. Except for those who actually participated, it was not "by invitation." Anna Porter and I both paid our own way. I phoned other publishers and asked them to attend. I phoned both associations and asked them to urge the publishers to attend. As a matter of fact, I even tried to get some French publishers to attend and some American publishers to attend, and in fact one did.

3. Regarding Canada Council money, Margaret, that has to be a joke. Let me tell you exactly what they did. They put up, I think, something like $4,000 to support the book display. How this money was actually spent, I don't know. I don't think the publishers who displayed were reimbursed in any way. Perhaps they paid for the space and the tables and that sort of thing. In addition, according to the best of my knowledge, they put up another $8,000, which paid the expenses of participants, by which I mean chairmen, panelists and authors who were participating.

So that's a vast amount of money?

I wonder if it was noticed by any of these detractors that neither Anna nor I spoke at any of the sessions or at any of the events. The same can't be said for Doug Gibson.

There aren't too many other points that I want to make but there are a few:

1. I have absolutely no regret or remorse about anything I did to create and push this conference.

2. If the conference appeared to be pushing M&S authors and M&S books, it is mainly because the conference was about Canadian literature and the Canadian novel, and M&S authors and M&S books just happen to form a very substantial part of what is Canlit.

3. If pushing the list lends support to my detractors and lends credence to the suspicions raised by a lot of small people, I can't for the life of me think why that should trouble me. Margaret, I am not running a popularity contest and never have tried to do so except with the people we publish. To hell with these people who resent M&S.

The list may be an embarrassing thing to you because you are at the head of it. That, in fact, is where you belong. These lists have been prepared in England and France and in fact in most cultured countries of the world. Such lists have been prepared relating to film, relating to plays, relating to art, relating to all cultural activities, in fact all athletic activities. What is wrong with such a list?

You probably know better than anyone else why such a list is needed. The academics don't know what the hell they are talking about, for the most part. The teachers sure as hell know very little about Canadian literature, and the public knows far too little. So I should be upset because some frightened

academics get nervous, because some critics attack the
principle (perhaps because they weren't invited to vote), because
some writers who are perhaps afraid that they won't be included
get nervous, and some publishers get nervous because some of
the books they published in the last five years haven't been
accepted as instant classics—this is all bullshit. Should I get
nervous because Mordecai Richler jokes about such a list? That's
his role in life. He can ignore the fact that such lists have long
been available in every culture of the world.

Leaving aside your personal feelings, is it bad for Canada to
have *The Stone Angel* recognized as the top Canadian novel of all
time? I don't think so. Is it bad to have *The Tin Flute* recognized as
a close second? I don't think so. I don't understand all this
bullshit. Perhaps you can straighten me out. Otherwise, I am
prepared to be the sacrificial lamb. I push this thing because I
believe it is for the good of the country.

So there it is. It is a long letter, but I am glad that I have done
it. It has served the purpose—giving the matter all this further
thought—of reaffirming my faith that I was right to begin with
and that I am still right. I won't take any action for the moment.
I'll give you some further opportunity for rebuttal. Before I do,
let me say this. If in your rebuttal you come up with one solid,
sensible and reasonable reason why such a list should not exist
and be used, it will be the first one I have heard. Novels should
not be classified? That's a joke. I may be a publisher, but I did
study English literature at the University of Toronto. Novels
shouldn't be compared with each other? That, too, is a joke. We
don't have a large enough body of literature? That's a joke. It is a
McClelland and Stewart promotion? To me, at least, that is a
joke. Okay, Margaret, give me your best shot.

Despite all the foregoing, Margaret, I love you dearly. May I
suggest that I leave the writing to you and you leave these much
less important matters to me.

Cheers!

Jack McClelland

1. Richard Wright (b. 1937): novelist whose books include *The Weekend Man* (1970), *In the Middle of a Life* (1973), *Final Things* (1980), and *The Age of Longing* (1995). Alice Munro (b. 1931): short story writer. Her *Selected Stories* appeared in 1996.

2. Willa Cather (1876-1947): American novelist. Her novels include *O Pioneers* (1913), *The Professor's House* (1925) and *Death Comes for the Archbishop* (1927).

TO DOUGLAS CREIGHTON

Douglas Creighton (b.1956): newspaper publisher.

March 3, 1978
Mr. Douglas Creighton
Publisher
The Toronto Sun
333 King Street East
Toronto, Ontario

Dear Doug:
As per our telephone conversation, I enclose a copy of the novel I referred to, *A Casual Affair* by Sylvia Fraser. It is being published tomorrow, Saturday, March 4.

As I reported to you, there is a rumour circulating in Toronto at the moment to the effect that the male protagonist is Jack McClelland. According to the information I have, the story is being pushed by a female journalist whose name I won't mention but whom I identified in our conversation. After talking to you, I learned that she had been successful to the degree that my name appeared in the *Globe* review of the book but was killed at the editorial desk.

I have a number of areas of concern. First, the story is untrue. Second, it is extremely damaging to the literary reputation of the author, who is a serious artist. Third, and obviously most important to me, it could cause a great deal of embarrassment to my family.

The worst part of the whole thing is that if such a story

appeared, no apology could undo the damage. I would be bound to sue. While it is no secret that McClelland and Stewart could use the large sum of money that such a suit would produce, I would rather avoid it. Obviously it is not easy for me to write this letter. I am not interested in circulating the story any further. On the other hand, my lawyer has advised me that since I could not accept an apology, it is wise to state in advance that I would consider any reference to me in connection with the book as malicious.

I would be grateful to you for anything you can do to avert any references to this matter in your columns. The simple fact is that an unavoidable action would be brought into being that would be extremely damaging to me and even more damaging to the newspaper.

Needless to say, it is embarrassing to have to write this letter. I thank you for hearing me out.

Best personal regards.

Sincerely,

Jack McClelland

TO PIERRE BERTON

March 29, 1978
Mr. Pierre Berton
My Country Productions
21 Sackville Street
Toronto, Ontario

Dear Pierre:
I have been asked to approach you by a distinguished group of Canadians who ask if you would be willing to run in the next election as an independent nationalist. The group includes a lot of serious people who care a great deal about this country—Peter Newman, Margaret Atwood, Mel Hurtig, etc.—and I am

sure that I don't have to spell out who the others are. They are not asking you to run as part of an official movement, as I interpret it, but what they are saying instead is that the country is in dire straits and needs people like you in the House of Commons. The approach, as I understand it, implies support financial and otherwise.

As a post-nationalist, I am by no means certain that I could share the specific aspirations of this group. I believe in Canadian unity and the survival of the country, but I am no longer satisfied that it can be achieved with the freight of any consideration of economic and political independence.

Nonetheless, I am totally in accord with this group in believing that you could do a great deal to ensure that Canada has a future by trying your hand at politics. Your election would be a certainty. Given the scenario that could develop, I am prepared to believe that you could become prime minister as head of a Coalition to Save Canada. I hope you will think about it.

Because you know that I do not admire our political system, that I do not support or belong to any political party and, in fact, that I abhor party politics, you may well believe that I am routinely passing on a request that was made of me. Initially this was true, but the more I think about it, the more convinced I become that the proposal that I am passing on makes sense. I believe we are headed for a minority government. I believe there are a number of distinguished independents running in the next election. There is evidence everywhere that a lot of party candidates are prepared to jump in a new direction after election if given the opportunity. I believe there is no party now in existence that can pull Canada together. Given that speculative scene, I can tell you quite honestly, Pierre, that I can think of no other Canadian who has the public image, acceptance and ability to pull the whole goddamn thing together. It is a mad scenario, but these are mad times for Canada. You believe Joe Clark will be elected. The thought appals me and I hope you are wrong. I believe Trudeau will be re-elected and that thought appals me too. By the way, read Peter Newman's piece "The Wizard of Ottawa" in the April 3 *Maclean's*. It is a devastatingly good piece. So Ed Broadbent becomes our next prime minister? Forget it. Why not Pierre Berton? The pieces are all there. Why don't you pull them together.

Cheers!

Jack McClelland

TO MATT COHEN

Matt Cohen (b. 1942): prolific short-story writer and novelist best known for *The Disinherited* (1974), *The Sweet Second Summer of Kitty Malone* (1979), *The Spanish Doctor* (1984), *The Bookseller* (1993) and *Last Seen* (1995).

October 3, 1978
Mr. Matt Cohen
Toronto, Ontario

Dear Matt:
There is absolutely no way for *Sunrise* [as a title]! For Godssake, Matt, let's not go through all that again. There is nothing wrong with *The Sweet Second Summer of Kitty Malone*. Everybody here likes it. If you don't want to use it, however, do come up with another title because I simply do not want to let you call the book *Sunrise*. I am so certain that it will kill off the sales potential of the book that I am sure it would be a damn foolish thing to do, so either agree to *Kitty Malone* or come up with another title, please.

All the best.

Sincerely,

Jack McClelland

FROM AL PURDY

R.R. 1
Ameliasburgh, Ontario
October 4, 1978

Dear Jack:

I'm sorry you feel so disturbed over the review I did of [Leonard] Cohen's book [*Death of a Lady's Man*].[1] I should mention: I did not write the headings for the review, and those made it seem worse than it actually was. Actually, I paid Cohen many compliments for his earlier books, and even one or two for the present book. However, I do not think it a very good book, and being so honest yourself, I am sure you would want me to say what I feel and think.

What? Do I hear you say you don't want me to say what I feel and think? I must have heard wrong. Surely you don't want me to be a yes-man, somebody who always agrees with you? I know you have a special feeling for Cohen, and believe he is a special human being. I can understand that, and hope you can remain feeling that way. It is a good feeling, this admiration of "difference" in someone else, and I'm sure that Cohen welcomes it from someone in your position: his publisher.

However, and it's a big "however," I calls 'em as I sees 'em, and I don't intend to be influenced by anyone either way. I thought you knew me well enough to know that.

The Cohen reviews I've seen have been interesting: one in the *Vancouver Sun* was a pretty flat dislike: Geddes[2] in the *Globe* thought *Lady's Man* was a comic book, one which ridiculed itself; another review apparently didn't care for it much; and mine, which said that Cohen had written much better previously, and that this book was not up to his earlier standard. I haven't seen any raves yet and don't expect to. *It is not a good book.*

Again, I'm sorry you feel so personally affronted, as appeared when I met you briefly at Hollinger House. Whether you know or believe it or not, I have quite a lot of admiration for you—for reasons I don't intend to specify. And I do hope we can be more or less civil to each other most of the time. If not, well—I accept that too, and can get used to it.

Best wishes,

Al Purdy

1. The review appeared in the *Toronto Star*, September 30, 1978.

2. Gary Geddes (b. 1940): anthologist and minor poet (*Rivers Inlet*, 1971).

TO AL PURDY

October 16, 1978
Mr. Al Purdy
R.R. 1
Ameliasburgh, Ontario

Dear Al:
For years I have been told that few people can tell when I am being serious and when I am not. It has even been suggested that I should carry a sign in my pocket which I could hold up and which would say something like, "I'm only kidding." I would say this to you. If you were not an old friend and had I been in any way serious, I would not, even for a minute, have considered assaulting you in such harsh terms. Had I been serious, it is conceivable that I might have ignored you, more likely that I would have written you, but the last thing I would have considered would be a performance of that sort.

In my trade, reviews are of little significance except for any effect they may have on the psyche of the author. But that's the author's problem, not the publisher's. I don't think reviews, pro or con, have any profound effect on the immediate or future sales of any book. In fact, I would prefer a negative review with a lot of space to a short positive review. I measure the value in column inches. The only type of review that irritates me is the lightweight, silly review. A case in point would be Barbara Amiel's spoof of the Merle Shain[1] book in a recent issue of *Maclean's*. I don't know whether you saw it or not. Instead of reviewing the book, Amiel wrote a piece in the form of a confession from Merle Shain as to how she put the book together. It was a silly review. Yours was anything but silly and, of course, you had some kind things to say about Cohen.

It is true that I don't agree with your evaluation of the book. So what else is new? I seldom agree with other people's opinions anyway. I happen to think this is one of the finest things Cohen has ever written. One thing I don't understand, however, is why, in the very small literary community that we have in Canada, important writers like yourself risk their own personal relationships—and here I am thinking of you and Leonard, although Leonard would be one of the last people in the world to harbour a grudge because of a review—when it would be so much easier to read the book and tell the paper "I don't want to review it." In other words in this very small community, I think it would be far better for all the major writers to say no— considering the pittance they get for doing a review anyway— unless they can be positive about the book by one of their peers. So why should I single you out for this comment? Everybody does it. It is just something that I don't understand. Life is too short.

Cheers!

Jack McClelland

1. Barbara Amiel (b. 1940): journalist and columnist with *Maclean's* (1976–), *Toronto Sun* (1983–85), *London Times* (1986–90) and *Sunday Times* (1991–94). Merle Shain (1935–1989): author of *Some Men Are More Perfect than Others: A Book about Men, hence about Women* (1973), *Love and Dreams* (1973) and *When Lovers Are Friends* (1978).

TO CHARLES TEMPLETON

Charles Templeton (b. 1915): a former evangelist, Templeton has written
several popular novels, none of which has yet made it into *The Oxford
Companion to Canadian Literature* (*Act of God*, 1977; *The Third Temptation*,
1980). He has also written *Farewell to God: My Reasons for Rejecting the
Christian Faith* (1996).

November 17, 1978
Mr. Charles Templeton
Apt. 3708
44 Charles Street West
Toronto, Ontario

Dear Charles:

I do want to put on record that I am most optimistic about your
new novel *[The Third Temptation]*. It is my guess that it has superb
market potential. Certainly for North America, and because it
has it for North America, it probably exists for the world
market. The theme is a good one. Your two principal characters
are strong, colourful and interesting. Quite honestly, although it
is far from the easiest novel that anyone has tried to pull off—
which may be an understatement—I think you can do it and I
think it is going to turn out really well.

Whatever you do, don't begin to overestimate the
intelligence of the reading public. You have developed the
ability to write readable, popular fiction. In my opinion you are
already doing it more successfully than many of the most
celebrated names in the field. The great, popular novelists of
our time did not achieve their reputations or their markets by
making things difficult for their readers. You have the market
running for you. It is my view that it is not a good time to
become too philosophical, too pedantic, too precious. In fact, it
is the very wrong time to do that. Other writers have
succumbed to that temptation and been burned, and it
shouldn't happen to you.

So in the end what is my message? My message is that you have developed a fine craft. You are into an exceptional novel. Don't let anything divert you. This one will be worth all the effort that you have and will put into it.

All the best.

Sincerely,

Jack McClelland

FROM PIERRE BERTON

21 Sackville Street
Toronto, Ontario
November 29, 1978

Dear Jack:

I have your letter re the film of *The Dionne Years*. You are in error when you say no credit was given to the book. Immediately after the opening title, the words "based on *The Dionne Years* by Pierre Berton" appeared in large type. You were probably out in the kitchen having a drink at the time.

Best wishes.

Sincerely,

Pierre

TO KENNETH TAYLOR

Kenneth Taylor (b. 1934): the Canadian ambassador to Iran during the 1979 revolution against the shah, who helped rescue six Americans after the American embassy had been overrun and more than a hundred Americans taken prisoner. He did not write a book about the experience.

SECTSTATE HULL

FEBRUARY 1, 1979

AMBASSADOR KENNETH TAYLOR
C/O THE HON FLORA MACDONALD

WELCOME BACK AND CONGRATULATIONS
PLEASE SIGN NO BOOK DEAL WITHOUT
TALKING TO ME FIRST

JACK MCCLELLAND
MCCLELLAND AND STEWART LIMITED

25 HOLLINGER ROAD
TORONTO ONTARIO

TO MARGARET ATWOOD

February 7, 1979
Ms. Margaret Atwood
14 Belgrave Crescent
Edinburgh, Scotland

Dear Peggy:
The thing you don't realize, my dear girl, is that I have been
forced by the economic realities to start taking publishing very
seriously. For example, it has been brought to my attention that
our ability to continue to pay the hordes of people employed[1] by
M&S (God knows how many mouths have to be fed) depends
directly on the number of copies of your new novel [*Life Before
Man*] that we are able to sell between September and Christmas.
In the past I have been able to treat this whole thing as a fun
game. I have never been troubled by the cavalier explanations
about lost manuscripts and fuck-ups of various sorts. Now I

have learned that this is a deadly serious game. I don't laugh at jokes about the Canadian postal service. I cry. We will let you know when the manuscript arrives.

What's that about Barbara Amiel? I haven't seen her say anything kind about anything Canadian. You have to be more specific. She will lose her job immediately if she says anything nice. I have been trying to have her fired for years and I realize now that is her great strength. The more I persist in getting her fired, the more valuable she becomes. Unless she agrees to pay me a commission, I'll pull out the rug from under the whole scene.

Cheers!

Jack McClelland

1. Economic pressures in 1979 forced M&S to lay off fifteen employees.

TO WALTER STEWART

Walter Stewart (b. 1931): journalist and columnist (*Maclean's*) who has written several books on business or economic issues: *Canadian Newspapers: The Inside Story* (1980); *The Golden Fleece: Why the Stock Market Costs You Money* (1992); *Belly Up: The Spoils of Bankruptcy* (1995).

June 26, 1979
Mr. Walter Stewart
Shrug Limited
43 Chaplin Crescent
Toronto, Ontario

Dear Walter:
I wouldn't touch a book on Canadian chartered banks with a ten-foot pole. First, to be read it would have to be fairly critical. Let's face it. The bank situation is a fairly easy and pleasant one. It could not be a kind book. I have learned the hard way

through the years that a book publishing house—one that is dependent on the good will [of banks]—doesn't mess around with such a subject. They have no sense of humour. I have, from time to time through the years, had occasion to make anti-bank speeches particularly in relation to my role with the Committee for an Independent Canada. I don't ever remember making an adverse comment anywhere, either here or in the United States, that didn't get back to one of the two banks we use. I don't remember ever making such a speech without hearing from them about it and being warned. In other words, when it comes to banks, I am a coward. I think the idea is a good one, but it ain't a good one for M&S. That is probably a terrible admission, but when it comes to dealing with banks, I am a coward and I am not interested in rocking the boat. In any case, I will be back in touch.

All the best.

Sincerely,

Jack McClelland

FROM SYLVIA FRASER

The book referred to by Sylvia Fraser is Sheila Watson's *The Double Hook* (1959).

[early November 1979?]

Dear Jack:
I met a gentle, shy and lovely person in Ottawa who spoke glowingly of her publishing experience with you, as if it had happened yesterday though it had taken place many years ago. She said her book had been turned down heartbreakingly, and even insultingly, over seven years. You read it, said instantly that you would publish it, and did so, with great sensitivity and style, and without changing a word. She said she'd never met you, and

that you didn't know it, but that she loved you. I thought it the
sort of confidence well worth breaking: from Sheila Watson.
Her whole life, since then, has been defined by the good things
flowing from that one perfect publishing experience. Bouquets,
Old Jake. Not many people can make that sort of difference to
the lives of other people.

Love,

Sylvia

TO PIERRE ELLIOTT TRUDEAU

Pierre Elliott Trudeau (b. 1919): former prime minister (1969–79;
1980–84).

December 12, 1979
The Hon. Pierre Elliott Trudeau
House of Commons
Ottawa, Ontario

Dear Prime Minister:
Forgive the salutation. It is deliberate. I continue to think of you
in those terms and I don't really feel that symbols can be all that
transient.

I did my first draft of a letter to you on the day that you
announced your resignation. The purpose of the letter was
straightforward enough. It was an almost automatic routine
letter from a serious book publisher for the purpose of
recording the fact that we would have a great interest in being
the publisher of your memoirs or any other work that you
might decide to write.

Unfortunately I found that I could not write such a letter. I
found that I was, as a Canadian, wound up in an emotional
situation that led me to write a much more complex letter than

I had originally intended. My initial purpose became obscured. I tore up several drafts and decided to wait until more direct exposition was possible.

The time lapse has not helped. Let me say this to you. As a Canadian I feel greatly in your debt. For more than a decade, you have given this country great pride, great hope and I believe a serious sense of purpose. For a great part of that period, the external odds against any substantial achievement were overwhelming. I would guess the things you gave Canada during that period are the important things and all else is irrelevant.

I deplore the timing and the fact of your resignation, but I can't fault you on either count. I have never had a party affiliation and I guess I never will have. I seem to be one of the few people not stunned by the recent Gallup Poll. To me it seemed inevitable, but let me not ramble. My purpose here is to thank you with sincerity for what you have done for Canada.

My other purpose is to say very simply that I do want to be your publisher. I have devoted most of my energy to one objective—that of becoming the best book publisher in the country. I may or may not have achieved that aim. There is only one thing I ask. Before you make any publishing arrangement of any sort, do give me the opportunity to explain our services.

With great admiration.

Sincerely,

Jack McClelland

THE EIGHTIES:
The End of an Era

After the financial and emotional dust had settled and M&S had been sold to Avie Bennett, Jack McClelland looked back at the history of the company and summed it up in a comparison of its two CEOs.

My father and I presided over the affairs of the first eighty-seven years of McClelland and Stewart for almost an equal amount of time, with the advantage slightly in his favour. We also presided over the financial calamities to which Canadian publishing is prone, in somewhat equal measure, but the advantage here was clearly mine.

From 1979 to 1981, as the country lurched from election to election and Pierre Trudeau (imitating Frank Sinatra) retired, made a comeback and then retired again, M&S stumbled from financial crisis to financial crisis. The books kept appearing at a rate of at least eighty a year, but what was left of McClelland's legendary chutzpah and energy seemed to go more and more into keeping the firm afloat with various loans, restructurings and shifts in personnel. He was shadow-boxing and he knew it.

Reflecting the problems on the financial side was his announcement in 1979 that while M&S books would still be Canadian, "there would be a steady movement towards popular, commercial fiction—less emphasis on literary and intellectual books and a greater preponderance for mysteries, adventure and science fiction." While sales and the number of books published were high, a survey of the catalogues reveals if not complacency then at least an understandable conservatism. Each season reads like a list of the usual suspects guaranteed to provide the usual pleasures. Berton, Mowat and Charlotte Vale Allen are nearly annual fixtures; Richler, Laurence and Peter Gzowski are regulars; and Atwood's novels punctuate the list. But only occasionally, as with Michael Ondaatje's *Running in the Family* (1982), Michael Bliss's *Banting: A Biography* (1984) or Dennis Lee's anthology of *The New*

Canadian Poets (1985), does one have the impression that the book is important enough or good enough to outlast the season. McClelland's letters to close friends confess exhaustion, disillusionment and the absence of new ideas.

Particularly unsettling are the letters in which he questions his own nationalism or refers to himself as a post-nationalist, as if sensing that the economic and political nationalism of the sixties, which had been an implicit impetus behind his entire enterprise, was either a spent historical force or had been co-opted by the feel-good North American multiculturalism of the seventies and eighties. In 1978, for instance, he wrote Pierre Berton that "as a post-nationalist ... I believe in Canadian unity and the survival of the country, but I am no longer satisfied that it can be achieved with the freight of any consideration of economic and political independence." As a businessman who had studied international trade agreements, he must have known that without "economic and political independence" Canadian nationhood was probably meaningless.

Where earlier honours and honorary degrees had celebrated an achievement in progress, the award of the Molson Prize in 1982—a very safe lifetime award almost always given in the last years of the recipient's career—implicitly confirmed that McClelland's work was done. The 1983 bankruptcy of Clarke, Irwin, the house that had published Robertson Davies's novels in the 1950s, was a reminder of what could happen to a publishing house that couldn't put its affairs in order. The sale of M&S in December 1985 to Avie Bennett, a Toronto real-estate developer, was inevitable and a godsend, both providing the company with a solid financial foundation and over the next decade breathing new life into the creative side.

But if Jack McClelland had the clear "advantage" over his father in "financial calamities," he also had the advantage in books published that have made a significant or lasting contribution to the country. The major books of the fifties, sixties, seventies and eighties are still in print, and the fiction and poetry he published are both in the canon and in the New Canadian Library, which M&S recently reissued in a new format.

TO M&S SALES DEPARTMENT

February 21, 1980
MEMO TO: Sales Department
FROM: Jack McClelland
RE: PHYLLIS GROSSKURTH'S' *HAVELOCK ELLIS*

I am returning the purchase order herewith along with an
earlier memo on the subject. I really don't want to discuss this
one, but I do propose one change in the purchase order. I think
we should amend it to say 2,000 copies bound, 1,000 copies
printed sheets. Please hold for instructions.

There are a number of reasons for my feeling this way about
this title:

1. Although I am prepared to believe that the book trade in
Canada is in some trouble at the present time, I am not
prepared to believe that it has come to a complete stop. I may
be wrong. One of the few things I have learned to believe is a
truism in this industry—and it is almost a never-fail rule—that
a good book by a good author on a reasonable subject will
probably succeed in the marketplace.

2. I could be wrong about this rule. I realize that I probably am,
but a few extra thousand dollars—if I am not wrong—is not
going to change very much.

3. This is a book by a highly respected professor of English at the
University of Toronto. She is respected as a literary critic, as a
writer, as a member of the literary community. Her last book, a
biography which is a relatively rare category in Canada, won the
Governor General's Award and a great deal of international
critical acclaim. She was selected some thirty years after his
death to write the official biography of the greatest sexologist
of his day (greater than Freud) and given exclusive access to his
papers for that purpose. She has written an important book, and

I can think of few books that have had more publicity in advance of publication than this one. It is a book of quality. I don't believe it is the greatest book that has come down the pipe, but I do believe that it will sell.

4. As yet our sales department has not been able to sell it. I don't know what the hell that means. It may be because many of our sales people and many of the book buyers in the country have never been to university and have never heard of Havelock Ellis. It could be that. It is also true that they haven't had a chance to read the book. I doubt that they will sell many more after they have read it, or it may be that I was right the first time—the book business has come to a dead stop. I can't answer that one.

5. I do know that we made some weeks ago, from my reading of the situation, a commitment to buy the paper. Since we have bought the paper and since we may not be able to get more copies in a hurry, it makes sense to me to print them. If the hardbound book bombs because we don't know how to promote and sell it, then we can bind those sheets up in a paper edition and get rid of them.

6. By the way, I should mention that as a young man I read a good deal of and about Havelock Ellis. The only significant thing I learned from this book is that the greatest pioneer sexologist got his kicks from watching women pee. Would you believe!

1. Phyllis Grosskurth (b. 1924): author and former professor of English at the University of Toronto. Grosskurth has published widely on Victorian life and literature as well as on psychoanalysis (*The Secret Ring: Freud's Inner Circle and the Politics of Psychoanalysis*, 1991). Her first book, *John Addington Symonds* (1964), received a Governor General's Award. *Byron, the Flawed Angel* (1997) is her most recent. Her relationship with J.M. and M&S was made difficult by the fact that the company lost the papers and manuscripts pertaining to *Havelock Ellis* (1980) that she had left with them for storage.

FROM FARLEY MOWAT

Brick Point
July 14, 1980

Dear J:
And the place is singularly aptly named. On the night of July 12
God spoke. He sent a fucking great lightning bolt that exploded
our chimney as efficiently as would an eight-inch naval shell,
and then, by jasus, he poured a six-inch rainfall (that's right—*six*
inches) through the hole. We liked to have drowned after we
finished liking to have been incinerated and electrocuted. David
Blackwood[1] was here for a rest. The blast tossed him clean out
of bed onto his ass. The shrapnel (brick chips) did a job on my
Volvo like you wouldn't believe. Great fun.

Do you think Someone is trying to tell me Something?

Shit, I feel much as you do. Brassed off, fed up, fucked out
and finished. Thinking of abandoning this place and sticking
myself into Port Hope in a wheelchair and drinking myself to an
early grave. The reasons are different, the net result much the
same.

Another book? Are you kidding? Not unless I'm born again.

Pretty good piece of you in *Toronto Life*. Make a good
obituary...

Cheers, you old prick,

F.

Like fuck I'm "growing old gracefully." I'm going down the
drain snarling all the way!

1. David Blackwood (b. 1941): Canadian artist who collaborated with Mowat on *The
Wake of the Great Sealers* (1973).

TO FARLEY MOWAT

July 22, 1980
Mr. Farley Mowat
R.R. 1
River Bourgeois
Richmond Co
Cape Breton Island, N.S.

Dear Farley:
The thing that you don't really understand is that [my secretary] Marge Hodgeman is desperately trying to arrange things so that we all end up in a wheelchair in Port Hope in the fall of this year. She knows very well that I don't read my letters. She is supposed to read them to make sure that they make sense. Well, screw that.

As to the lightning and the explosion—that was directed from here. That was from me. That was a signal that you should be fucking well writing a book. I have it scheduled for 1981.

I have decided that you had better stay down there through October. I may get down in September, but it is much more likely that I will get down in October. Things are lousy everywhere. The weather is terrible. The business pressures are beyond belief. I am drinking myself into an early grave. I like the drinking but I don't particularly want the early grave, so for Christ's sake, Farley, hang in.

Cheers!

Jack McClelland

FROM ROBERTSON DAVIES

Massey College
University of Toronto
September 9, 1980

Dear Jack:
It is dreadful of me to have waited until now to reply to your
letter of May 30 about Pierre Berton's new book, *The Invasion of
Canada*. The only excuse I can offer is that I have been writing
another novel [*The Rebel Angels*] and have only got as far as the
first revision; you will know better than most people what
ruthless demands such work makes. However, I have read
Pierre's book and enjoyed it enormously because, for the first
time, the War of 1812 made sense to me. I have always been
interested in it because a lot of my own forebears fought in it
and one or two of them are named on the Brock monument. I
am also very proud of the fact that the Battle of Stoney Creek
was fought on a family farm, though I am furious that in the
museum which has been made out of the farmhouse the
descendants of the original owners stopped with my older
brother and I just missed being included—one of the great
injustices of history.

When you see Pierre, will you give him my thanks and good
wishes because I think that the book is a first-rate addition to
our Canadian history about a subject which has, for so long,
been spread over a great variety of books and is thus inaccessible
to anybody except a researcher.

With good wishes,

Yours sincerely,

Rob Davies

TO ROBERTSON DAVIES

September 30, 1980
Professor Robertson Davies
Massey College
The University of Toronto
Toronto, Ontario

Dear Rob:
Many thanks for your note and your very good words about
Pierre's new book. I have, of course, passed on your comments
to him and he is pleased. He did not, however, agree to work a
mention of your forebears into the Battle of Stoney Creek, so
one of the great historical injustices will have to remain.
Sincerely,

Jack McClelland

TO MATT COHEN

October 21, 1980
Mr. Matt Cohen
P.O. Box 401
Verona, Ontario

Dear Matt:
The material that you have sent as an outline for *The Jewish Doctor*
[*The Spanish Doctor*] is fine in terms of content. In fact, in terms of
content, it turns me on completely. This is going to be a great
book. I have no reservations in believing—as I have said to
you—that this is going to be your breakthrough novel and I
think establish you as a major international author.
Having said that, though, I must tell you that this is one of
the worst outlines I have ever read. Will you please rethink it?
Forget formality, forget form, and write for me a three- or four-

page outline in which you are trying to sell the book idea and its content. Potential buyers are publishers. I can have this done for you, but I think that would be a mistake. You write extremely well, but you are being inhibited by the need to provide a formal outline.

   Look on it as a selling piece. Forget that you are the author. Your name won't be attached to the presentation. So let me give you the challenge. The challenge is to write a review of the book for a popular journal, or if you prefer, write extensive copy. As I say, forget modesty or anything of that sort. Describe the book in the most favourable possible terms. That's what I need.

Cheers!

Jack McClelland

FROM ARITHA VAN HERK

Aritha van Herk (b. 1954): professor of English at the University of Calgary and author of the novels *Judith* (1978), *The Tent Peg* (1981) and *No Fixed Address* (1986).

2764 West 2nd Avenue
Vancouver, B.C.
November 6, 1980

Dear Jack:
Lily[1] has already told you about our problems in the search for a new title; we haven't managed to come up with anything, although we've both tried—everything from *Sex and Violence in the Canadian North* to *Virgin Rock*s. Or something. I truly do understand your objection to the title *The Tent Peg* and I can see why you are worried about it; I'm willing to do the wildest kind of publicity to counter the impression that this novel is about camping. (But take heart, Jack—pegs aren't so bad—didn't *The Last Spike* sell marvellously well?)

Anyway, I've suggested to Lily that we treat the tent peg as the phallic symbol it is and put a suggestive cover on the book (a woman superimposed on a tent peg being screwed into the ground?); you have my tacit agreement to go along with whatever you think will work. Maybe a disclaimer: "This book is *not* about camping, it is about ..." [My husband] tells me there are at least 20,000 geologists/mining people in the country who are a good potential market. Maybe some advertising aimed at them?

I'll be in Toronto from November 20 to 23. Can we have dinner? I'd love to see you. Also, I owe you a big hug for the success *Judith* has had. I'm so happy the returns have covered the advance. I'll do everything I can so that this book does as well

Take care and I hope to see you in Toronto.

love,

Aritha van Herk

1 Lily Miller, M&S editor.

TO JOHN REEVES

John Reeves (b. 1938): Toronto photographer; his "Literary Portraits" appeared in *Canadian Fiction Magazine* No. 34/35 (1980).

February 4, 1981
Mr. John Reeves
Photographer
11 Yorkville Avenue
Toronto, Ontario

Dear John:
Thank you for your note and for sending me a copy of "John Reeves' Literary Portraits." I am stunned by it. It is beautiful. There is only one notable omission—myself. If you had

included me, I would have gone out and bought a dozen copies of *Canadian Fiction Magazine* at the full retail price.

Seriously though, John, it is beautiful. I know all the people and think it is a superb job. I haven't yet had a chance to read the accompanying text, but you have done it. It is great and I treasure it. It does, however, bring a very important issue to a head. We have been discussing for some months the 1982 project that you refer to. To be completely candid about it, John, I don't know how in God's name we can bring this off. If we could, I would like to do it, but I don't think we can. I think it needs a massive subsidy. I am one of your greatest admirers, and we are old friends, but I simply do not know how we can successfully publish the sort of book that you have described without a huge subsidy.

Our thinking goes along these lines. First, there is no international market. That is not your fault and has nothing to do with the quality of the work. It has to do with the fact that your subjects are Canadian and very few of them are of international interest. Our second problem is that we don't see a large Canadian market. You are a big name in Toronto, but you are not a household word in Vancouver or Halifax. How do we deal with that? Finally we deal with another truth, which is that the work has to be produced superbly, which costs a lot of money. Without subsidy it almost certainly means that we are pricing ourselves out of the market. *Canadian Fiction Magazine* did a good job—the quality is good, not great—but it is good. To tell you the truth, I don't know how they did it. We don't have subsidies for this sort of thing.

Best personal regards.

Sincerely,

Jack McClelland

FROM FARLEY MOWAT

Ode to a Publisher Who Did His Duty by the World

[1981?]

The curfew tolls the knell—
Alack!
Poor Jack
Is off to hell.
Pitchforked to Hades by these most hellish of all hellers,
The Book-sellers.

Sackcloth upon our heads, and ashes in our mouth
We hold our gay carouse.
Toast him in boiled tea,
And weep—for all the vanished royalty
That he
Had promised me.
And that we'll never see.

Our Golden Boy, the Heaven Sent
Of struggling authors, now is went.
No more the Granite Club shall echo to his cry:
"Two stiff martinis—quick!—and make them dry!"

Sadly his chiefest mourners go,
Led by the chairman of the LCBO
While in the roaring depths below,
Satanic scribes rush to and fro,
Piling a mountain of remainders round the stake,
In preparation for a grand McClelland Bake.

The curfew tolls the knell—
Alack, poor John
Is gone.
And never shall we see his like again.
At least this is the pious prayer I fondly pen!

FM.

If you'd like to make an advance on this ...?

TO CHARLOTTE VALE ALLEN

Charlotte Vale Allen (b. 1941): popular author of romances such as *Love Life* (1976), *Leftover Dreams* (1982) and the memoir of sexual abuse *Daddy's Girl* (1980).

March 31, 1981
Ms. Charlotte Vale Allen
29 Scarth Road
Apt. 2
Toronto, Ontario

Dear Charlotte:
Would you believe you are creating a very difficult problem for me? First, I do appreciate the proposed acknowledgement, and I thank you very much for it. The problem is that I decided as a matter of policy more than twenty-five years ago that there would be no such acknowledgements in books published by us. As a consequence, there have been none, and I have laid a very heavy trip on a great many authors through the years to keep it that way. If I make an exception now, they are going to feel that I have let them down, and I don't really think that is fair. I kid you not when I say that I have laid a really heavy trip on them. In fact, in some cases I have arranged for the acknowledgement to mysteriously disappear.

The reason for the policy was very simply that if you visualize it as something that might have (indeed, would have) become moderately frequent, it would then theoretically become something that a lot of authors might feel obliged to do. I think the policy has worked very well. I really believe it should be perpetuated, and I would be grateful to you if you would agree to have it dropped. I love you dearly, and I will love you even more dearly if you do agree to drop it.

Cheers!

Jack McClelland

TO EDWARD SCHREYER

Edward Schreyer (b. 1935): premier of Manitoba (1969-77), governor general of Canada (1979-84). This open letter appeared as a column in *Maclean's* (May 18, 1981) with the title "A Novel Suggestion."

The Right Honourable Edward Schreyer
Governor General of Canada, CC, CMM, CD
Government House
1 Sussex Drive
Ottawa

Your Excellency:
With the greatest respect, sir, I must tell you that you have a problem. It concerns the Governor General's Literary Awards. You should be the first to know that the innovations introduced into the program during your term of office have failed lamentably.

The first innovation was the decision to move the awards ceremony away from the nation's capital. The purpose of that move, as I understand it, was to strengthen the curtain of secrecy that has been drawn over these proceedings in the past. With the advance in communications technology, it has become more difficult to maintain secrets in Ottawa. There are just too many newspeople around Parliament Hill. But I must tell you that I am concerned about the choice of Moncton for this year's May 11 ceremony. Is it sufficiently remote? Is it not possible that despite every care, there will be a news leak? There are more secure places that could be found—outports still exist in Newfoundland.

Another innovation is the issuing, before the winner is announced, of a so-called short list of candidates in final contention. This way everyone knows that the judges are competent, take their work seriously, and missed no leading contenders. This, I think, was a sound idea. But please consider what your lunkhead judges have done! In only the second year under this new program, they have issued a short list of final contenders that must be the ultimate irritant. They have failed to include what many consider to be Hugh MacLennan's finest book (*Voices in Time*), Pierre Berton's finest book (*The Invasion of Canada, 1812-1813*), Richard Gwyn's finest book (*The Northern Magus*), Phyllis Grosskurth's finest book (*Havelock Ellis*), Mordecai Richler's finest book (*Joshua Then and Now*), and I won't even mention the authors that they have failed to include in the poetry category because that situation has already been categorized on the CBC as a national disgrace. Have the rules and the policies been changed? Is the purpose, now, to deliberately stir up controversy? Or is the purpose to denigrate the Governor General's Literary Awards to such a degree that the program can be quietly discontinued in the future? Please, Your Excellency, may I be informed of the new objective? Authors expect me to know about these things.

Your Excellency, do you doubt the fact that these ceremonies have been held almost in secret in the past? About fifteen years ago, I arose uninvited, on two successive Governor General's Awards Dinners (long since eliminated), to make a plea that these ceremonies should be made into news events. I was told by the then-chairman of the Canada Council that I would not be invited back unless I gave prior written assurance that I would refrain from such controversial outbursts. After all this time, I have been given only one reason for secrecy—that the Governor General's office is involved, and that controversy must be avoided at all costs. I say to hell with stuffy protocol. Let's celebrate our authors. I guarantee that the impact of these awards could be increased tenfold without the expenditure of an extra dollar if a sensible approach were taken.

Another problem with the Governor General's Awards relates to the Canada Council. I am not in any general sense critical of the work of the council. I think it has been a great force for good in Canada. It is in that context that I say unequivocally that their handling of these awards has been abysmal. Their performance in the selection of the award-winning books has been almost beyond comprehension. Small, elitist juries have been appointed in each category. The juries consist, for the most part, of writers in the categories to be judged. Do you think for a minute that this is a fair system? Let me tell you from my experience of over thirty-five years, in which most of my waking hours were spent with authors, that this is nonsense. The intrigues, the petty jealousies, the vendettas, the cliques—well, the lamentable results through the years speak for themselves. I would not employ an author to referee a Ping-Pong match. By their very nature they are biased and bloody-minded. Better put a fox in a henhouse than ask an author to judge his peers.

Let us set up a broad, representative jury comprised of critics, reviewers, booksellers, librarians, teachers, professors, publishers and readers—let's bring it out in the open and let's lay down the rules. Let's understand what are, in the opinion of a reasonable cross-section, the most worthy books. Let's pick the winners properly, and then let's celebrate them.

Now, Your Excellency, I am going to make a rude suggestion. I believe that it is time for you to get out of the literary awards business. I am sure that you do not want to preside over the liquidation of the Governor General's Awards, but it is time to do so. Let's call them the Canadian Literary Awards. Let us get the Canada Council out of the act. Please insist that they continue to supply the funds and, in fact, double the amount of the awards. Let the book industry, through its various associations, decide the how, when and where of these literary prizes. It is finally time that we gave suitable and ample recognition to the handful of Canadians who contribute more to this country than anyone else.

Respectfully submitted,

Jack McClelland

TO MARGARET TRUDEAU

Margaret Trudeau (b. 1948): the prime minister's wife who preferred the company of Mick Jagger to that of the governor general. The book in question in this letter is *Consequences* (1982), described accurately and efficiently in the National Library catalogue as about "Prime Ministers - Canada - Spouses - Biography."

October 27, 1981
Mrs. Margaret Trudeau
95 Victoria Street
Ottawa, Ontario

Dear Margaret:
I am enclosing a copy of a letter from Bantam's corporate lawyer sent to Roloff Beny's lawyer with respect to the photographic session he had with you some months ago. I also enclose a copy of my response to that letter, which was sent voluntarily to clear the air.

Margaret, let me make it clear that the last thing in the world I want to do is have a fight with you about this matter. In fact, I don't intend to have a fight with you. However, the matter is not quite as simple as your deciding that you do not like the pictures taken by Roloff Beny.' Let me give you the background.

First, whatever you or any of your advisers may think, Roloff Beny on his record must be considered as one of the top photographers in the world. No photographer—and I mean just that, no photographer—has even come close to his success with books in the international marketplace. His record stands on its own, and while some people may say they don't like his photography, the acceptance of his books at the top end of the price scale and on an international level supports Beny, not his detractors.

The problem is further complicated by the fact that we commissioned Beny to take your portrait and also by the fact that he is a personal friend of mine. Looked at from his point of view, the situation we have is that a photograph has been tentatively accepted by two professional art departments in book publishing houses and is then rejected by the subject. If he wanted to, he could probably argue that this is injurious to his reputation.

But that is not really the point, Margaret. Because you did not like any of the pictures, we agreed not to use them. Technically and legally I believe we had a perfect right to use them, as I think my letter to Bantam indicates.

Normally that would have been the end of the matter, but in this case it may not be. Bantam, because they negligently damaged some of the transparencies, is trying to limit their liability (or the liability of their insurance company) to Beny by claiming that the photographs having been rejected by the subject are valueless. It is not an opinion I share, but for the moment at least, I think it important that you be kept informed of the matter. It is a tricky issue. For example, should anyone, until the dust settles, ask you about the photographs that Roloff Beny may or may not have taken of you, it would I think be best to say no comment.

I think the book is going to be a big success. I hope in the

meantime that the television show is proceeding very well.
    All the best.

                                Sincerely,

                            Jack McClelland

1. Roloff Beny (1924–1984): photographer and author; his books included *The Thrones of Earth and Heaven* (1958), *To Everything There Is a Season* (1967) and *Persia: Bridge of Turquoise* (1975).

TO THE *GLOBE AND MAIL*

November 24, 1981
The Editor
The Globe and Mail
444 Front Street West
Toronto, Ontario

Dear Sir:
The record indicates that most people find Ben Wicks[1] to be amusing. Some don't. I can't quarrel with those who don't. Humour is a most subjective matter. I do take serious issue with your Eve Drobot,[2] who in a review of his new book (*Ben Wicks' Etiquette*) describes him as "racist, sexist, puerile."
    This is an astounding accusation. It is rather like describing Wayne Gretzky as an exhibitionist because he scores a lot of points in the National Hockey League. Wicks is a humorist. That is his role in life. Through satire, irony, and improbable exaggeration, he tries to introduce a little humour into our lives. If he fails—this most gentle, most considerate and most thoughtful of all individuals—if he fails, he fails totally. That seems unlikely.
    As for Eve Drobot, I am not sure. Until today I assumed her column ("Current Coin," *Fanfare*) was about money. Now I find it

is about "manners, mores and things."

I learned in that same November 21 issue of the *Globe* (where she reviewed Wicks) in her account of a book by an erstwhile butler (whose credentials seem to impress Ms. Drobot) that "most delicious are his sly reminders that servants are human, too." Now that really is good news! And after that Ms. Drobot has the effrontery to call Ben Wicks "racist, sexist." Truly, she is putting me on.

Sincerely,

Jack McClelland

1. Ben Wicks (b. 1926): Toronto-based cartoonist whose work has been collected in books and has been the basis for several television shows ("World of Wicks", "Dear Mum", "Wicks"). He is also the author of *Book of Losers* (1978) and *The Boys Came Marching Home (1991)*.

2. Eve Drobot (b. 1951): columnist and reviewer with the *Globe and Mail*, and author of *Amazing Investigations: Money* (1987).

TO MARGARET ATWOOD

December 22, 1981
Ms. Margaret Atwood
73 Sullivan Street
Toronto, Ontario

Dear Peggy:
First, I want to thank you again for the tremendous contribution that you have made to the sales and marketing success of *Bodily Harm* through your travels, personal appearances, interviews, autographing appearances, etc. It has used up a tremendous amount of your time and energy—over the last few months—time that you could have been spending, in an ideal world, writing new books.

I deplore the fact that this has become an inescapable part of the publishing procedure. I remember many years ago, Gabrielle Roy, after the major success of her first book, saying to me, "Let's make a deal. I will write the books—that's my job. You will market and publicize the books—that's your job." She was absolutely right and it was a fair agreement at the time. Unfortunately things have changed. She has through the years steadfastly refused to make any personal appearances. The books, although they have in no way diminished in quality, reach today only about 15 per cent of their former sales levels. If there is any doubt that the personal appearance is an essential part of the game today, that experience alone should confirm it.

One of the things that troubles me as a publisher is that there really is no compensation for the time and energy, and I am prepared to believe that at least 60 per cent of your sales result directly or indirectly from that promotional contribution. Do you keep track of the number of hours and the extra expense— sitters, phone calls, general dislocation—that our travel budget doesn't cover? Is there any way that you can utilize this for a tax credit?

Sincerely,

Jack

TO MARGARET LAURENCE

March 11, 1982
Mrs. Margaret Laurence
8 Regent Street, P.O. Box 609
Lakefield, Ontario

Dear Margaret:
Because I consider you a very good friend, and because you are one of the relatively small group of people whom I love and admire—and if that sounds like a form letter, it ain't—I want to tell you about a special event that will take place on March 18.

We have a board meeting that day—I wish you were still on that board. I shall resign as president of the company. Our new president and publisher will be Linda McKnight.

I want you to know that I have thought about all this for a long period of time. I think the change is not only in my best interest personally, but I think it is in the best interest of the company. Linda has had a long and useful apprenticeship. She is one of the most reliable people I have ever met in the book world. She is totally dedicated. She has a great feeling for what is important. She recognizes what M&S has tried to stand for. She recognizes that the author is the most important person in the publishing equation. She will, I believe, run the company effectively. I don't mind admitting, too, that in the year 1982 I am particularly delighted to be appointing a woman to head Canada's most prestigious publishing house. I am not a women's libber in any sense of the word, but at the same time I think it appropriate and right that a woman should take over as boss of our company.

She is not going to be a fake boss, she will be the real boss. I will be here. I will be chairman of the board and will work on a lot of projects, and I intend to retain a direct connection with a small handful of people whom I care about, like Farley and Pierre and Mordecai and Margaret—but not all that many. I am going to work on other projects—all publishing related—and I will back Linda up when she needs it, but she is going to be the operational head of the company.

I don't think that this will usher in a new era in Canadian publishing. If I thought it was going to do that, I wouldn't have appointed Linda McKnight. I want her to do a better job than I did—and quite honestly I think she will do a better job than I have done in recent years. I want her to improve the internal management of the company. I haven't the slightest doubt that she is going to do that because I have been too bored to pay much attention to that. Promotional flair is not her strongest point, but she knows enough about promotional flair to hire people who will be able to do it for her, but I think she is smart enough to realize that she had better be the central core of that, and I think she will be.

Cheers!

Jack McClelland

FROM MARGARET LAURENCE

8 Regent Street
Lakefield, Ontario
March 16, 1982

Dear Jack:

Thanks very much for your letter, which I received two days ago. This is my third attempt to answer it! It's difficult to say exactly what I mean.

I do approve of your decision to make Linda McKnight president and publisher. I have known her a long time, and I respect her efficiency and her ability to work with writers. I've given a statement to this effect for the PR in connection with the announcement of her appointment. I'm also very glad that you will remain chairman of the board. You are very much needed there.

The announcement will obviously cause quite a stir in Canadian literary and publishing circles, and you will probably get some flak, but then, you are used to that, if anyone can ever be said to get used to that kind of thing. So I wanted to let you know my own personal feelings on the matter.

The main reason I approve your decision really has to do with you yourself. You have worked far too hard, frequently under terrible pressure, for a long time. You have kept the firm afloat mainly owing to your determination, will power and tremendous sense of caring. I think you bloody well have earned the right to simplify your life to some extent and to have sufficient time for various projects that truly interest you. Never fear, your life will continue to be busy as hell because that is the kind of person you are. But you have paid your dues many times over. The day-to-day operation of the firm, and day-to-day decisions *should* be handed over to someone else at this point, not because you can't do them but because I think you owe it to yourself and your family to take life a bit easier from now on.

I made a similar kind of decision about my own life two years ago. I felt the need to simplify and to quit running as hard as I had been doing for more than twenty years. I sold my cottage. I sorted through all my papers (in case I kick the bucket suddenly, and also for—let's face it—a certain amount of money). I got a form letter, which I often use now to refuse invitations for readings, etc. (I enclose a copy for your amusement—I really am asked to do all those things!). I still answer stacks of mail, but I'm trying to make it as easy as possible for myself. I'm trying to keep fairly regular writing hours, but the fact that the thing is coming very slowly no longer bothers me a great deal. There are ways in which I, too, have paid my dues. Not that my life will ever be boring or overly quiet—I'm not that kind of person, either.

But I must take friendly issue with you when you say Linda will be able to do the job better than you have in late years. Rubbish. She will do a splendid job, but so did you, throughout very trying times. Please do not *ever* underestimate what you have done in your years as publisher, Jack. Damn near singlehandedly, you transformed the Canadian publishing scene from one of mediocrity and dullness to one of enormous interest and vitality. Had it not been for M&S, I wonder if a whole lot of people such as myself, Mordecai, Al Purdy, Farley, Pierre, Peggy Atwood, and on and on and on would have found the wide audience of readers that we have. I doubt it. Your great talent has always been your ability to spot good writers and your willingness to take a chance on them. Lots of people who now think of some of us as household names, or at least, in Mordecai's words, "world famous throughout Canada"(!), forget that there was a time when we were all beginning and unsure of ourselves. At least this is true of myself, anyway, and I'm sure it must be true of others. You and

Malcolm dreamed up the NCL, and that series in itself has revolutionized our publishing industry and made it possible for Canlit to be taught in our universities and high schools. (By the way, I love the new format ... very classy.)

I've known you as my publisher and friend for twenty-three years now. Seems impossible, but there it is. I first met you in 1959, when M&S had just accepted my first novel, *This Side Jordan*. You certainly took a chance on that one, as it was set in Africa (indeed, was one of the first books about Africa at the time of a country's independence and transition). This was before the upsurge of African writers themselves and also before books about the "new" Africa became popular subjects. In those twenty-three years, you have published twelve of my books—all of them, in fact, except a small book of Somali translations published years before, and my book on Nigerian writing, which I did not expect you to publish, in any event. I have not forgotten, also, that it was very largely through your efforts that Knopf was persuaded to take on my books, and that was a major turning point in my career.

I recall also some of our magnificent battles, usually through letters. The battle over the title of *The Fire-Dwellers*, which was *not* through letters that time. You visited Elm Cottage in England briefly that year, and I sat you down in my study and talked at you for about three hours, explaining in boring detail just why my title was the right one! At the time I didn't realize that the firm was in dire straits financially and you had a hell of a lot more on your mind than the title of one author's book. I also recall the famous battle over the Writers' Union contract, when I angrily wrote to all the board members. Ye gods, I now think the union contract is far too ambitious and complicated and needs to be simplified and made more realistic (I think this is being done). Also the fight re the [Roloff Beny] Iran book. Nostalgiasville, at this point.

Well, we have disagreed a lot throughout the years, Jack, but the main thing is that I have always felt I could express my views, and that although you might disagree with them, you would always take them seriously. I know quite well that a great many other M&S writers feel the same way.

It has been a long association, and a valuable one, I think, to both of us. That association won't end now, of course. But I just wanted to say some of these things, and to wish you all the best in whatever new ventures you'll be undertaking.

God bless—

Margaret Laurence

TO MARGARET LAURENCE

March 23, 1982
Mrs. Margaret Laurence
8 Regent Street
Lakefield, Ontario

Dear Margaret:
All things considered, I guess that is the nicest letter that I have ever received, and I thank you for it. There is a lot of fiction in your assessment, but one expects fiction from Canada's greatest novelist. Dear Margaret I thank you for what you have said. Our association over the years is one of the things that I value most in any retrospective of my life as a publisher, which in effect was the course of my life.

I wish I could believe that today was the start of a new life— it ain't, but it is the start of clearing up a backlog and eventually, if not a new life, then a slightly different one; you are quite right. We are both the same in that respect. It is possible to disengage in some areas, but it is not possible to disengage entirely.

I hope I see you very soon, and thanks again.

Cheers!

Jack McClelland

1

FROM MICHAEL ONDAATJE

Department of English
University of Hawaii at Manoa
April 6, 1982

Dear Jack:
First of all, thank you for all connected with *Running in the Family*. Your offer, the personal interest, all meant a great deal to me, and make me understand why you have such a faithful following among writers.

This letter is, I guess, prompted by your decision to move up to a less intense involvement with M&S, and just is a note of appreciation for the various things you have done for me, even though I've tended to circle outside the fence of M&S for many years, working with Coach House and Anansi, etc. But I did and still do appreciate your defence of me over the Cohen monograph years ago, when there was some question of the language used, and also your quick interest in *Trick with a Knife* when I phoned you about it. Even the semi-drunk conversation after a Writers' Union gathering in Toronto. You have always been very straight with me, and I value that greatly.

Anyway, thank you for that and much else to do with Canadian literature.

Michael

P.S. I enclose on a separate page a less personal note in response to what the hell *Running in the Family* is to be called.

FROM MICHAEL ONDAATJE

Department of English
University of Hawaii at Manoa
April 6, 1982

Dear Jack:
In response to your question of what do we call *Running in the Family* ...

Well, quite honestly, I don't know. My tendency would be to be evasive if asked officially. But I realize that your sales people do have a problem. What category do you place it in, etc.

In many ways, like *The Collected Works of Billy the Kid* and *Coming through Slaughter, Running* ... tends to fall between countries, or falls into several countries, maybe provinces. Apart from safely saying it is "a new prose work by M.O.," it probably won't be safe to say too much. If we call it a *novel*, then critics will spend most of their time arguing with that. I have never called it one and wouldn't. Along with the other two books, it is a mongrel. I slip into whatever form I can to try and capture what I am after—whether it is essay, fiction, non-fiction, poem or memoir. A friend called it a "fictional memoir."

So my tendency/suggestion would be to admit, up front, that we don't know and don't care *what* it is. Why categorize it; it will only limit the book and us. It is a sort of "soup," partly liquid, partly solids.

Hope this helps, though it probably won't.

I will be back sometime in June, so if you would like me to meet with your salespeople then I would be happy to.

all the best,

Michael Ondaatje

TO MARGARET LAURENCE

June 17, 1982
Mrs. Margaret Laurence
8 Regent Street
Lakefield, Ontario

Dear Margaret:
I think I have not responded to your letter about the Writers'
Development Trust Dinner. I am now about to respond. Let me say
this. I lay very few personal trips on you. This time I am laying a
really personal trip on you. I want you to come to the dinner. In
fact, I insist that you come to the dinner.

I want you at the dinner so much, Margaret, that I will, if
necessary, drive to Lakefield and pick you up and bring you back,
take you to the dinner, have you live at my place. I will do all that
or part of it or whatever. It is one night and we need you.

A few things you should remember. First, you were one of the
founders of the Writers' Development Trust. Second, it is in
financial trouble. Third, in order to save it, I have put my
reputation and my energy on the line and we are going to save it.
In order to save it, we have to raise a lot of money. In order to raise
a lot of money, we need Margaret Laurence at the dinner. It really
is that simple.

Your presence has been sold to Donald Early, who has bought a
table so that he will have Margaret Laurence as the guest. You may
not remember Donald Early, but I hope you will. He is the
chairman of the executive committee at McClelland and Stewart.
You have met him at board meetings in days gone by. A very
charming man. He is a partner in Greenshields and Company. You
will like the people with him. It will be old-home week. It will be a
very pleasant evening.

Who else is going to be at the dinner—a lot of people that you
like. Farley, Pierre Berton, Peter Newman, Mordecai Richler, on
and on. Well, they are sold as you are but I am doubly committed. I
am committed to selling a hundred tables, and I am also

committed privately in not embarrassing any authors. In other words, I don't want anybody left out. It is going to be a fantastic night, but, Margaret, we really need the stars and you are the top star in the whole Canadian galaxy and I have got to have you.

I don't want to be a real shit and embarrass you, but let me tell you that another star, not in your galaxy at all but another star, can't be there. She is going to be in Australia. Her name is Margaret Atwood, but would you believe what she is doing. She is making a goddamn Atwood effigy. I enclose a description of it. I mean this is a total commitment thing.

Margaret, I love you but my reputation depends on you being at the bloody dinner and it is not too big a price to pay. I would love to have you stay at our place in Kleinburg. It really is very comfortable and you would enjoy it. You will go to the dinner with Elizabeth and myself and you will come back with us. It will be easy. You will love our new place, and quite literally, I will drive down and pick you up and drive you back if necessary. So help me God, I want to issue a press release saying that Margaret Laurence will be there. You are a modest lady and you don't really understand how many people that will attract. Believe me, that is what the whole thing is about and we need Margaret Laurence. Think back how many times I have laid a trip on you. Not very often. This time I am laying a real trip. Come. Please phone Marge on receipt of this letter and say, "Okay, tell the boss or old Jake that I will be there. I will be there reluctantly, but I will be there."

Can I really tell you how it is? I want it to be a major success. It is a simple fact of life that the dinner can't even come close to my aspirations unless Margaret Laurence is present. I have conned Farley into coming all the way back from Cape Breton on the same pretext—well, I phoned him. The reason I have written you rather than phoned you is that I like getting your letters, and besides our mutual correspondence is saleable at both ends. I sell your letters. You should be selling mine.

Cheers!

Jack McClelland

MY STORY OF JACK McCLELLAND

All of Jack's writers, those whom he published and gave a start to, and believed in through so many years, have a favourite "Jack" story. Mine is different from many.

I first met J.G.M. in 1959, when he had accepted my first novel, *This Side Jordan*. He visited Vancouver, where I then lived, and I was very young and frightened until I met him, when I knew that here was someone who really knew how to read. Our association has gone on since then. We have differed in viewpoints, and have exchanged many an angry and witty letter and have always somehow made up, because basically we were on the same side. I used to call him, for years, ironically, "Boss," an irony that we both appreciated.

Jack McClelland is known for his panache, his flamboyance. My best story of him is the reverse. In 1968, when my novel *The Fire-Dwellers* had been accepted by M&S in Canada, by Knopf in the U.S.A. and by Macmillan in England, Jack was in England and came briefly out to my home, Elm Cottage, in Buckinghamshire. He was there just for an afternoon, during which he was subjected to a fantastic attack by me. He said, "Margaret, I love the novel but I hate the title ... it's awful!" I sat him down in my study and told him for hours why this title was the only right one. Finally, he said wearily, "Okay, Margaret, we'll go with your title." I had been yelling and roaring, explaining all the nuances of that miraculous title (and it is a good title). What I did not know until much later was that at that particular time he had been trying to get a loan from the Ontario government to keep the firm afloat, and was worried out of his mind. He never told me that. He listened while I went on, and he respected my views. Restraint is not usually associated with him, but I can tell you he has had it, in relation to many writers, myself included.

He is a Canadian pioneer. He has risked his life for us,

Canadian writers. I think we have proved him right. Thanks, Boss.

Margaret Laurence
LAKEFIELD, 1986

Editorial Note

1. Though I have edited many of the letters, I have decided not to mark the cuts. This is not a scholarly edition, the letters are available at McMaster University, and anyone can obtain a photocopy of the relevant original without difficulty. In almost all cases, the cuts involved material that was redundant or not particularly interesting.

2. In Jack McClelland's letters, I have often added material, placed in square brackets, to clarify a detail or point. In the choice between occasional square brackets or a footnote, I have been on the side of the brackets. I have also silently corrected some errors of grammar or spelling.

3. The letters are arranged chronologically, with one or two exceptions where I have tried to keep together some letters that are thematically related.

4. The letters give the addresses of McClelland's correspondents but not his because his is always the same, the M&S editorial offices in Toronto. I have assumed that most readers would like to know where an author is writing from (Cohen in Greece, for instance) or the address to which McClelland is sending the letter (Laurence in England).

5. With headnotes and footnotes, an editor can choose between Holly Stevens's minimalism in *Letters of Wallace Stevens* (Knopf, 1966) or the meticulous and exemplary work of William Toye in *Letters of Marshall McLuhan* (Oxford, 1987). Though I have identified almost all the correspondents in the headnotes and footnoted all the references, my procedure has been closer to Stevens's. Readers wishing for more information about the individuals named should turn to Toye and Eugene Benson's indispensable *Oxford Companion to Canadian Literature*, the annual *Canadian Who's Who* (University of Toronto Press), *The International Who's Who 1996-7* (Europa Publications) or *The Writers Directory 1996-8* (St. James Press). If no date of birth is noted, the reader should assume that I have been unable to find one.

6. I have imposed a standard style or format on the dates and

addresses, but have retained the idiosyncrasies of the correspondents' styles. This is most obvious in the letters from Earle Birney, Farley Mowat and Al Purdy.

Readers wanting more information about M&S and Jack McClelland's career should consult the Introduction and the Chronology in Carl Spadoni and Judith Donnelly's *Bibliography of McClelland and Stewart Imprints, 1909-1985: A Publisher's Legacy* (ECW, 1994).

All that remains is to thank some people who made the task easier and more enjoyable than it might have been. I am particularly grateful to Jack McClelland for not telling me which letters to include, for not offering any advice about editing and for not "censoring" any of the letters. His tact has been exemplary. My research assistant, Annick Hillger, was invaluable in helping with every aspect of the editing, from choices to annotations. I owe a substantial debt to Carl Spadoni, Charlotte A. Stewart and the staff at the William Ready Division of Archives and Research Collections, McMaster University, for their help, interest and friendly concern over several weeks. James King, Jack McClelland's biographer, kindly shared some ideas and offered some guidance about the papers over a Faculty Club lunch that made me feel welcome at McMaster. Douglas Gibson of McClelland and Stewart provided information about authors and executors. I am grateful to William Toye for his encouragement and example. Anna Porter made it all possible by inviting me to edit the book; and Janice Weaver, my editor at Key Porter Books, made this a better book than it otherwise would have been with her editorial eye and pencil. I am especially indebted to Catherine Porter for her preliminary research in the McMaster archives. T.H. Adamowski, Chair of the Department of English at the University of Toronto, provided vital support in the early going.

And a special continuing thank you to those who keep the candle burning in the darkness: Susan Addario, Elena Sarno, Lydia Powers, Karen Mulhallen, Andrea Werner-Thaler, Elias Polizoes and André and Vanessa Solecki.

Sam Solecki

Index